T0334030

Rethinking Macroeconomics with Endogenous Market Structure

Rethinking Macroeconomics with Endogenous Market Structure

MARCO MAZZOLI
University of Genoa

MATTEO MORINI
University of Torino

PIETRO TERNA
University of Torino

CAMBRIDGE
UNIVERSITY PRESS

CAMBRIDGE
UNIVERSITY PRESS

University Printing House, Cambridge CB2 8BS, United Kingdom

One Liberty Plaza, 20th Floor, New York, NY 10006, USA

477 Williamstown Road, Port Melbourne, VIC 3207, Australia

314–321, 3rd Floor, Plot 3, Splendor Forum, Jasola District Centre,
New Delhi – 110025, India

79 Anson Road, #06–04/06, Singapore 079906

Cambridge University Press is part of the University of Cambridge.

It furthers the University's mission by disseminating knowledge in the pursuit of
education, learning, and research at the highest international levels of excellence.

www.cambridge.org
Information on this title: www.cambridge.org/9781108482608
DOI: 10.1017/9781108697019

© Marco Mazzoli, Matteo Morini and Pietro Terna 2019

First published 2019

Printed in the United Kingdom by TJ International Ltd. Padstow Cornwall

A catalogue record for this publication is available from the British Library.

Library of Congress Cataloging-in-Publication Data
Names: Mazzoli, Marco, author. | Morini, Matteo, author. | Terna, Pietro, author.
Title: Rethinking macroeconomics with endogenous market structure / Marco
Mazzoli, Matteo Morini, Pietro Terna.
Description: First. | New York : Cambridge university press, 2019. |
Includes bibliographical references and index.
Identifiers: LCCN 2019029309 (print) | LCCN 2019029310 (ebook) |
ISBN 9781108482608 (hardback) | ISBN 9781108697019 (epub)
Subjects: LCSH: Macroeconomics – Mathematical models. | Equilibrium (Economics)
Classification: LCC HB172.5 .M3649 2019 (print) | LCC HB172.5 (ebook) |
DDC 339.01/51922–dc23
LC record available at https://lccn.loc.gov/2019029309
LC ebook record available at https://lccn.loc.gov/2019029310

ISBN 978-1-108-48260-8 Hardback

Contents

Illustrations

Tables

Notes on Contributors

Marco Mazzoli is associate professor of Economic Policy at the University of Genoa (Italy). He holds a PhD in Economics from the University of Warwick. He has published various papers in international journals and, with Cambridge University Press, he published in 1998 the research monograph *Credit, Investments and the Macroeconomy*. His research fields include macroeconomics, monetary economics and financial markets.

Matteo Morini got his PhD at the Ecole Normale Supérieure de Lyon, France; he works on complex networks, and develops agent-based and econometric models at the University of Torino. He is also employed at the Institut für Wirtschafts- und Verwaltungsinformatik at the Universität Koblenz-Landau, teaches courses on complex systems in the Carlo Alberto postgraduate programme and sits in the board of directors (as vice-president) of the Swarm Development Group. He co-authored and co-edited two books on complexity and ABMs. For more of his work, see http://perso.ens-lyon.fr/matteo.morini.

Pietro Terna is a retired professor of the University of Torino (Italy), where he was a full professor of economics. His research work is in the fields of (i) artificial neural networks for economic applications and (ii) social simulation with agent-based models (where he has been pioneering the use of Swarm, www.swarm.org). He has prepared a new agent-based simulation tool in Python (Swarm-Like Agent Protocol in Python), SLAPP (https://terna.github.io/SLAPP/), deriving it from the Swarm project. He is currently teaching a course on econophysics for the master degree in physics for complex systems at the University of Torino. His publications and projects can be found at https://terna.to.it.

Simone Lombardini is a PhD student at the University of Genoa, Italy, where he got his master's degree in economics and financial institutions, and is currently visiting the University of Oslo, Norway. Recently, he published a book on *Inequality and Poverty in Modern Capitalism*, in Italian. His research interests include business cycles, finance, inflation and income distribution.

Introduction

Do entry, exit and changes in market structure affect the macroeconomy? Is there a link between the strategic interactions among oligopolistic firms and the macroeconomic equilibrium? The question is certainly not trivial in modern economies, where large oligopolistic firms play a relevant role and so many meetings among statesmen have the explicit scope of promoting contracts for some large and important firms of their countries. However, surprisingly enough, the most popular theoretical models in the modern macroeconomic literature hardly see any explicit formalization for the macroeconomic effects of changes in market structure, entry, exit and strategic interactions among oligopolists, if not as mere mechanic and secondary effects of the usual technology shocks, commonly invoked as the cause of business cycle. Do we really think that the sophisticated strategies of large firms' decision makers do not carry any macroeconomic consequences? The market structure and strategic interactions among oligopolists are not necessarily associated with scale economies or technology shocks. In order to better focus on this point, the theoretical model of this book describes, like some of the most important original contributions in the conventional DSGE literature, an economy where the labor is the only production input.

This book deals with all these issues by introducing a new macroeconomic approach: Part 1 provides its theoretical background and modeling framework, and Part 2 its implications by running some simulations and comparing the results with the US macroeconomic data.

A feature of our model is endogenous market structure, explicitly built to account for its feedback with the aggregate variables: in particular, changes in market structure are a potential cause of macroeconomic fluctuations and business cycle, and this is formalized by plugging into a macromodel a theoretical mechanism of entry and exit that also allows to keep track of aggregate output, market size, social mobility and income distribution. What we mean to create is a general framework that may be adapted (by specifying less general and more detailed features) to model specific assumptions and phenomena. In this sense, the perspective of our book is different from the contributions focused on the statistical properties of oligopolistic markets or on the statistical distribution of firm size.

Our framework also provides a theory to interpret markups over the business cycle according to the feasibility of entry: in particular, Chapter 4 also includes a simulation where countercyclical markup emerges as a consequence of large entry and disappears in the case of blocked entry.

Lee and Mukoyama (2018) introduce a general equilibrium model to account for entry and exit over the business cycle, assuming that the entry costs are cyclical. While the only point in common with our work is that the entry and exit rates are determined by an endogenous mechanism, we focus instead on the fact that in an oligopolistic economy entry and exit cannot be explained without explicitly considering and modeling the strategic interactions among the oligopolistic firms. Therefore, without loss of generality, we do not need to assume that entry costs are cyclical, we do not need to make any specific assumption on the statistical or empirical configuration of firms' size and we mainly model the logical links between macroeconomic facts and decisions of the entrepreneurs and potential entrants. In this regard, we introduce a theory of information spreading and individuals decision making consistent with a fairly general notion of rationality and, more specifically, even with the notion of rational expectations.

We believe that introducing this perspective as the theoretical background of agent-based macroeconomic simulations constitutes an interesting point in itself. Apart from introducing a new microfounded theoretical model that explains the business cycle as an effect of entry/exit, interpreted as strategic decisions of the firms and introducing, in this regard, a general notion of rationality also broadly consistent with the assumption of rational expectations, we produce simulations and appropriate predictions for the macroeconomic fluctuations based on the agent-based methodology.

To develop the last paragraph, let us describe the Agent-Based Models (ABMs) field in a few steps. We follow – with some modifications – the specifications of two of the pioneers of the field, Robert Axtell and

Joshua M. Epstein, particularly in the description of the ABMs that they introduce in Axtell and Epstein (2006).

i) The starting point is a population of agents, representing individuals or, more generally, *entities* as the component of a generic system that we construct using small parts of computer code operating in dedicated software environments.

ii) The goal is to search for regularities at the macro level generated by the behavior of the agents (micro level, if individuals; *meso* level, if more complex entities).

iii) An ABM does not introduce equations governing the effects of the agents' behavior at the macro level, but it allows us to observe the emergence of those effects (i.e., summing up the outcomes of the actions and interactions of the agents).

iv) Agents, on their side, can use equations to assume their decisions; equations can be very complicated (e.g., produced via artificial neural networks or other artificial intelligence algorithms). Agents can also learn from their errors, modifying the internal equations or artificial neural networks. In this book, their action is based on the sequence described in Chapter 3, and particularly in Figure 3.1.

v) Heterogeneity is usual in ABMs, and as a consequence, the agents have different internal structures.

vi) With ABMs we can manage boundedly rational behavior, non-equilibrium dynamics, and spatial processes.

vii) Regularly, the coding techniques are based on object-oriented programming and build the agents using *instances* of *classes*, where a good class synonym is *set*.

In our model, the agent-based technique allows us to emphasize the role of strategic interaction among oligopolistic firms, as the consequence of subjective decision making, formalizing in the most appropriate way the implication and results of these decisions. We produce all the actions and reactions designed by the model equations via the behavior of heterogeneous agents actually acting in the simulated time. We remark that between (*a*) the formal presentation of the model in the equation based way, strictly necessary to be consistent with the literature upon which our work is grounded, and (*b*) the agent-based implementation, the consistency is deeply satisfied, but with a few inevitable distinctions. The same kind of differences that we run up against when we compare (*a*) the formalization of a phenomenon and (*b*) the related observation of the reality (here: an artificial one, simulated).

We hope that the framework introduced in this book may be a useful tool for further research and extensions, where the endogeneity of market structure in a macromodel and its potential implications is a distinguished feature.

Rationale, Scope and Contribution of the Book to the Existing Literature

The last decade has seen a lively debate in macroeconomics, with an increasing criticism on the model that seemed to be dominant in literature since the end of the 1990s, the Dynamic Stochastic General Equilibrium (DSGE, hereafter), and, consequently, the birth of some new theoretical approaches and methodologies.

In spite of the *heroic* defense of the DSGE approach introduced by Christiano et al. (2018), the serious drawbacks of that class of models is clearly described by Romer (2016), who explicitly talks about lack of scientific background. However, we believe that the general notion of general equilibrium, in dynamics terms, is not ill-based, and for this reason, our theoretical model has still the nature of a general equilibrium model, although its premises are completely different from those of the conventional DSGE literature.

On our side, we have the double feature of ABMs: to be close to a narrative of the reality, thanks to their flexibility, but most of all, to be close to a mathematical model, thanks to a rigorous representation via a computer code.

With Lengnick (2013) we can argue that

[...] agent-based modeling is an adequate response to the recently expressed criticism of macroeconomic methodology because it allows for aggregate behavior that is more than simply a replication of microeconomic optimization decisions in equilibrium. At the same time it allows for absolutely consistent microfoundations, including the structure and properties of markets. Most importantly, it does not depend on equilibrium assumptions or fictitious auctioneers and does therefore not rule out coordination failures, instability and crisis by definition. A situation that is very close to a general equilibrium can instead be shown to result endogenously from non-rational micro interaction.

Important contributions in this direction come from Di Guilmi et al. (2017). A different criticism on the DSGE paradigm is expressed in Wiesner et al. (2019), where the questionable role of DSGE models is inserted in an analysis of the stability of democracies in a complex systems perspective.

Consistent with the last context is the famous Trichet (2010) observation, when he was close to leave the role of President of the European Central Bank:

As a policy-maker during the crisis, I found the available models of limited help. In fact, I would go further: in the face of the crisis, we felt abandoned by conventional tools. [...] We do not need to throw out our DSGE and asset-pricing models: rather we need to develop complementary tools to improve the robustness of our overall framework. [...] First, we have to think about how to characterise the homo economicus at the heart of any model. The atomistic, optimising agents underlying existing models do not capture behaviour during a crisis period. We need to deal better with heterogeneity across agents and the interaction among those heterogeneous agents. We need to entertain alternative motivations for economic choices. Behavioural economics draws on psychology to explain decisions made in crisis circumstances. Agent-based modelling dispenses with the optimisation assumption and allows for more complex interactions between agents. Such approaches are worthy of our attention.

Ghorbani et al. (2014), whose article has the descriptive title *Enhancing ABM into an Inevitable Tool for Policy Analysis*, work in the same direction, proposing to use a coordinated rich set of instruments for policies.

The novelty of our book is also that of introducing a completely new theoretical framework whose purpose is modeling a stylized fact that has been partly neglected in macroeconomic research: the reciprocal interactions between industrial structure and the macroeconomy in an economy with large oligopolistic firms. Entry and exit in an oligopolistic economy are phenomena with a large enough magnitude to affect the macroeconomic equilibrium, and most economists would agree with the fact that the birth and death of firms is an empirical phenomenon associated with the business cycle or, perhaps, one of the main empirical features of the business cycle.

Our theoretical framework is also useful to analyze the behavior of the firms' markups over the cycle in a (realistic) world where individuals are heterogeneous in their budget constraints: they can be workers, or new entrant entrepreneurs, or incumbent entrepreneurs or unemployed and may change their status when they take a *drastic* decision (i.e., using the language and metaphors of economists, when they are *affected by informational shocks*). The aggregate demand is micro-founded and explicitly modeled as the sum of the individual demands. Another *realistic* feature of our theoretical model is that oligopolistic firms and heterogeneous agents have, in general, diverging incentives (Aoki and Yoshikawa, 2007). The algebraic structure of our model may also be used as an analytical framework for the links among entry/exit, social mobility and the macroeconomy.

In Chapter 5, we report actual data related to our main research pattern, i.e., the emergence of the countercyclical markup. We aware of the open issue of ABMs validation and the methodological contribution of Fagiolo et al. (2007), but we remark that out main purpose here is to build a *reasoning machine*. Broadly, these might be summarized as a pattern oriented modeling approach, and we can do many-leveled, qualitative logical *validations*. For an interesting open discussion on validation, refer to Malleson (2018).

We could do a many leveled, qualitative validation. We can check that the outcome distributions are the right shape (or other known facts about people) to simultaneously constrain the simulation in many aspects, dimensions and scales at once.

This work is a research book, mainly addressed to postgraduate students, PhD students, professional economists and researchers. If you are not interested in the full details, please simply read the Introduction and Chapters 1, 2 and 4. If possible, refer to Appendix A.

An overview

In Chapter 1, we briefly discuss the rationale and the premises for the theoretical model of the book and how our theoretical model relates to the existing and related literature. The model describes an economy with an oligopolistic industrial sector, and our purpose is to analyze the interactions between the market structure and the macroeconomy – in particular, how the equilibrium among the oligopolistic firms impacts the macroeconomy and how the macroeconomy in turn impacts the equilibrium among the oligopolistic firms.

In Chapter 2, we have the structure of the model, built plugging the entry/exit decisions into a macroeconomic system, by using a notion of statistical distribution of expectations that is consistent with the idea of rational expectations (at least in its original formulation) to model the entry decision of potential entrants. The theoretical framework is also useful to analyze, on a theoretical ground, the behavior of the firms' markups over the cycle and is employed for the agent-based simulations. In particular, we model a macroeconomic system with oligopoly, entry/exit and heterogeneous individuals.

In Chapter 3, starting from the equation based construction introduced in Chapter 2, we build a macroeconomic simulation model of an economic using the agent-based technique; the model is microfounded, and so our explanation starts from the behavior of the agents and of the market frameworks where they behave. The structure of the simulation model is well represented via the sequence of the 12 items of Figure 3.1.

In Chapter 4, we analyze the simulation results, considering both the dynamic of the time series of the main economic variables of the model and their correlation structure. The attention is mainly related to the emergence of the countercyclical markup phenomenon and to the dynamics of the market structures, ranging from tight oligopolistic constructions to the development of large atomistic markets.

In Chapter 5 we propose some actual data related to the GDP cycle and to the income components, to search for the presence of the countercyclical markup.

Appendix A is dedicated to a digression on decentralized market based on agents, and it is useful to understand the background of Chapter 4.

Appendix B introduces the collection of the parameters (names and values) used in the book.

Appendix C explains how to run the code, with some documented exception for the different cases of Chapter 4.

Online Resources

The code has a reference handbook, *Oligopoly: the Making of the Simulation Model*,[1] that describes the details of the program, complying with the *AEA Data Availability Policy*.[2]

---

[1] Online at https://terna.github.io/oligopoly/Oligopoly.pdf.
[2] https://www.aeaweb.org/journals/policies/
data-availability-policy.

Online we have also the whole *oligopoly* code,[3] and the SLAPP shell,[4] employed to run the model in the way pointed sub vii) above.

Acknowledgments

First of all, a huge thanks to Eleonora Priori,[5] for her thorough and passionate comments and suggestions. We are also deeply grateful to a special reader, Dr. Simone Landini,[6] for his precious review of the manuscript. The very valuable comments from the Cambridge University Press anonymous referees have been extremely useful to improve our work and are gratefully acknowledged.

Thanks for their suggestions and encouragements to Giorgio Rampa and Federico Boffa.

Thanks to the Italian scholars in agent-based simulation, for creating a favorable environment for this kind of research. We remind the groups quoted in Dosi and Roventini (2017): the *Scuola Superiore Sant'Anna (Pisa)*; the so called *CATS family*, developed between Ancona and Milano; the *EURACE model*, born in the University of Genova. A group has also been alive in Torino.

[3] https://github.com/terna/oligopoly.
[4] At https://terna.github.io/SLAPP/ or at https://github.com/terna/SLAPP.
[5] Currently (2018) a student of the Vilfredo Pareto doctoral school in Economics of the University of Torino
[6] I.R.E.S Piemonte, Torino, Italy

PART ONE

Theory

1 | Industrial Structure and the Macroeconomy: A Few Premises for a Macromodel

MARCO MAZZOLI

1.1 Introduction

This chapter briefly discusses the rationale and the premises for the theoretical model of this book and how our theoretical model relates to the existing and related literature. As discussed in the next chapter, our model describes an economy with an oligopolistic industrial sector, and our purpose is to analyze the interactions between the market structure and the macroeconomy. In particular, how does the equilibrium among the oligopolistic firms impact the macroeconomy, and how does the macroeconomy impact back on the equilibrium among the oligopolistic firms?

The birth and death of firms is not just an empirical fact associated with the business cycle: it is the heart of the business cycle and the macroeconomic effects of the equilibrium and strategic interactions emerging among the firms operating in an economy with oligopolistic markets are likely to be non-negligible.

More generally, we state that diverging incentives between oligopolistic firms and heterogeneous agents may play a relevant macroeconomic role. Entry and exit respectively generate or eliminate new entrepreneurs with firms and workers. In this sense, a macro-model that explicitly models the causes or incentives for entry/exit, markups, employment/unemployment may shed a new light for understanding the possible causal links among market structure, social mobility and the macroeconomic trends if one removes the assumption (rather conventional in the DSGE literature) that individuals are at the same time entrepreneurs and workers and therefore each of them, rather hilariously, negotiates with himself his wage. A model with these features could also provide a general framework to analyze the behavior of markups over the business cycle.

Each individual's expectation constitutes a point along the curve of frequency of the distribution of expectations. The average of such frequency distributions corresponds to the market's rational expectation. In this sense, the model is consistent with the rational expectation idea that the individuals' expectations are "on average" correct in predicting the relevant market variables. The agents, in their rationality, are aware of the existence of a distribution of expectations (i.e., a distribution of individually heterogeneous expectations but with a "correct average") and, for this reason, make the adjustment attempts described in Chapter 3. In this sense, the agent-based simulations constitute a link between theory and reality that actually explains how they attempt to know the "correct" market average of expectations (not known a priori by them) by making sequences of attempts.

The theoretical premises of this book, therefore, are rather different from those of the "behavioral new Keynesian model," introduced in the seminal works by De Grauwe (2011), De Grauwe and Kaltwasser (2012), Branch and McGough (2010), and Branch and McGough (2016), who incorporated the agent-based computational techniques into conventional DSGE models.

The next section and all its subsections briefly discuss why the theoretical premises of our model could not be developed within a conventional DSGE framework and in what regards our model is different from that class of models and from other existing macroeconomic approaches.

The last section of this chapter contains some final remarks and introduces the basic assumptions contained in the model of the next chapter.

1.2 Why a New Theoretical Approach

Discussing how the literature on agent-based computational economics relates to the DSGE models and analyzing all the various forms of criticism toward the DSGE models is well beyond the purpose of this book, and several excellent surveys exist in this regard, like, for instance, Dilaver et al. (2018) or, for what concerns the policy implications, Fagiolo and Roventini (2017). In this chapter, we focus instead on a specific causal link and modeling feature that has been relatively neglected by the conventional macroeconomic and DSGE literature: the (reciprocal) link between industrial structure and the macroeconomy.

The class of models sometimes denominated as "macroeconomics from the bottom up" (Delli Gatti et al., 2005, 2010, 2011; Gaffeo et al., 2008) follows the evolutionary economics approach, includes agents' heterogeneity and bounded rationality and often refers to complexity theory. More precisely, these models usually focus on the macroeconomic outcomes emerging from firm heterogeneity in the transmission and amplification of shocks. Instead of focusing the analysis on the notion of equilibrium, it is the concept of "emergence" of a macroeconomic state that is the leading methodological concept.

Lee and Mukoyama (2018) provide a very remarkable paper, where stochastic productivity shocks affect the dynamics of plant investments and, in this way, the business cycle. Like in the conventional business cycle literature, the productivity shocks are the very cause of business cycle and, as a consequence, of the rate of entry, which are then ultimately still related to productivity shocks. Clementi and Palazzo (2016) extend Lee and Mukoyama's model (as it appears in a previous version) by including capital stocks, which play the important empirical role of generating a propagation mechanism. Previous contributions, like Veracierto (2002, 2008), assumed exogenous entry and exit, while Comin and Gertler (2006), in a model with endogenous innovation and technology adoption, endogenously explain entry, while exit is still exogenous. In this sense, Lee and Mukoyama, by associating entry and exit to productivity shocks, certainly provide a significant contribution, although they do not explicitly model capital stock and land (Lee and Mukoyama, 2018, p. 10). Differently from them, in our model, entry and exit are associated with the (heterogeneous) profits level and not with the mere productivity shock, while entry and exit interact with the macroeconomic equilibrium, and, as a consequence, the macroeconomic price level is not only determined by wages.

Dosi et al. (2006, 2008, 2010) introduce a new class of models, sometimes denominated "Keynes meets Schumpeter." Instead of focusing on complexity, they put their emphasis on the heterogeneity of agent types. Their critique of the real business cycle and "New Keynesian DSGE" is based on the fact that the explanation of the macroeconomic fluctuations in these two approaches mainly rely on exogenous and stochastic technology shocks and undervalue the relevance of endogenous technology innovation. Having introduced a high degree of sophistication in modeling and plugged endogenous technology innovation in macroeconomic models, this class of models usually formalized pricing as a markup over unit cost and modeled the markup evolution in a very simplified way, similar to the following:

$$\mu_{j,t} = \mu_{j,t-1} \left\{ 1 + \left[(f_{j,t-1} - f_{j,t-2})/f_{j,t-2} \right] \right\}$$

where $\mu_{j,t}$ is firm j's markup at time t and $f_{j,t-1}$ is firm j's market share at time t.

In this book, we focus instead on the macroeconomic implications of the strategic interactions among oligopolistic firms. Complexity, of course, may emerge from the decentralized interactions among individuals (and our model explicitly formalizes them), but first we have to settle down a microfoundation of the strategic interactions among oligopolistic firms. Complexity may emerge by extending the model with suitable assumptions. The model introduced in the next chapter allows then for more flexibility in the markup behavior, which emerges from a Nash equilibrium in mixed strategies among the oligopolistic firms.

1.2.1 *Microfoundation*

The models following the original DSGE framework (see, for instance, Walsh, 2017, ch. 8), given the assumption of monopolistic competition (which requires the introduction of a continuum of imperfectly substitutable goods), introduce the metaphorical notion of "composite consumption good," which also enters the household's utility function, but whose macroeconomic behavior is qualitatively indistinguishable and not different from the one of a generic homogeneous good. In other words, each consumer buys a unit of the composite bundle of goods, and the aggregate output is composed of the bundle of composite goods. The market form implemented in the model, i.e., monopolistic competition, a priori both (i) drastically simplifies the market structure and (ii) rules out any macroeconomic implication of the strategic interactions among large oligopolistic firms.

In the DSGE, the composite consumption good is defined as follows (see Walsh, 2017, ch. 8):

$$C_t = \left[\int_0^1 c_{jt}^{(\theta-1)/\theta} dj \right]^{\theta/(1-\theta)} \tag{1.1}$$

where C_t is, of course, the consumption level that enters the utility function to be maximized in an intertemporal problem, with disutility of labor and money in the utility function of this kind:

$$E_t \sum_{i=0}^{\infty} \beta^i \left[\frac{C_{t+i}^{1-\sigma}}{1-\sigma} + \frac{\gamma}{1-b} \left(\frac{M_{t+i}}{P_{t+i}} \right)^{1-b} - \chi \frac{N_{t+i}^{1+\eta}}{1+\eta} \right] \tag{1.2}$$

where M_{t+i} is nominal money stock, P_{t+i} is the aggregate price level, σ, b, χ and η the usual elasticity constant parameters. As shown in (1.2), using an aggregate composite consumption good amounts to a formal metaphorical assumption, since it is C_t that enters all the microfounded macroeconomic equations. In this sense, it is equivalent to use, as we are doing in our model, a generic undifferentiated good, which has, on the other hand, the advantage of allowing to formalize an oligopolistic industrial sector and its strategic interactions with the macroeconomy.

In our oligopolistic economy producing a homogeneous good, each individual may earn financial remuneration by investing in bonds, but, due to the oligopolistic nature of the economy, cannot be at the same time worker and entrepreneur, although each individual may change their status on the basis of a stochastic decision-making process of the workers, who are assumed to be potential entrants. This assumption also allows us to introduce in the model the wage negotiations, trace out the income distribution between aggregate wages and profits and remove the implicit DSGE "schizophrenic" assumption that each individual is negotiating with herself the wages as an entrepreneur and a worker.

However, introducing in a macromodel the assumption of quantity (Cournot) competition might raise the problem of how prices are determined without referring to an auctioneer or, equivalently, what prevents the firms from implementing price undercutting and price competition. A possible way to deal with these problems is assuming a quantity precommitment à la Kreps and Scheinkman (1983), whose results can be extended under the fairly general conditions shown by Madden (1998), whose results are invoked in our model to justify the equilibrium in the oligopolistic industrial sector.

Some problems in the conventional use of the representative agent lies in the aggregation of heterogeneous agents, as already pointed out many years ago by Forni and Lippi (1997), who show that many statistical features associated with the dynamic structure of a model (like Granger causality and cointegration), when derived from the micro theory, do not, in general, survive aggregation. This means that the parameters of a macromodel do not usually bear a simple relationship to the corresponding parameters of the micromodel. Of course, this kind of problem cannot be solved without explicitly formalizing a statistical aggregation process and individuals' externalities, and this is actually done in our model, which also explicitly formalizes the aggregate demand function as the sum of the individual demand function of different individuals with heterogeneous budget constraints.

A long-lasting criticism to the representative-agent methodology was raised in an earlier contribution by Blinder (1986), who pointed out that microfounded models with a representative agent, by assuming that the observable choices of optimizing individuals are "internal solutions" may yield biased econometric estimates when the choices of a relevant portion of individuals are actually corner solutions: "For many goods, the primary reason for a downward sloping market demand curve may be that more people drop out of the market as the price rises, not that each individual consumer reduces his purchases" (Blinder, 1986, p. 76).

Finally, a last point raised here is associated with the interpretation of the representative agent utility function: following Kirman (1992), logically speaking, what does the representative agent utility function represent? If we look at it with the criteria of "hard sciences," can it really be interpreted as a proper microfoundation of a macroeconomic system composed of a high number of heterogeneous individuals without formalizing any statistical law of aggregation that accounts for externalities and agents' rational interactions? Is it not instead a sort of "aggregate utility function," and if so, is it not a "macroeconomic" preference function? In other words, if the utility function of the representative agent is metaphorically meant to model all the consumers of an economy, is it not subject to the Lucas critique? Why not explicitly modeling agents' (rational) interactions by means of some statistical principles of aggregation? In this regard, Aoki and Yoshikawa (2007, p. 28) point out that

the standard approach in "microfounded" macroeconomics formulates complicated intertemporal optimization problems facing the representative agent. By so doing, it ignores interactions among nonidentical agents.

Also, it does not examine a class of problems in which several types of agents simultaneously attempt to solve similar but slightly different optimization problems with slightly different sets of constraints. When these sets of constraints are not consistent, no truly optimal solution exists.

Furthermore, for what concerns the role of microfoundation,

Roughly speaking, we de-emphasize the role of precise optimization of an individual unit while emphasizing the importance of proper aggregation for understanding the behavior of the macroeconomy. The experiences in disciplines outside economics such as physics, population genetics and combinatorial stochastic processes that deal with a large number of interacting entities amply demonstrate that details of specification of optimizing agents (units) frequently diminish as the number of agents become very large. Only certain key features of parameters such as correlations among agents matter in determining aggregate behavior. (Aoki and Yoshikawa, 2007, pp. 28–9).

Of course, one may object that even an "aggregate utility function" still allows to build the aggregate behavior on some rigorous, logical and consistent axiom of preference. Therefore, in this paper, the utility function of the representative agent, which is the basis for the derivation of the aggregate demand, will be employed as the basis for the microfoundation of the aggregate demand. However, our demand function is explicitly formalized as the aggregation of demand functions of heterogeneous agents, and the rest of the model explicitly accounts for interactions, conflicts and externalities. In this sense, this book follows, in spirit (although not always in each formalization), Aoki and Yoshikawa's (2007) approach, since several phenomena (like entry, as discussed below and as shown in the next chapter) are formalized in terms of statistical aggregations and the theoretical model accounts for the existence of individuals with different (and sometimes conflicting) targets.

Our aggregate demand is built by summing up each individual's demand, which is explicitly derived from a problem of intertemporal optimization of this kind of preferences

$$\max U_t = E_t \left[\sum_{i=0}^{\infty} \left(\frac{1}{1+\rho} \right)^i u(c_{t+i}) \right]$$

with c_{t+i}, c_{t+1}, for each $i = 0, 1, \ldots \infty$
subject to the following constraint:

$$E(b_{t+i+1}) = (1 + R_{t+i})E(b_{t+i}) + E(y_{t+i}) - c_{t+i}$$

where $u(c_{t+i})$ are the individual's preferences for each period $t + i$, defined over the undifferentiated generic good c_{t+i} demanded and consumed by the individual i, R_{t+i} is the nominal interest rate at time $t + i$, b_{t+i} is the risk-free financial asset and ρ is the subjective rate of intertemporal preference. The wealth distribution among individuals follows a random pattern, and the optimization problem of each individual generates the individual demand, which is the following:

$$c(X_{j,t}) = \left[1 - (1 + R_t)^{\frac{1-\gamma}{\gamma}} (1 + \rho)^{-\frac{1}{\gamma}} \right] (b_{j,t} + g_{j,t})$$

$X_{i,t}$ is the sum of the financial and human wealth.

And the aggregate consumption and demand is the sum of the demands of each individual:

$$C_t = \sum_{j=1}^{l} c_i (R_t, X_{i,t})$$

The other assumptions of the model (explained in the next chapter) allow one to avoid any problem that may derive from tracing out the wealth and income distributions by summing up the consumption and behavior functions of each individual.

Unlike Delli Gatti et al. (2005, 2010), we are not introducing heterogeneous preferences (although we do agree with the fact that preferences' heterogeneity might be a relevant element to explain several macroeconomic stylized facts) because the focus of this book is on the macroeconomic implications of strategic interactions among firms and/or potential entrants (in our model, the workers) and, as a purely logical consequence, this specific concern is better tackled by introducing heterogeneity in the budget constraints instead of the individuals' preferences. Explaining entry or exit as an effect of heterogeneous preferences (i.e., as an effect of a greater or smaller propensity to risk) would look like an "ad hoc" assumption, not suitable to capture the phenomena we intend to describe in our work.

1.2.2 Market Structure

The DSGE framework originally departed from the Real Business Cycle models by introducing some nominal rigidities and monopolistic competition, i.e., a market configuration where the effects of entry/exit are not explicitly modeled and the producers of differentiated goods are formalized as a continuum of firms in the normalized space [0, 1].[1]

For the sake of simplicity, by taking the version with labor only as an input, each firm j has a production function of this kind:

$$c_{j,t} = Z_t N_{j,t} \tag{1.3}$$

where $c_{j,t}$ is the specific output of firm j and Z_t is a normalized random technology shock.

The relative price of the specific product of firm j, emerging from the first order conditions in the firm's decision problem, is a function of the price demand elasticity of the firm specific good, of the firm's real marginal costs and of the probability of "not adjusting the prices" for the specific firm.

By modeling all the firms as a continuum in the unit normalized space, each of the firms is assumed to be infinitesimal, and in this way, the effects of entry/exit of each of these infinitesimal firms cannot affect, by definition, the production capacity of the economy. Such a peculiar modeling feature, a priori, reduces the space and scope for monetary policy (since the magnitude of the entry/exit effect, in spite of being one of the main empirical features of the business cycle, is not computed and normalized to one). Furthermore, in the standard DSGE models, the monetary policy can only affect the "output gap," i.e., the gap between the actual price equilibrium and the benchmark case of flexible prices, although price rigidity and price behavior might be also related, in principle, to the market structure, rather that to a policy-generated equilibrium, unless one introduces some very restrictive assumptions on the strategic interaction among the firms.

Etro and Colciago (2010) introduce a model of business cycle with differentiated goods, market structure, full employment, and

---

[1] See, for instance, the seminal works by McCallum and Nelson (1999), Galí (2002) and Walsh (2017, ch. 8).

different industrial sectors, where two separate benchmark cases of price (Bertrand) competition and quantity (Cournot) competition are extensively analyzed. They show that with no product differentiation and with a unique homogeneous good, markups only survive in the case of quantity (Cournot) competition, while they vanish in the case of price (Bertrand) competition, which degenerates into a conventional real business cycle model. In their model the interaction between business cycle and market structure goes as follows: an exogenous technology shock affects output and consumption, increases profits and, as a consequence, triggers entry. They do not explicitly refer to oligopoly (the word "oligopoly" never actually appears in their paper), and introduce instead a more general framework of "imperfect competition," which may include several sub-cases according to the pricing mechanism and/or to the value of the elasticity of substitution among commodities. In that context, the assumption of full employment and intrasectoral competition, in an economy whose production capacity and potential output is still only driven by technology shocks, amplifies the stochastic technology shocks, which generate changes in the firms' markups and profits and, only as a consequence, entry/exit and market structure endogeneity. Although Etro and Colciago provide an appealing explanation for a number of empirical stylized facts, such as countercyclical markups and pro-cyclical business creation, they do not discuss whether and how can the economic system move from a Cournot to a Bertrand equilibrium or vice versa.

Bilbiie et al. (2012) also introduce entry in a model with the business cycle, but still within the standard and conventional framework of a continuum of monopolistic competitive firms (whose set is normalized in the unit segment), without formalizing the strategic interaction among firms and their macroeconomic implications and with a representative agent that does not display any significant element of heterogeneity.

Gabaix (2011) provides strong evidence for the macroeconomic role of large firms shocks and behavior: while the conventional macroeconomic literature focuses on aggregate shocks, by assuming that idiosyncratic shocks vanish out by aggregating the individual data, he proves instead that individual shocks to large firms generate aggregate macroeconomic fluctuations when large firms account for a large portion of the GDP (like the United States, where in 2010 the sales of the top 100 firms represented 29% of the GDP). He also shows that shocks on large firms output and behavior explain up to one-third of Solow residuals and generate a significant share of aggregate output variance. This result, called by Gabaix "granular" hypothesis (since a relevant portion of output can be associated with "large grains" of economic activity), turns out to be particularly significant when the distribution of firm size is fat-tailed, as empirically documented by Gabaix for the US economy. A fat-tailed statistical distribution for firm size seems to exist not only for the United States, but for many countries and industries, as shown, for instance, by Corbellini et al. (2010) for the Italian manufacturing sectors, whose size is modeled by a "Pareto II" distribution.

Grassi and Carvalho (2015) provide a theoretical model for firms and new entrant dynamic decisions employed as a basis for aggregating individual firms behavior and generalizing Gabaix (2011) contribution. Their calibration, built in a way to match Gabaix (2011) fat tail of firm size distribution, shows that when the number of firms increases, the rate at which aggregate volatility decays is slower than what a central limit argument would predict (i.e., volatility displays a stronger persistence that does not disappear with aggregation if large firms occupy a large market share). Acemoglu et al. (2012) look inside the "black box" of the transmission of the firms idiosyncratic shocks from an individual level to a macroeconomic level by providing a theory of intersectoral input-output linkages entirely consistent with Gabaix (2011) findings. Carvalho and Gabaix (2013) provide a similar kind of result by showing a strong evidence to interpret the data of the US and other four major economies during the "great moderation" and its end with a model that again associates the macroeconomic fluctuations to microeconomic idiosyncratic shocks.

Moreover, our purpose to formalize entry and exit within a macromodel by explicitly endogenizing the market structure requires a change of perspective from the empirical literature in industrial organization and, more in general, from the empirical literature on firms size for several reasons. First of all, the just mentioned class of models is focused on productivity shocks or technology shocks, while our work is focused on another nature of shocks, determined by the strategic interactions among oligopolistic firms in an oligopolistic economy. Secondly, we are ideally proposing a general theory and framework for a macromodel with endogenous market structure that may be adapted to account for specific empirical contexts by introducing specific assumption for detailed contexts.

Entry decisions are, in general, modeled as the outcome of strategic interactions among incumbent and potential entrants, described by game-theoretical models. Aguirregabiria and Mira (2007) provide a method of sequential estimation of dynamic discrete games of incomplete information and introduce, for this purpose, a class of estimators that they call "pseudo maximum likelihood" (PML) estimators, for which they analyze the asymptotic and finite sample properties. For the sake of our theoretical macromodel with endogenous market structure, the use of some specific statistical properties of entry and exit would entail some loss of generality: as Sutton (1998) pointed out, while commenting the results of two decades of Industrial Organization research, the majority of the results emerging in the game-theoretic literature were critically relying on some specific, if not arbitrary, model assumptions introduced by researchers. Looking at specific issues, Sutton (2002) analyzes the link between the firm's size and its growth rate and, in order to interpret the fact that large firms do not seem to be much more stable than small firms, he introduces a model that he calls "partition of integers." This model is further extended in Sutton (2003), while Sutton (2007), investigates the duration of industry leadership and reports an empirical relationship between a firm's current market share and the standard deviation of market share changes by using a Japanese set of 45 industries for 23 years.

A methodologically interesting example of agent based simulation in an oligopolistic market is provided by Weidlich and Veit (2008) analysis of the German electricity market, based on the assumption that markets should be designed by means of engineering tools, such as experimentation and computation, instead of statistical assumptions. In their framework, agent-based modeling methodology offers the flexibility suitable to specify complex scenarios for market analysis and decision making.

The specificity of these empirical analyses and results, extremely relevant for the research shows in any case a different perspective from the one of this book, focused, as we said, on the construction of a general macroeconomic framework with endogenous market structure rather than firms' size statistical analysis.

1.2.3 Expectations and Implications for the Simulations

Our model does not deviate from the notion of rational expectations, but recalls instead its original interpretation of a prediction "on average" correct expressed by the market. Of course, in conventional models this idea does not rule out the idiosyncratic prediction mistakes, modeled as an additive stochastic shock with zero mean. We use the same concept in slightly different formulation, by stating that the individuals' expectations are modeled as a frequency distribution, whose average correctly predicts the relevant variables, but where each individual's predictions are interpreted as a distribution of individual idiosyncratic information random shocks. The individuals can be workers, or new entrant entrepreneurs, or incumbent entrepreneurs, or unemployed, and may change their status due to informational shocks associated with the process of entry and exit and to prediction mistakes. It is assumed that there is skill loss, so that the individuals who have been unemployed lose their skills to become entrepreneurs, which means that the only potential entrants are the current workers, who can also observe the production process of their firms. The decision of entry consists of comparing the expected value of their future expected income as workers and their future expected income as entrepreneurs. On average, all the workers formulate correct expectations on the expected value of their income as workers and their potential income as entrepreneurs if they decide to enter the market. However, although the average expectation of all the workers are correct, some workers are more optimistic (and expect higher incomes than the average expectation as entrepreneurs if they decide to enter the market) and some workers are pessimistic (and therefore believe they are better off as workers and do not enter the market).

In other words, the probability of entry (which can be considered as the information shock that triggers entry) can be interpreted as follows:

$$\Pr(\text{entry})_t = \int_0^{n_t(1-h_t)} \Pr(w_t < E_{t-1,i}(\Phi_t))_i di$$

where $n_t(1 - h_t)$ is the number of workers (potential entrants), since n_t is the total amount of employed individuals and h_t is the fraction of entrepreneurs over the employed individuals; w_t is the wage (set before the entry decision is taken) and $E_{t-1,i}(\Phi_t)$ is the idiosyncratic expectation of the worker i, in case she decides to enter the market and become an entrepreneur. We assume that the expectations expressed by the whole of workers are correct (and in this sense we do accept the notion of rational expectations) but we interpret the expectations as a frequency distribution.

The way one models expectational shocks carries significant implications for the interpretation of macroeconomic fluctuations. In this paper, informational shocks on workers' expectations determine entry, while in conventional models the expectations are associated with the behavior of the aggregate demand. Lorenzoni (2009) introduces a model of business cycles driven by shocks to consumer expectations regarding aggregate productivity and where the agents are hit by heterogeneous productivity shocks: they observe their own productivity and a noisy public signal regarding aggregate productivity, and these "noise shocks," mimic the features of aggregate demand shocks. News shocks (together with other shocks) are the focus of Jaimovich and Rebelo (2009) model, which generates both aggregate and sectorial co-movement in response to both contemporaneous shocks and news shocks about fundamentals.

The issue of interaction between market structure and entry/exit decisions lead by the agents' expectations in a macromodel is not an exclusive concern of large industries and large firms. For instance, Dunne et al. (2013) empirically analyze the short-run and long-run dynamics of an oligopolistic sector and the role of entry costs and toughness of short-run price competition, by using micro data for the US dentists and chiropractors industries, certainly not two sectors characterized by giant firms.

The modeling features are discussed in detail in the next chapter; however, it may be useful to anticipate and introduce a few points in the present discussion.

The aggregate demand is microfounded and explicitly modeled as the sum of the individual demand functions. The way the aggregate demand is formulated allows to account (although in a simplified way) for the wealth distribution and income distribution among workers, incumbent entrepreneurs, new entrant entrepreneurs and unemployed. As shown in the next chapter, this specific modeling feature derives from assuming that the agents are heterogeneous in their budget constraints.

The number of workers, entrepreneur or unemployed individuals is logically connected to the process of entry/exit, determined by information shocks and may potentially generate (as a consequence) distributional shocks on the aggregate demand. In the model it is assumed that the workers are potential entrants and are perceived as such by the incumbent entrepreneurs; this generates an interaction between the labor market equilibrium and the entry/exit decisions. This last assumption aims at characterizing our model as a general equilibrium model unless we had a price frequency distribution (with different prices set by different oligopolistic firms.) In this sense, since the law of one price does not applies to our model, on the one hand we avoid to a great deal the typical DSGE problem of not having a unidirectional causal structure within the period (and ambiguity of events time ordering), since in DSGE the endogenous variables are the solution of a system of simultaneous equations. On the other hand, the very nature of our microfoundation, with heterogeneous agents in their budget constraints and the assumption that agents' expectations are modeled as a distribution whose mean corresponds to the rational expectations, is clearly more consistent with an agent based computational economics approach than with numerical equations simulations. This is what we are going to do, after introducing in detail the theoretical model, in the next chapter.

2 | Industrial Structure and the Macroeconomy: The Macroeconomic Model and Its Algebraic Framework

MARCO MAZZOLI[1]

2.1 Introduction

The previous chapter introduced the rationale and premises for the theoretical model of this book, which is based on the idea that in a world of large corporations, with economies characterized by oligopolistic industries, the equilibrium emerging among oligopolistic firms may carry significant macroeconomic implications. The birth and death of firms are some of the most relevant empirical phenomena in the business cycle, and our model is microfounding the strategic interactions among the firms in a macroeconomic system with oligopolistic features, without referring to the simplifying assumptions of monopolistic competition that characterize most DSGE models. To the extent that very large firms play a relevant role in an oligopolistic economic system, not modeling their interactions would leave aside a big part of the story, ignoring causal links between the industrial structure and the macroeconomy.

The interdependence between the sectorial rates of entry and exit is a well-established empirical fact in the applied research on industry dynamics, as shown by Manjón-Antolín (2010), among others, and this model provides a general theoretical framework where the interdependence between entry and exit is a sub-case that may be reproduced and traced out in a microfounded macroeconomic context.

The model introduced here plugs the entry/exit decisions into a macroeconomic system by using a notion of statistical distribution of expectations that is consistent with the idea of rational expectations

---

[1] I would like to dedicate this chapter to the memory of Prof. Keith Cowling (1936–2016), a long-standing economist at the University of Warwick. His course "Industrial Structure and the Macroeconomy" has been a great source of inspiration for many PhD students of my generation at Warwick. It has been a great privilege and honor for me to be one of them.

(at least in its original formulation) to model the entry decision of potential entrants. The theoretical framework that we are going to introduce is also useful for analyzing, on a theoretical ground, the behavior of firms' markups over the cycle and is employed for the agent-based simulations contained in the chapters that follow. In particular, we model a macroeconomic system with oligopoly, entry/exit and heterogeneous individuals.

The individuals are heterogeneous in their budget constraints: they can be workers, or new entrant entrepreneurs, or incumbent entrepreneurs or unemployed and may change their status due to informational shocks associated with the process of entry and exit and with prediction mistakes. The aggregate demand is microfounded and explicitly modeled as the sum of the individual demands. Diverging incentives between oligopolistic firms and heterogeneous agents are also explicitly modeled: in particular, entry is determined by informational shocks randomly affecting some workers. Entry and exit respectively generate or eliminate new entrepreneurs who have to hire workers in order to produce and are therefore associated with a change in the social status of the individuals. In this sense the model provides a theoretical interpretation of the links among entry/exit, social mobility and the macroeconomy.

This is rendered by a particular modeling feature, consisting of the fact that the labor market interacts with the process of entry/exit, since the latter has the obvious consequence of determining the number of employed people (number of existing firms hiring workers) and, consequently, macroeconomic fluctuations.

The aggregate demand is explicitly determined by the sum of individual demand functions, and also explicitly takes into account (although in a simplified way) the distribution of financial wealth, since the agents are heterogeneous in their budget constraints.

The number of workers, entrepreneurs or unemployed individuals is logically connected to the process of entry/exit, determined by information shocks and may potentially generate (as a consequence) distributional shocks on the aggregate demand. In this regard, it is assumed that the workers are potential entrants and are perceived as such by the incumbent entrepreneurs: this generates an interaction between the labor market equilibrium and the entry/exit decisions. This last assumption characterizes this model as a general equilibrium model.

Bertoletti and Etro (2016), in a context of partial equilibrium, provide an approach where, for given technological conditions and for the three cases of monopolistic competition, where, for given technological conditions and for the three cases of monopolistic competition, both Cournot competition (in quantities) and Bertrand competition (in prices) endogenize some elements of the market structure. Differently from the contribution by Bertoletti and Etro (2016), we do not provide a partial equilibrium analysis and assume that the firms' decisions and strategies may determine a macroeconomic impact and obtain feedback from the macroeconomic equilibrium. Finally, while in Bertoletti and Etro (2016) the Cournot and Bertrand benchmarks are basically consistent with pure strategies equilibria in a game among the existing firms, our Cournot oligopolistic equilibrium in the goods market has the nature of an equilibrium in mixed strategies, since the purpose of our research is to track out the macroeconomic impact of the unpredictable outcome (i.e., stochastic shocks) of the rivalry among the oligopolistic firms. In particular, our model explicitly links the Cournot and Bertrand equilibria by assuming quantity precommitments. The oligopolistic firms produce a homogeneous good, and the individuals cannot be workers and entrepreneurs at the same time but may change their status as a consequence of different kinds of stochastic shocks. Introducing in a macromodel the assumption of quantity (Cournot) competition might raise the problem of how prices are determined without referring to an auctioneer or, equivalently, what prevents the firms from implementing price undercutting. We solve this problem by assuming an oligopolistic industrial sector with quantity precommitment à la Kreps and Scheinkman (1983), with the modified and extended assumptions provided by Madden (1998) We use Madden (1998) existence theorem of a Cournot-Nash equilibrium in mixed strategies to formalize the stochastic nature of the firms' markups, explained as follows.

2.2 The Algebraic Derivation of the Aggregate Demand

Since we are modeling an economy with an oligopolistic industrial sector, the producers choose a point along the demand curve, and, given their outputs and their production decisions, they determine, at the same time, their profits. The individual demand functions are derived from (and therefore consistent with) the optimizing behavior of the consumers, and the aggregate demand function is explicitly modeled as the aggregation of the individual demands as shown in the next section.

The banking and financial sector is modeled in a simplified way or, should we say, with a degree of simplification (in particular, the way banking and financial intermediaries are modeled) broadly corresponding to the first-generation DSGE models, such as represented by Galí (2008) or Walsh (2017, ch. 8).

The nominal variable A_t at time t, here defined as "financial assets," does not include the firm ownership, and, for the sake of simplicity, it is assumed to be risk free. It includes government bonds and deposits (i.e., it corresponds to M3). We also assume that deposits are remunerated and that the interest rate on risk-free government bonds is equal to the interest rate on deposits, since they are both assumed to be risk-free financial assets. The monetary policy consists of interest rate setting. Exogenous changes in the money stock can be easily formalized as changes in the nominal amount of risk-free financial assets, since M3 is a function of the money base, but they will not be considered in this work. Since the focus of this model is not on the financial sector of the economy, in order to simplify the algebra, we may assume that the banking sector instantaneously performs all the transactions among individuals, with no specific need for cash. The banking system charges the transactions concerning all the individuals' incomes (excepting the transactions concerning consumption of the unemployed individuals, performed by spending the lump-sum tax that covers all the unemployment subsidies) a transaction, fee ς. ς is a constant portion of all the transactions, and its magnitude is extremely small compared to all the other parameters and variables of the model. These transaction fees (that may also be interpreted as banking commissions) represent the cost of banks' intermediation and, in this model with a perfectly competitive banking and financial sector, determine the income of the banking and financial sector, so that the interest rate on bank lending at time t is equal to the nominal interest rate R_t (r_t in real terms) on the asset A_t, exogenously controlled by the policy makers. The banking sector perfectly diversifies its lending risk to the firms, and any risk of financial distress is handled by the lender of last resort, although the monetary authorities are not in the focus of our analysis.

The entrepreneurs can be incumbent, earning at time $t+i$ the incumbent nominal profits Π_{t+i}^{in} (Π_{t+i}^{inR} in real terms) or new entrants, earning the new entrant nominal profits Π_{t+i}^{e} (Π_{t+i}^{eR} in real terms). Π_{t+i}^{e}, in general, diverges from Π_{t+i}^{in} because the new entrants bear some entry costs (as explained later). All the agents have the same preferences (i.e., their preferences are represented by the same utility function), but their main source of earnings may be divergent and be given either by wages, or profits or transferals to the unemployed individuals, assumed to be financed, for the sake of simplicity, by a nominal lump sum τ (τ_R in real terms).

The entrepreneurs hire the workers for the period going from t to $t+1$ and pay them the nominal wages W_t. They also pay themselves the same nominal wage W_t (w_t in real terms) and get the residual nominal profits, so that the remuneration for the entrepreneurs is W_t plus Π_{t+i}^{in} if the entrepreneur is an incumbent or W_t plus Π_{t+i}^{e} if she is a new entrant. When $\Pi_{t+i}^{in} < 0$ or $\Pi_{t+i}^{e} < 0$, (or, equivalently, as shown below $\Pi_{t+i}^{inR} < 0$ and $\Pi_{t+i}^{eR} < 0$), the incumbent or the new entrant for the period going from t to $t + 1$ goes bankrupt (which happens with a probability to be specified later), the entrepreneur and the workers become unemployed and, until they are hired again by a new firm, they receive a transferal given by a portion of the total unemployment subsidies, entirely financed by a lump-sum tax τ on the incomes of the employed individuals. We assume that the labor contract is such that each worker receives the nominal wage W_t for the period going from $t + i$ to $t + i + 1$, for a fixed amount of hours of work. Let l be the total labor force (assumed to be exogenous and constant), n_{t+i} the number of employed individuals at time $t + i$, h_{t+i}^{in} (with $0 < h_{t+i}^{in} < h_{t+i}$) the portion of incumbent entrepreneurs at time $t + i$ and h_{t+i}^{e} (with $0 < h_{t+i}^{e} < 1$) the portion of new entrants at time $t + i$ (with $h_{t+i} = h_{t+i}^{in} + h_{t+i}^{e}$ and $0 < h_{t+i} < h_{t+i}$). This means that the portion of workers over the total employed labor force is given by $1 - h_{t+i}^{in} - h_{t+i}^{e} = 1 - h_{t+i}$.

$(n_{t+i}W_{t+i} + n_{t+i}h_{t+i}^{in}\Pi_{t+i}^{in} + n_{t+i}h_{t+i}^{e}\Pi_{t+i}^{e})\varsigma$ are the transaction fees to the banking system at time $t + i$, since each employed individual pays a nominal lump-sum tax τ (τ_R in real terms) to finance the unemployment subsidies. $n_{t+i}\tau_R(1 - \varsigma)$ is the overall amount of real unemployment subsidies (net of the transaction fees to the banking system). We assume that τ_R and ς are constant and very small in their magnitude, so that τ_R is assumed to barely cover the survival expenses of the unemployed individuals.

The model displays a form of skill loss: being an entrepreneur requires some skills that are lost by not working and being unemployed for one period or more. On the other hand, being a worker is not assumed to require any particular skill. On the basis of our assumptions, we may simplify out the effects of tax transferals and bank commissions and formalize the aggregate demand as follows:

$$Y_{t+i} = n_{t+i}(W_{t+i} + h_{t+i}^{in}\Pi_{t+i}^{in} + h_{t+i}^{e}\Pi_{t+i}^{e} - \tau)(1 - \varsigma) +$$

$$+ n_{t+i}\tau(1 - \varsigma) + n_{t+i}(W_{t+i} + h_{t+i}^{in}\Pi_{t+i}^{in} + h_{t+i}^{e}\Pi_{t+i}^{e})\varsigma$$

$$Y_{t+i} = n_{t+i}(W_{t+i} + h_{t+i}^{in}\Pi_{t+i}^{in} + h_{t+i}^{e}\Pi_{t+i}^{e}) \tag{2.1}$$

What is needed, for the sake of our model, is a proper formalization of an aggregate demand function, and we model it in such a way that it is explicitly formalized as the aggregation of the individual demands expressed by each consumer. We also explicitly show that such individual demands are consistent with (and therefore derived from) the optimizing behavior of the consumers.

We derive and microfound the aggregate demand in a rather conventional way, based on a standard optimization problem of the consumer. Given the overall forward-looking preferences $U_{j,t}$ for the generic consumer j, and defining the utility in each period t as $u(c_{j,t})$, a function of the amount of goods consumed for time t, we can now turn to the individual consumer problem, which is very similar to the one presented in (Bagliano and Bertola, 2004, ch.1). Its purpose is to define a microfounded aggregate demand, explicitly formalized as the aggregation of the individual demand functions of each consumer. Let us assume that the preferences of the individuals are represented by a CRRA utility function and the consumer problem is formalized as a standard intertemporal optimization problem:

$$\max U_t = E_t \left[\sum_{i=0}^{\infty} \left(\frac{1}{1+\rho} \right)^i u(c_{j,t+i}) \right] \tag{2.2}$$

$$c_{j,t+i}, i = 0, 1, \ldots, \infty \tag{2.3}$$

subject to the following constraint, where, as usual for the dynamic models, the interest rate is introduced in nominal terms,

$$E(b_{j,t+i+1}) = (1 + R_{t+i})E(b_{j,t+i}) + E(y_{j,t+i}) - c_{j,t+i} \tag{2.4}$$

and

$$c_{j,t+i} \geq 0$$

at every time $t + i$ from $i = 0, 1, \ldots, \infty$, where:

- $\left(\frac{1}{1+\rho}\right)$ is the subjective discount factor;
- R_t is the nominal interest rate on the financial asset at time t (controlled by the central bank);
- $c_{j,t}$ is the real consumption at time t for the consumers (defined as $c_{j,t} = C_{j,t}/P_t$, with $C_{j,t}$ as the nominal consumption and P_t as the price level at time t);
- $y_{j,t}$ is the consumer j's real income (defined as $y_{j,t} = Y_{j,t}/P_t$, where $Y_{j,t}$ is the nominal income at time t) and $b_{j,t}$ is the real financial wealth held by the individual consumer j at time t (again defined as $b_{j,t} = B_{j,t}/P_t$, with $B_{j,t}$ as the nominal financial wealth at time t), which may be defined as a random portion δ_j of the aggregate real wealth $a_{j,t}$ (i.e., $b_{j,t} = \delta_j a_{j,t}$ with $0 < \delta_j < 1$), so that summing up to all the l individuals, we have $\sum_j \delta_j a_{j,t} = a_{j,t}$ and $\sum_j \delta_j = 1$.

The price level P_t at time t is, of course, a macroeconomic variable also allowing one to determine the link between nominal and real variables and is the average of the frequency distribution of all the prices set by the oligopolistic firms.

The financial assets are risk free and do not include shares: in this simplified model, investing in shares is a time-consuming activity and implies being an entrepreneur. The budget constraint (2.4) also holds for any time $i = 0, 1, \ldots, \infty$. The transversality condition is as follows:

$$\lim_{j \to \infty} b_{t+j} \left(\frac{1}{1 + R_{t+j}}\right)^j \geq 0$$

Since the marginal utility of consumption is always positive, the transversality condition is always satisfied in terms of equality. The financial wealth $b_{j,t}$ and the individual human capital (let us define it $g_{j,t}$) are assumed to be valued at the beginning of period t, while $X_{j,t} = (1 + R_t)(b_{j,t} + g_{j,t})$ represents the individual total wealth, which is valued at the end of period t, but before consumption $c_{j,t}$, that absorbs part of the available resources. We also assume that both profits and wages are paid at the end of the period, when consumption takes place. The human capital valued at the beginning of time t is

$$g_{j,t} = \frac{1}{(1 + R_t)} \sum_{i=0}^{\infty} \left(\frac{1}{1 + E_t(R_{t+i})} \right)^i E_t(y_{j,t+i}) \tag{2.5}$$

and, as above,

$$X_{j,t} = (1 + R_t)(b_{j,t} + g_{j,t}) \tag{2.6}$$

hence

$$E_t(X_{j,t+1}) = (1 + R_t) \cdot$$
$$\cdot \left[E_t(b_{j,t+1}) + \frac{1}{(1 + R_t)} \cdot \right.$$
$$\left. \cdot \sum_{i=0}^{\infty} \left(\frac{1}{1 + E_t(R_{t+i})} \right)^i E_t(y_{j,t+1+i}) \right] \tag{2.7}$$

Substituting in the budget constraint the definition of $b_{j,t+1}$, we get:

$$E(X_{j,t+1}) = (1 + R_t)[(1 + R_t)b_{j,t} + y_{j,t} - c_{j,t+i} +$$
$$+ \frac{1}{(1 + R_t)} \sum_{i=0}^{\infty} \left(\frac{1}{1 + E_t(R_{t+i})} \right)^i E_t(y_{j,t+1+i})]$$

Hence

$$E(X_{j,t+1}) = \left[(1 + R_t)(b_{j,t} + g_{j,t}) - c_{j,t+i} \right]$$
$$= (1 + R_t)(X_{j,t} - c_{j,t+i})$$

and, generalizing,

$$E(X_{j,t+i+1}) = (1 + R_{t+i})(X_{j,t+i} - c_{j,t+i})$$

where $X_{j,t+i+1}$ is the state variable.

$$g_{j,t} = \frac{1}{(1 + R_t)} \sum_{i=0}^{\infty} \left(\frac{1}{1 + E_t(R_{t+i})} \right)^i E_t(y_{j,t+i}) \tag{2.8}$$

where, again, summing up over the all population, we get the aggregate human wealth G_t (i.e., $\sum g_{j,t} = G_t$) and, as above,

$$X_{j,t} = (1 + R_t)(b_{j,t} + g_{j,t}) \tag{2.9}$$

where $X_{j,t}$ is the overall (human and financial) wealth of the individual j at time t. Like in (Bagliano and Bertola, 2004, ch. 1), it is assumed that consumption takes place at the end of each period.

Let us assume now that the instantaneous utility is represented by the following function:

$$u_{j,t} = \frac{c_{j,t}^{1-\gamma}}{1-\gamma} \tag{2.10}$$

with $0 < \gamma < 1$.

Therefore the consumer problem boils down to the following Bellman and Euler equations, respectively:

$$V(X_{j,t}) = \max_{c_{j,t}} \left[\frac{c_{j,t}^{1-\gamma}}{1-\gamma} + \left(\frac{1}{1+\rho} \right) E(V(X_{j,t+1})) \right] \tag{2.11}$$

$$u'\left(c_{j,t}\right) = \frac{1+R_t}{1+\rho} E_t u'_{j,t}\left(c_{j,t+1}\right) \tag{2.12}$$

subject to

$$E(X_{t+1}) = (1+R_t)(X_t - c_{j,t}) \tag{2.13}$$

where X_{t+i+1} is the state variable.

Now we assume (and later prove) that the value function has the same analytical form of the utility function, i.e.,

$$V(X_{j,t}) = \Theta \frac{X_{j,t}^{1-\gamma}}{1-\gamma} \tag{2.14}$$

where Θ is a positive constant whose exact value will be shown later. By using the definition of $V(\omega_t)$ (2.14), the Bellman equation can be rewritten as follows:

$$\Theta \frac{X_{j,t}^{1-\gamma}}{1-\gamma} = \max_{c_t} \left[\frac{X_{j,t}^{1-\gamma}}{1-\gamma} + \frac{1}{1+\rho} E \left(\Theta \frac{X_{j,t}^{1-\gamma}}{1-\gamma} \right) \right] \tag{2.15}$$

Hence, using the constraint (2.13) and deriving with respect to $c_{j,t}$, we get the first order condition:

$$c_{j,t}^{-\gamma} = \frac{1+R_t}{1+\rho} \Theta \left[(1+R_t)(X_{j,t} - c_{j,t}) \right]^{-\gamma}$$

and solving for $c_{j,t}$, we get the individual consumption (demand) function:

$$c_{j,t} = \frac{1}{1 + (1+R_t)^{\frac{1-\gamma}{\gamma}} (1+\rho)^{-\frac{1}{\gamma}} \Theta^{\frac{1}{\gamma}}} X_{j,t}$$

where Θ is the constant to be determined.

To complete the solution, we still use the Bellman equation (2.15), substitute the consumption function in it and we set:

$$M \equiv (1 + R_t)^{\frac{1-\gamma}{\gamma}} (1 + \rho)^{-\frac{1}{\gamma}}$$

just to simplify the notation. Then we get:

$$\Theta \frac{X_{j,t}^{1-\gamma}}{1 - \gamma} = \frac{1}{1 - \gamma} \overbrace{\left(\frac{X_{j,t}}{1 + M\Theta^{\frac{1}{\gamma}}} \right)^{1-\gamma}}^{c_{j,t}} + \qquad (2.16)$$

$$+ \frac{1}{1 + \rho} \frac{\Theta_t}{1 - \gamma} \underbrace{\left[(1 + R_t) \frac{M\Theta^{\frac{1}{\gamma}}}{1 + M\Theta^{\frac{1}{\gamma}}} X_{j,t} \right]^{1-\gamma}}_{X_{j,t+1}}$$

The value of Θ satisfying equation (2.16) can be obtained by equating the coefficients of $X_{j,t}^{1-\gamma}$ in the two sides of the equation and solving for Θ:

$$\Theta = \left(\frac{1}{1 - M} \right)^{\gamma}$$

Under the condition $M < 1$, the consumption (expenditure) function is fully specified:

$$V(X_{j,t}) = \left(\frac{1}{1 - (1 + R_t)^{\frac{1-\gamma}{\gamma}} (1 + \rho)^{-\frac{1}{\gamma}}} \right)^{\gamma} \frac{X_{j,t}^{1-\gamma}}{1 - \gamma}$$

and

$$c(R_t, X_{j,t}) = \left[1 - (1 + R_t)^{\frac{1-\gamma}{\gamma}} (1 + \rho)^{-\frac{1}{\gamma}} \right] X_{j,t}$$

i.e.,

$$c(X_{j,t}) = \left[1 - (1 + R_t)^{\frac{1-\gamma}{\gamma}} (1 + \rho)^{-\frac{1}{\gamma}} \right] (b_{j,t} + g_{j,t})$$

where $c(w_t)$ can be interpreted as the individual demand function, i.e.,

$$c(R_t, X_{j,t}) = D_t(R_t, X_{j,t}) = \left[1 - (1 + R_t)^{\frac{1-\gamma}{\gamma}} (1 + \rho)^{-\frac{1}{\gamma}} \right] (b_{j,t} + g_{j,t})$$

$$(2.17)$$

Recalling that $b_{j,t} = \delta_{j,t} a_t$ and summing up for all the individuals, we have:

$$
\begin{aligned}
C_t &= \sum_{j=1}^{l} c_i(R_t, X_{i,t}) \\
&= \sum_{i=1}^{l} \left[1 - (1 + R_t)^{\frac{1-\gamma}{\gamma}} (1 + \rho)^{-\frac{1}{\gamma}} \right] (\delta_{i,t} a_t + g_{j,t}) \\
&= \left[1 - (1 + R_t)^{\frac{1-\gamma}{\gamma}} (1 + \rho)^{-\frac{1}{\gamma}} \right] \sum_{i=1}^{l} (\delta_{i,t} a_t + g_{j,t}) \\
&= \left[1 - (1 + R_t)^{\frac{1-\gamma}{\gamma}} (1 + \rho)^{-\frac{1}{\gamma}} \right] (a_t + G_t) \\
&= \left[1 - (1 + R_t)^{\frac{1-\gamma}{\gamma}} (1 + \rho)^{-\frac{1}{\gamma}} \right] W_t
\end{aligned}
$$

where W_t is the aggregate overall wealth. This is the aggregate demand.

We can rearrange the aggregate demand $D_t(\cdot)$ in order to account for income distribution and expected future variables, under rather general assumptions. Let us start by defining

$$
\Omega = \left[1 - (1 + R_t)^{\frac{1-\gamma}{\gamma}} (1 + \rho)^{-\frac{1}{\gamma}} \right]
$$

since ρ is constant and $0 < \gamma < 1$, then $\partial C(\cdot)/\partial R_t < 0$.

Defining the aggregate real income as y_{t+i}, we may write the aggregate demand as follows:

$$
D(\cdot)_t = \Omega(R_t) \left(a_t + \frac{1}{1 + R_t} \sum_{i=0}^{\infty} \left(\frac{1}{1 + E(R_{t+i})} \right)^i E(y_{t+i}) \right)
$$

Since we have

$$
\begin{aligned}
1 + R_t &= (1 + r_t)(1 + E(\iota_{t+i})) \\
a_t &= A_t / P_t \\
y_t &= Y_t / P_t
\end{aligned}
$$

if we make a temporary assumption that for each future time $t + i$, we have $E(P_{t+i}) = P_t$, we may re-write the aggregate demand function as follows:

$$D(\cdot)_t = \frac{\Omega(R_t)}{P_t} \left(A_t + \frac{1}{(1+R_t)} \sum_{i=0}^{\infty} \left(\frac{1}{1+E(R_{t+i})} \right)^i E(Y_{t+i}) \right)$$

(2.18)

which is a unit elastic aggregate demand function, where A_t is the nominal aggregate financial wealth and Y_t is the nominal aggregate income.

The reader might remark that if one assumed that the future expected price level had an increasing trend instead of being a stationary variable, we write the aggregate demand in the following way:

$$D(\cdot)_t = \frac{\Omega(R_t)}{P_t} (A_t + \frac{1}{(1+E(r_t))(1+E(\iota_{t+1}))} \cdot$$

(2.19)

$$\cdot \sum_{i=0}^{\infty} \left(\frac{1}{(1+E(r_{t+i}))(1+E(\iota_{t+i+1}))} \right)^i E(Y_t)(1+E(\iota_{t+i}))$$

where $E(\iota_t)$ is the expected inflation rate for time t and r_t is the real interest rate for time t.

We further assume that the expected inflation of all the individuals is defined as a "core inflation," contingent on the existing monetary policy regime. To the extent that the policy regime is not modified (even though temporary, short-run policy intervention might occur within a given policy regime), the "core inflation" (i.e., the expected inflation) is going to be constant. Indeed the other element suitable to affect the future inflation, the outcome of the interaction among the oligopolistic firms and its impact on the future price levels, could be positive or negative. Therefore, assuming that the expected future inflation is contingent on the monetary policy regime (and will not change unless the monetary policy regime is modified) is consistent with the idea that the individuals observe the past outcomes of the games among the oligopolistic firms, which determine (jointly with the aggregate demand) the price level, and the individuals consequently formulate their expectations of the long run inflation level, the "core inflation" ι. The current observable inflation may certainly deviate from the "core inflation" due to stochastic shocks (since the actual outcome of the rivalry among the oligopolistic firms may positively or negatively affect the price level), but the expectations of the "core inflation" are assumed to reflect the inflation target, which is common knowledge, since it is publicly announced by the authorities and is assumed (for the sake of our model, in this version) to be credible. The "core inflation" ι is therefore constant under a given monetary policy regime and henceforth we simply define it ι.

Equation (2.19) can be useful if we want to study the impact of monetary policy and future inflation path on the aggregate demand. However, for the time being, we refer to equation (2.18).

For what concerns the future values of the real income and nominal income, we have to take into account that they are affected by several elements: first of all, the outcome of the interactions among the oligopolistic firms (which jointly determine output quantities and prices); secondly, the expected inflation; thirdly, the decisions of the monetary authorities, who are not almighty, not omniscient, not present in each human heart and may only interact with all the subjects of the economy. Assuming the expected future aggregate real income to be equal to the current observable aggregate, real income is only one of the numerous assumptions we could make, and probably one of the most simplified ones. We could begin enriching the scenario by introducing some elements that affect the future value of the real and nominal aggregate income, i.e., the profits of the new entrants, the profits of the incumbents (both determined by the interactions in the oligopolistic goods market) and the wages. Therefore we may rewrite the aggregate demand function in the following way:

$$D(\cdot)_t = \frac{\Omega(R_t)}{P_t}\{A_t + ((1+r_t)(1+\iota)^{-1} \sum_{i=0}^{\infty}[(1 + E\,(r_{t+i})\,(1 + \iota)]^{-i} \cdot$$
$$\cdot E(n_{t+i}(W_{t+i} + h_{t+i}^e \Pi_{t+i}^e + h_{t+i}^{in} \Pi_{t+i}^{in}))\} \qquad (2.20)$$

That formulation is equivalent to (2.18), but, in addition:

a) it allows to account for the income distribution new entrant entrepreneurs, incumbent entrepreneurs and workers;
b) it is a unit elastic aggregate demand function in nominal terms.

The second property turns out to be extremely useful in determining the equilibrium among oligopolistic firms.

Let us begin, however, by keeping things as simple as possible and assume that the "core inflation" is null. This assumption can be easily removed for further analyses.

Let us define now the following notation, for a "shift parameter" in the aggregate demand curve:

$$\Psi_t = \sum_{i=0}^{\infty} (1 + E(R_{t+i}))^{-i} \cdot$$
$$\cdot E[n_{t+i}(W_{t+i} + h_{t+i}^e E(\Pi_{t+i}^e) + h_{t+i}^{in} E(\Pi_{t+i}^{in}))] \qquad (2.21)$$

The parameter Ψ_t, in other words, contains all the elements that might generate parallel shifts in the aggregate demand and may be affected by:

a) changes in the current or future expected monetary policy (i.e., changes in the current nominal interest rate R_t or in its future expected value R_{t+i} respectively);
b) changes in the expected inflation, affecting both the nominal interest rate and the nominal variables in the square brackets;
c) distributional shocks that may be generated by entry/exit or diverging incentives among workers and entrepreneurs.

The algebraic properties of the shift parameter Ψ_t turn out to be useful to analyze the nature of the various shocks affecting the model.

2.3 The Firms

The firms operate under regime of oligopoly by using the same production technology and produce the same generic good.

We assume that starting a new firm requires entrepreneurial skills (that are lost after being unemployed for at least one period) and exogenous nominal sunk costs of entry F (organizational costs and setting up costs) that the new entrant entrepreneur has to support just before entering the market.

We assume that only labor is employed in the production process, although the model can be extended by including capital. Because of skill loss, only the workers can enter the market as new entrepreneurs and are therefore perceived by the incumbents as potential entrants.

The labor contract establishes a fixed number of working hours for each worker, i.e., hiring a worker implies hiring a fixed number of working hours for the firm. This means that labor also is a sunk cost. The oligopolistic firms enter a two-stage game à la Kreps and Scheinkman (1983) with the modifications provided by Madden (1998), who extends the Kreps and Scheinkman (1983) results to the case of a uniformly elastic demand function.

Section 2.9 shows the conditions for the existence of a Cournot-Nash equilibrium in mixed strategies among the oligopolistic firms and also shows that these conditions are met by the assumptions of our model.

Let $\varphi_{i,t}$ be the individual real output planned by firm i at time t, and let the production function employed by each be the following:

$$\varphi_{i,t} = \Lambda L_{i,t}^{\alpha} + \psi_{i,t} \tag{2.22}$$

The production function is a Cobb-Douglas with labor only, where L_t is the (discrete) number of workers employed by the firm i at time t for the period from t to $t + 1$, Λ is the usual technology parameter, ψ_t is a discrete random variable with 0 average and uniform distribution containing the information on two stochastic phenomena: the first one is the stochastic nature of a mixed-strategy Cournot-Nash equilibrium existing among the oligopolistic firms. The second one is an "implementation" shock acting in the following way: the oligopolistic firms enter a two-stage game (briefly described in the next sections), where in the first stage they decide the amount of workers to employ (which determines a quantity pre-commitment), and in the second stage, the equilibrium price and output commitment. The output commitment is not necessarily the actual amount of output produced by the firm: it is just a contractual commitment that the firm undertakes with its customers, to provide them with an agreed quantity of output. Between the commitment and the actual production and delivery of the goods, unpredictable episodes of conflict with the workers might occur and prevent the firm to fulfill the contract and deliver the agreed amount of commodity to the customers. When this happens, some transactions with some customers do not take place, some of the customers get less commodities than planned and the firm sells less commodities than agreed. This detail (together with the stochastic nature of the mixed strategy equilibrium among the oligopolistic firms) is described by the stochastic variable ψ_t. The firms that suffer from the implementation shock are, in other words, getting a negative stochastic shock to their profits, because they sell less commodities than they were willing to.

As a consequence, other firms sell more than expected and get higher profits.

The firms first serve the customers with whom they have a commitment, then, residually, serve any possible residual customer whose demand was not satisfied because of the "negative implementation shock." The potential additional demand unexpectedly addressed to the "lucky" firms generates a random positive shock in their prices and profits, i.e., the firms can be affected by a shock that may be positive (for the "lucky" firms) or negative, and we model it as a uniform random variable with zero average.

For the sake of numerical simulations, in aggregate terms, we do have a macroeconomic ex post price level, which simply is the average market price.

The existence of the (positive or negative) production shock, that we define as $\psi_{i,t}$, is explicitly considered by the firms in their production function, allowing us to define the nominal aggregate output:

$$Y_t = P_t \Lambda \sum_{i=1}^{H_t} (L_{i,t}^{\alpha} + \psi_{i,t})$$

where P_t is the aggregate price level, which is the weighted average of the prices set by the individual oligopolistic firms. Since $\psi_{i,t}$ has a zero average,

$$E(Y_t) = P_t \Lambda \sum_{i=1}^{H_t} L_{i,t}^{\alpha} \tag{2.23}$$

Instead of the usual technology shocks, we do have here "implementation shocks" on the real output, arising both from the stochastic nature of a mixed strategy equilibrium in a game among the firms (as shown in the next section) and by "inside the firm" conflicts. They are conceptually different, but empirically similar.

Let us define the number of existing firms as $H_t = n_t h_t$, the new entrants as $H_t^e = n_t h_t^e$ and the incumbent as $H_t^{in} = n_t h_t^{in}$.

Since entry and exit modify the number of existing firms, this affects the production capacity. At any generic point t in time, we have $(H_t^e + H_t^{in})$ firms in the market. In this oligopolistic economy, there are exogenous fixed costs of entry F (F_R in real terms), which can be thought of as organizational costs and setting up costs; contrary to

Etro and Colciago (2010), we assume that the entry costs are given by the stock price of a generic incumbent firm.[2] Therefore, to enter the market at time t, the new entrant has to bear these costs at time $t - 1$, raise an amount F of financial funds and repay (at the end of period t) $(1 + E(r_{t-1})(1 + \iota))F$, where ι is the core inflation, defined above (constant, given the current monetary policy regime) and r_{t-1} the real interest rate, under the control of the monetary authorities. In other words, the potential entrants decide at time $t - 1$ whether to be in or out in the next period and decide whether or not to bet the amount of money $(1 + E(r_{t-1})(1 + \iota))F$ to get the expected future income of a new entrant (weighted with the probability of survival). Once the new entrants have entered the market, at time t, they enter the oligopolistic game. The new entrants discount the expected bankruptcy probability at the moment when they decide to enter, at time $t - 1$ for time t.

As shown below, in the price setting process taking place among the oligopolistic firms, we assume proportional rationing.

Since the workers may decide to become entrepreneurs, the wage and entry decisions are related to an incentive compatibility constraint: the labor market does not necessarily clear, due to oligopoly in the firms sector and to a particular kind of wage rigidity, which will be explained below. Starting a new firm requires some skills that only employed workers have and with the timing assumptions of our model, only employed individuals are perceived by the incumbent firms as potential entrants. With unemployment, the firms are wage setters and with full employment the workers are wage setters. The wages applying for the next period (from time t to time $t + 1$) are set before the potential entrants decide whether or not to enter the market. Although the oligopolistic entrepreneurs obviously want to keep the wages low, they do not want to push them so low to trigger entry by the workers. This assumption boils down into an incentive compatible constraint in wage setting, based on comparing the expected future income of a worker with the

---

[2] At the initial time t_0 the existence of entrepreneurs and firms (i.e., different social groups) can be thought of as being determined by a random initial distribution of wealth, allowing a subset $h_{in,0}$ of the labor force l at the initial time 0, to cover, once and for all, the initial exogenous sunk costs, at the initial instant of the whole economic process.

expected future income of a new entrant entrepreneur. If all the firms were respecting such an "incentive-compatible" constraint, entry would simply not occur, so there are two reasons for entry to occur:

1) the expectation on new entrant future profits is actually a frequency distribution of heterogeneous expectations: its average value is the "rational expectation" on new entrant future profits and, in this sense, the conventional assumption on rational expectations is respected, since "on average" the market expectations (i.e., the average of the frequency distribution of expectation) would be correct if there were no stochastic and unpredictable shocks; the portion of frequency distribution of new entrant future profits that is "above" the average expected profit is associated with "optimistic" potential entrants who actually enter the market;

2) changes in the variance of the frequency distribution of new entrant profits expectations generate an increase/decrease in entry; these changes in the variance, as shown below, are due to shifts in the aggregate demand or changes in policy, that increase the frequency of "prediction mistakes" (i.e., increase in the variance), for a given "correct" market expectation (i.e., rationale expectation) of the new entrant future profits.

Therefore if entry increases or decreases, it is because the variance of the expectation distribution of all the individuals is not constant. On the other hand, if the wages were irrationally set so low that their expected future value would be lower than the expected future value of the profits of a new entrant, then many workers would prefer to bear the risk of entering the market as entrepreneurs and large scale entry would take place until profits vanish out and the entrepreneurs would only earn the wage they pay themselves and get zero profits. This means that when the entrepreneurs are wage setters (i.e., when there is unemployment, due to market imperfections), the wages correspond to a level that discourages entry and entry is only due to the predictions errors distribution around the average of the workers' expectations. We call the wage that does not ex ante (and on average) trigger entry the "incentive compatible" nominal wage and denote it W^* (w^* in real terms).

Let us consider first the case of unemployment with wage setter firms. Between time $t - 1$ and time t the firms designate a common representative, who publicly announce the incentive compatible wage w^* (W^* in nominal terms).[3]

The unemployment subsidy τ (τ_R in real terms) is assumed to have a small magnitude compared to the all the other parameters of the model (and only barely allows the survival of unemployed individuals): with unemployment, all the incumbents have the same incentive not to offer a real wage greater or equal to w^*. Every worker who is offered w^* between time $t-1$ and t for the next period (from t to $t+1$) knows that by rejecting it, she would be substituted by an unemployed worker and become unemployed for the next period.

With full employment, the wage mechanism changes because the incumbents do not have any credible way to induce their workers to accept a "no entry wage": they cannot offer the same contract to unemployed individuals; therefore they have no longer any credible threat. This means that there is no longer incentive for the incumbents in coordinating themselves to offer a common wage. On the other hand, the rivalry among firms still exists and each rival has incentive to push a rival firm out of the market by stealing its workers by offering them a marginally higher wage. This rivalry may be interpreted as a one-shot game among the incumbents. The only way for each rival firm to prevent being pushed out of the market by its rivals is by offering a "zero-profit" wage, so that the entrepreneurs are only remunerated by the wage they pay themselves. Let us call this last wage w^{fu} in real terms (W^{fu} in nominal terms). Any lower wage offered by a firm to its workers would expose the entrepreneur to the risk of being pushed out of the market by her competitors, who could potentially steal her workers by offering them W^{fu}. In this case, W^{fu} is obviously a Nash equilibrium in a one-shot game among the oligopolistic incumbent firms, at the moment where wages are set.

Let us now turn to the case of unemployment. When the "incentive compatible real wage" W^* is announced (but still between time $t-1$

---

[3] We can imagine that no incumbent firm has incentive to deviate from this "publicly announced" incentive compatible wage by making the following assumption: since there is rivalry among the oligopolistic firms, the publicly announced wage is a form of coordination. If there were no coordination, each firm would have incentive to "steal" the workers from the rivals by offering them a marginally higher wage. We assume that this firm coordination is supported by a retaliation strategy against a firm that would deviate from the announced wage performed by all the other firms.

and time t), some employed workers may be affected by an "optimistic" idiosyncratic informational shock that make them decide to enter the market. Entry/exit affect the number of existing firms, and hence production capacity and aggregate employment.

The risk-free interest rate R_t is exogenous and under the control of the monetary authorities, and the revenue of the perfectly competitive banking and financial system is determined by the transaction fees and not by any interest margin; therefore R_t is also the interest rate that the firms have to pay to the banks on their loans.

In case of bankruptcy, the entrepreneurs lose their job, do not have the right to start a new firm next period, but keep their free financial assets A_t. This means, in aggregate terms, that it is irrelevant who is actually holding the financial assets A_t. Since any new firm has limited liability (and is a distinguished entity from the entrepreneur), any new entrant borrows from the banking and financial system in order to cover the cost of entry.

The expected remuneration of the entrepreneur is given by the profits (Π_t^e if it is a new entrant, Π_t^{in} if it is an incumbent) plus the wage W_t^* that the entrepreneur pays to herself.

The expected real payoff of the new entrant at time $t - 1$ for time t, $(E_{t-1}(\Pi_t^{eR}) + w_t^* - \tau_R - (1 + \iota)(1 + r_{t-1})F_R)(1 - \varsigma))$, is different, in general, from the expected real remuneration of the incumbent, $(E_{t-1}(\Pi_t^{inR}) + w_t^* - \tau_R)(1 - \varsigma))$.

Since entry and exit are determined by information shocks, with no modifications in the entry costs and for a given level of interest rate R_t, the survival of new entrants depends on their ability to substitute the firms that abandon the market, or by new equilibria configurations in the (oligopolistic) market for goods.

Having defined earlier the individual real output of the oligopolistic firm i at time $t + 1$ as $\varphi_{i,t+1}$, in equilibrium $\varphi_{i,t+1}$ and L_{t+1}^*, the amount of labor employed by firm i (which also determines the quantity pre-commitment among the oligopolistic firms) depends on the outcome of the game among the oligopolistic firms.

Since entry and exit are determined by information shocks, *ceteris paribus* (with no modifications in the entry costs and for a given level of interest rate r_t and a given "core inflation" rate ι_t), the survival of new entrants depends on their ability to substitute the firms that abandon the market, or by new equilibria configurations in the (oligopolistic) market for goods.

Therefore, the ex ante expected nominal profits for the incumbent i are:

$$E_t(\Pi_{t+1}^{in}) = [E_t(P_{t+1})E_t(\varphi_{i,t+1}) - W_{t+1}E_t(L_{i,t+1}^*) - \tau](1-\varsigma) =$$
$$= E_t(P_{t+1})[E_t\Lambda(L_{i,t+1}^*)^\alpha - w_{t+1}E_t(L_{i,t+1}^*) - \tau_R](1-\varsigma)$$

Where $E_t\Lambda(L_{i,t+1}^*)^\alpha$ is the expected real output, τ_R is the lump-sum tax expressed in real terms and w_{t+1} the real wage at time $t+1$.

This means that the prices (although they are stochastic, since they are the outcome of a Cournot-Nash equilibrium in mixed strategies) are likely to be set higher the higher are wages, incumbents' profits, unemployment subsidies and bank commissions.

The ex ante expected real profits for the incumbent i are:

$$E_t(\Pi_{t+1}^{inR}) = [E_t\Lambda(L_{i,t+1}^*)^\alpha - w_{t+1}E_t(L_{i,t+1}^*) - \tau_R](1-\varsigma)$$

As a consequence, the ex ante expected nominal profits for the new entrant j are:

$$E_t(\Pi_{t+1}^{e}) = E_t(P_{t+1})[E_t\Lambda(L_{j,t+1}^*)^\alpha - w_{t+1}E_t(L_{j,t+1}^*) - \tau_R -$$
$$- (1+\iota)(1+r_{t-1})F_R](1-\varsigma)$$

The ex ante expected real profits for the new entrant j are:

$$E_t(\Pi_{t+1}^{eR}) = [E_t\Lambda(L_{j,t+1}^*)^\alpha - w_{t+1}E_t(L_{j,t+1}^*) - \tau_R -$$
$$- (1+\iota)(1+r_{t-1})F_R](1-\varsigma)$$

The above definitions of real and nominal profits show that nominal profits are negative when real profits are negative and nominal profits are null when real profits are null. Obviously in real profits definitions, the output is at constant prices, normalized to one.

The ex post interaction among the oligopolistic firms yields a mixed-strategy Cournot-Nash equilibrium in the firms' commitment to provide the customers with commodities. This is a stochastic outcome where, for a given market price, each firm might get a (positive or negative) random shock in its profits.

The wage W_{t+1}^* is set in advance before time $t+1$ by a contract applying between time t and $t+1$. With no information shocks, the expected values $E_t(\varphi_{t+1})$ and $E_t(L_{t+1}^*)$ would be equal to their actual observable values at time t.

Let us now turn to the definition of the probability of a generic new entrant to stay in the market, which can be interpreted (since the firms are price makers) as the probability distribution function that Π_t^{eR} be greater than or equal to zero.

We now introduce an algebraic tool that is going to be very useful for our model formalization: the probability of survival of the new entrant and incumbent firms.

Having specified that these probabilities of survival are defined in real terms, the ex ante probability of the new entrant $\Pr(\Pi_t^{eR} \geq 0)$ and of the incumbent $\Pr(\Pi_t^{in} \geq 0)$ can be respectively defined as follows:

$$\Pr(\Pi_t^{eR} \geq 0) = \Pr\{[\Lambda E_t(L_{j,t}^*)^\alpha - w_t E_t(L_{j,t}^*) - \tau_R - $$
$$- (1 + \iota)(1 + r_{t-1})F_R](1 - \varsigma) \geq 0\}$$

$$\Pr(\Pi_t^{inR} \geq 0) = \Pr\{[\Lambda E_t(L_{i,t}^*)^\alpha - w_t E_t(L_{i,t}^*) - \tau_R](1 - \varsigma) \geq 0\}$$
$$(2.24)$$

The definition of (2.24) shows that a change in the interest rate r_{t-1} between time $t - 1$ and time t decided by the monetary authorities affects Π_t^{eR} and Π_t^{eR} by affecting the wage setting, through (2.24).

For the sake of simplicity, let us assume that $\Pr(\Pi_t^{eR} \geq 0)$ can be approximated as

$$\Pr(\Pi_t^{eR} \geq 0) = \Pr\left\{[\Lambda E_t(L_{j,t}^*)^\alpha - w_t E_t(L_{j,t}^*) - \tau_R] \geq 0\right\} - $$
$$- \xi[(1 + \iota)(1 + r_{t-1})F_R] + \psi_{j,t}$$

where $\psi_{j,t}$ is a random variable with zero mean, the price level (in real terms) is normalized to 1 and ξ is a linear parameter and $\Pr\{[E_t\Lambda(\lambda_{j,t}L_{j,t}^*)^\alpha - w_t E_t(L_{j,t}^*) - \tau_R] \geq 0\}$ is the probability of the incumbent to survive. Since the decisions are forward looking and are taken at time t, we assume that the expected future variables are equal to the last observable variable, so the expected future interest rate is set equal to r_{t-1} and, as we said, the expected future inflation ι_{t+i} is constant for a given monetary policy regime.

The expectations of future variables do not include stochastic shocks and, as a consequence of the previous assumptions, ex ante, we have $\Pr(\Pi_{t+i}^{inR} \geq 0) = \Pr(\Pi^{inR} \geq 0)$ for every i. Obviously, the actual number of incumbents that go bankrupt in each period might deviate from those implied by $\Pr(\Pi^{inR} \geq 0)$, and such is also the case with the volatility of the number of incumbents that go bankrupt, but this does not contradict the fact that *on average* the probability of incumbents going bankrupt (and its prediction formulated by rational agents) is equal to $\Pr(\Pi^{inR} \geq 0)$. This amounts to assuming that the probability of the incumbents to go bankrupt is a constant associated with their propensity to collude. Indeed this is different from saying that prices and profits are subject to stochastic shocks (since they are affected by the stochastic equilibrium in mixed strategies of the game among the oligopolistic firms): to put it another way, for the sake of simplifying the calculus, we are introducing the assumption that $\Pr(\Pi^{inR} \geq 0)$ is an exogenous variable, subject to stochastic shocks with zero mean.

Then, given our simplifying assumptions, the probability $\Pr(\Pi_t^{eR} \geq 0)$ of the new entrant to survive is the following:

$$\Pr(\Pi_t^{eR} \geq 0) = \Pr(\Pi^{inR} \geq 0) - \xi(1 + \iota)(1 + r_{t-1})F_R \qquad (2.25)$$

Incidentally, it is interesting to note, from (2.25), that a restrictive monetary policy (i.e., an increase in the nominal interest rate) reduces the probability of survival of the new entrants and, as a consequence, is expected to reduce entry. This is broadly consistent with the results by Chu and Ji (2016).

2.4 The Incentive Compatible Wage, the Probability of Entry and Exit and the Employment Level

At time t the new entrant survives with probability $\Pr(\Pi^{eR} \geq 0)$, goes bankrupt with probability $\left[1 - \Pr(\Pi^{eR} \geq 0)\right]$ and, in that case, both the entrepreneur and the workers will get the unemployment subsidy $\tau \cdot n_t\, (l - n_t)^{-1}$. At time t, the new entrant has two possible outcomes, or "future paths." At time $t + 1$, if successful, she will be an incumbent and survive with probability $\Pr(\Pi^{inR} \geq 0)$ or fail with probability $\left[1 - \Pr(\Pi^{inR} \geq 0)\right]$; still at time $t + 1$, the unsuccessful new entrant will be unemployed and have a certain probability of still being unemployed and another probability of being hired as a worker, and so on. In other words, at time $t = 1$ there will be two possible outcomes (or "future paths") for the new entrant, at time $t = 2$ there will be four possible "future paths," at time $t = 3$ there will be eight possible "future paths," and at time $t = n$ there will be 2^n possible "future paths." Similarly, the worker who decides not to enter the market as an entrepreneur, with probability $\Pr(\Pi^{inR} \geq 0)$, will earn the real wage w_t and (in the event that her firm goes bankrupt) loses the job with probability $\left[1 - \Pr(\Pi^{inR} \geq 0)\right]$ and earn the unemployment subsidy $\tau \cdot n_t\, (l - n_t)^{-1}$. However, if we move on in time, for instance, at time $t + 2$, the surviving entrant will eventually be incumbent and get with probability $\Pr(\Pi^{inR} \geq 0)$ the wage and the profit of the incumbent Π_t^{inR} and with ex ante probability $\left[1 - \Pr(\Pi^{inR} \geq 0)\right]$ the unemployment subsidy. Valuating the expectation of future profits for the new entrant means valuating a tree of outcomes where from $t + 1$ onward, in each period the firm can survive (with a certain probability) or going bankrupt (with the complementary probability). Going bankrupt in period $t + 1$ can be followed by the event of being hired as a worker by a new firm or remaining unemployed, and so on. In other words, the rational forward-looking decision maker that makes plans at time t for times $t + 1, t + 2, t + 3, \ldots, t + n$ (i.e., for all the future periods from t onward, faces 2^k different "future paths" for every k−periods interval in her future. For instance, when $t = 3$ (i.e., three periods ahead from the moment where the decision is taken), there will be $2^3 = 8$ possible "future paths," each of them with a given sequence of conditional probabilities.

The further away the expectations formulated at time t, the higher the number of combinations of possible "future paths" that characterizes the future of the decision maker. This boils down into a degree of ongoing uncertainty, which is increasing in the length of future time expectations and in the number of possible outcomes on which expectations are formulated, since at every future time, each agent can be in one out of several states that depend on the decisions simultaneously taken by all the other agents. Therefore, the variance of such expectations, in general, are higher the further away in the future is the forecast.

Let us define as J_{t+1} the expected future stream of income from time $t + 1$ onward for the successful entrant at time t, and let us define as Γ_{t+1} the expected future stream of income from time $t + 1$ onward for the worker who decides not to enter the market. We introduce then an approximation and define as Υ_{t+1} the expected stream of income from time $t + 1$ onward of an individual unemployed at time $t + 1$.

If the new entrant at time t is successful, her expected stream of future real income, from time $t + 1$ onward, is

$$J_{t+1} = \frac{1}{1 + \rho}\{[\Pr(\Pi^{inR} \geq 0)][E_t(\Pi_{t+1}^{inR}) + E_t(w_{t+1}) - \tau_R + J_{t+2}] +$$

$$+ [1 - \Pr(\Pi^{inR} \geq 0)][\tau_R \cdot n_{t+1} (l - n_{t+1})^{-1} + \Upsilon_{t+2}]\}$$

Υ_{t+1} positively depends on the probability of being hired as a worker by a firm the next period, and negatively on the number of unemployed individuals. Therefore the term $\{1 - \Pr(\Pi_t^{eR} \geq 0)]\}$ $(1 + \rho)^{-1} \cdot E_{t-1}[(\tau \cdot n_t \, (l - n_t)^{-1} + \Upsilon_{t+2}]$ is the expected future stream of income for the unsuccessful entrant from time t onward, weighted with the probability of going bankrupt in the first period.

Since we have assumed that ex ante, for what concerns the expected variables, we have $E[\Pr(\Pi_{t+1}^{inR} \geq 0)] = \Pr(\Pi_t^{inR} \geq 0)$, $E_t(\Pi_{t+1}^{inR}) = \Pi_t^{inR}$ and $E(n_{t+1}) = n_t$, then:

$$J_{t+1} = \frac{1}{1 + \rho}\{[\Pr(\Pi^{inR} \geq 0)][E_t(\Pi_{t+1}^{inR}) + E_t(w_{t+1}) - \tau_R + J_{t+2}]+$$

$$+ [1 - \Pr(\Pi^{inR} \geq 0)][\tau_R \cdot n_{t+1} \, (l - n_{t+1})^{-1} + \Upsilon_{t+2}]\}$$

On the other hand, if the potential new entrant at time t decides not to enter the market (i.e., to remain a worker), we define her expected stream of future income, from time $t + 1$ onward as Γ_{t+1}.

As we said earlier, the expectations of future variables, obviously, cannot possibly include any stochastic shocks and – since entry (as shown below) is determined by stochastic informational shocks on the stream of future income for the worker – at the moment where the worker decides not to enter the market, she perceives her decision as permanent, although she can turn entrepreneur in the future (if she is going to be subject to informational stochastic shocks). In other words, the event of turning an entrepreneur (since it would violate the "incentive compatible" wage that discourages entry) and her expected stream of future income, weighted with a probability notion of entry, is not included in Γ_{t+1}. Therefore,

$$\Gamma_{t+1} = \frac{1}{1 + \rho}\left\{\left[\Pr(\Pi^{inR} \geq 0)\right]\left[E_t(w_{t+1}) - \tau_R + \Gamma_{t+2}\right]+\right.$$

$$+ \left[1 - \Pr(\Pi^{inR} \geq 0)\right]\left[\tau_R \cdot n_{t+1} \, (l - n_{t+1})^{-1} + \Upsilon_{t+2}\right]\right\} =$$

$$= w_t \cdot \left[\sum_{i=1}^{\infty}(1 + \rho)^{-i} \cdot \Pr(\Pi^{inR} \geq 0)^i\right]-$$

$$- \tau_R \cdot \left[\sum_{i=1}^{\infty}(1 + \rho)^{-i} \cdot \Pr(\Pi^{inR} \geq 0)^i\right]+$$

$$+ \sum_{i=1}^{\infty}(1 + \rho)^{-i} \cdot \left[1 - \Pr(\Pi^{inR} \geq 0)\right]^i \cdot$$

$$\cdot \left[\tau_R \cdot n_{t+i} \, (l - n_{t+i})^{-1} + \Upsilon_{t+1+i}\right] \qquad (2.26)$$

Thus J_{t+1} may be also defined as follows:

$$J_{t+1} = \Gamma_{t+1} + \sum_{i=1}^{\infty} \left[\left(\frac{1}{1+\rho} \right)^i E_t \left(\Pi_{t+i}^{inR} \right) \left[\Pr \left(\Pi^{inR} \geq 0 \right) \right]^i \right] \quad (2.27)$$

We are now enabled to write the incentive compatibility constraint for wage setting with unemployment. In this case, the wage is set by the oligopolistic firms in such a way to discourage entry, i.e., it has to satisfy the incentive compatibility constraint saying that the expected future discounted stream of income from time $t + 1$ onward for the worker employed by an incumbent surviving at the beginning of time $t + 1$ has to be greater than or equal to the expected future discounted stream of income from time $t + 1$ onward for the new entrant.

$$\Pr(\Pi_t^{eR} \geq 0) (1 - \varsigma) (1 + \rho)^{-1} [E_{t-1} \left(\Pi_t^{eR} \right) + w_t - \tau_R + J_{t+1}(\cdot)] +$$
$$+ \Pr(\Pi_t^{eR} < 0) (1 - \varsigma) (1 + \rho)^{-1} \cdot$$
$$\cdot \left\{ E_{t-1}[\tau_R \cdot n_t (l - n_t)^{-1}] + \Upsilon_{t+1} \right\} \leq$$
$$\leq (1 + \rho)^{-1} (1 - \varsigma) \{ [\Pr(\Pi^{inR} \geq 0)] \cdot$$
$$\cdot [w_t - \tau_R + \Gamma_{t+1}(\cdot)] + (1 - \varsigma) (1 + \rho)^{-1} \cdot$$
$$\cdot [\Pr(\Pi^{inR} < 0)] \cdot E_{t-1}[\tau_R \cdot n_t (l - n_t)^{-1} + \Upsilon_{t+1}] \}$$
$$(2.28)$$

The term $(1 + \rho)^{-1} \cdot \Pr(\Pi^{inR} \geq 0) \cdot [w_t (1 - \tau_R - \varsigma) + \Gamma_t(\cdot)]$ is the expected stream of future income for the worker who decides to remain worker and whose firm survives. The term $\{ \Pr(\Pi^{inR} < 0) \cdot E_{t-1}[\tau_R \cdot n_t (l - n_t)^{-1} + \Upsilon_{t+1}] \}$ is the expected stream of future real income for the worker who decides to remain worker and whose firm goes bankrupt. As said earlier, for τ_R that is very small and negligible, the term $E_{t-1}[\tau_R \cdot n_t (l - n_t)^{-1}]$ also will be very small and negligible and the term Υ_{t+1} will be very small too. The incentive compatible constraint (2.28) yields the following wage setting rule with unemployment:

Simplifying our inequality (2.28) and remembering that $\Pr(\Pi_t^{eR} \geq 0) = \Pr(\Pi^{inR} \geq 0) - \xi(1 + \iota)(1 + r_{t-1})F_R$, we get:

$$[\Pr(\Pi^{inR} \geq 0) - \xi(1 + \iota)(1 + r_{t-1})F_R] \cdot [E_{t-1} \left(\Pi_t^{eR} \right) +$$
$$+ w_t - \tau_R + J_{t+1}(\cdot)] + [1 - \Pr(\Pi^{inR} \geq 0) +$$

$$+ \xi(1+\iota)(1+r_{t-1})F_R] \cdot \left\{ E_{t-1}[\tau_R \cdot n_t \, (l-n_t)^{-1}] + \Upsilon_{t+1} \right\} \leq$$

$$\leq [\Pr(\Pi^{inR} \geq 0)] \cdot [w_t - \tau_R + \Gamma_{t+1}(\cdot)] + [1 - \Pr(\Pi^{inR} \geq 0)] \cdot$$

$$\cdot E_{t-1}[\tau_R \cdot n_t \, (l-n_t)^{-1}] + \Upsilon_{t+1}]$$

Then, substituting (2.26) and (2.27) in the above inequality and simplifying out again, we get the following:

$$w_t \xi(1+\iota)(1+r_{t-1})F_R \cdot \left\{ 1 + \sum_{i=1}^{\infty} [\Pr(\Pi^{inR}0)]^i (1+\rho)^{-i} \right\} \geq$$

$$\geq [\Pr(\Pi^{inR} \geq 0) - \xi(1+\iota)(1+r_{t-1})F_R] \cdot$$

$$\cdot \left\{ E_{t-1}(\Pi_t^{eR}) + \sum_{i=1}^{\infty} (1+\rho)^{-(i+1)} \cdot E_{t-1}(\Pi_{t+i}^{inR}) \cdot [\Pr(\Pi^{inR} \geq 0)]^{i+1} \right\} +$$

$$+ \xi(1+\iota)(1+r_{t-1})F_R \cdot \left\{ 1 + \sum_{i=1}^{\infty} [\Pr(\Pi^{inR} \geq 0)]^i \cdot (1+\rho)^{-i} \right\} +$$

$$+ \xi(1+\iota)(1+r_{t-1})F_R \cdot \{ E_{t-1}[\tau_R n_t (l-n_t)^{-1} + \Upsilon_{t+1}] -$$

$$- \left\{ \sum_{i=1}^{\infty} [(1+\rho)^{-i}[1 - \Pr(\Pi^{inR} \geq 0)]^i \cdot \right.$$

$$\left. \cdot E_{t-1}[\tau_R n_{t+i}(l-n_{t+i})^{-1} + \Upsilon_{t+i+1}] \right\}$$

Then, using the properties of the geometric series for the terms:

$$\left\{ 1 + \sum_{i=1}^{\infty} [\Pr(\Pi^{inR} \geq 0)]^i (1+\rho)^{-i} \right\},$$

$$\left\{ E_{t-1}(\Pi_t^{eR}) \sum_{i=1}^{\infty} (1+\rho)^{-(i+1)} \cdot E_{t-1}(\Pi_{t+i}^{inR})[\Pr(\Pi^{inR} \geq 0)]^{i+1} \right\},$$

$$\xi(1+\iota)(1+r_{t-1})F_R \left\{ 1 + \sum_{i=1}^{\infty} [\Pr(\Pi^{inR} \geq 0)]^i (1+\rho)^{-i} \right\},$$

$$\left\{ \sum_{i=1}^{\infty} (1+\rho)^{-i} \left[1 - \Pr(\Pi^{inR} \geq 0) \right]^i \cdot E_{t-1} \left[\tau_R n_{t+i}(l-n_{t+i})^{-1} + \Upsilon_{t+i+1} \right] \right\}$$

and remembering that, ex ante, with no unexpected shocks, $E_{t-1}(n_t) = E_{t-1}(n_{t+1}) = E_{t-1}(n_{t+1+i})$ and $E_{t-1} \left(\lim_{t \to \infty} \Upsilon_{t+1} \right) = E_{t-1} \left(\lim_{t \to \infty} \Upsilon_{t+i+1} \right)$, since, with no unexpected shocks, $E_{t-1}(\Upsilon_{t+1})$ and $E_{t-1}(\Upsilon_{t+i+1})$ can also be represented as a geometric series; then, taking the limit for $t \to \infty$, we can further simplify and get:

$$w_t^* \geq \frac{E_{t-1}(\Pi_t^{eR})\left[\Pr(\Pi^{inR} \geq 0) - \xi(1+\iota)(1+r_{t-1})F_R\right]}{\xi(1+\iota)(1+r_{t-1})F_R \frac{1+\rho}{1+\rho-\Pr(\pi^{inR} \geq 0)}} +$$

$$+ \frac{E_{t-1}(\Pi_t^{inR}) \cdot \Pr(\Pi^{inR} \geq 0)}{\xi(1+\iota)(1+r_{t-1})F_R(1+\rho)} \cdot$$

$$\cdot \left[\Pr(\Pi^{inR} \geq 0) - \xi(1+\iota)(1+r_{t-1})F_R\right] +$$

$$+ \tau + \frac{1+\rho-\Pr(\Pi^{inR} \geq 0)}{1+\rho} \cdot E_{t-1}\left[\tau_R n_{t+1}(l - n_{t+1})^{-1} + \Upsilon_{t+1}\right] \cdot$$

$$\cdot \left[1 + \frac{1 - \Pr(\Pi^{inR} \geq 0)}{\rho + \Pr(\Pi^{inR} \geq 0)}\right] \qquad (2.29)$$

which is the wage determination equation with unemployment (2.29). Considering (2.29) as a binding equality, for a given exogenous value of $\Pr(\Pi^{inR} \geq 0)$, reminding that, on the basis of our assumptions, $\Pr(\Pi^{inR} \geq 0) - \xi(1+\iota)(1+r_{t-1})F_R = \Pr(\Pi_t^{eR} \geq 0) \geq 0$, and reminding that, being w_t set between time $t-1$ and time t, with no stochastic shocks, the expected values for Π_t^{inR}, Π_t^{eR}, n_{t+i} are equal to their observable values at time $t-1$, then w_t^* displays a set of rather intuitive properties:

$$\frac{\partial w_t^*}{\partial r_{t-1}} < 0; \quad \frac{\partial w_t^*}{\partial R_{t-1}} < 0; \quad \frac{\partial w_t^*}{\partial n_{t-1}} > 0; \quad \frac{\partial w_t^*}{\partial \Pi_{t-1}^{inR}} > 0; \quad \frac{\partial w_t^*}{\partial \Pi_{t-1}^{eR}} > 0$$

As explained above, τ_R is assumed to be constant and to have a very small magnitude, which also makes small the magnitude of Υ_{t+1}. This implies that the magnitude of $\partial w_t^*/\partial n_{t-1}$ is also small.

We have in this case $\partial w_t^*/\partial R_{t-1} < 0$ regardless of any "Fisher effect."

From (2.29), we also have $\frac{\partial w_t}{\partial \iota} < 0$ and $\frac{\partial w_t}{\partial \tau_R} > 0$, but these two inequalities are not relevant for our analyses, since we have assumed both τ_R and the core inflation ι to be constant. This means that this algebraic framework has to be slightly modified for macroeconomic and policy analyses with accelerating inflation. However, while doing this, one has to take into account that the price level is also jointly determined by the strategic behavior of the oligopolistic firms.

Defining the right-hand side of inequality (2.29) as Φ_t, we can introduce the probability of entry, $\Pr(\text{entry})_t$, which may be interpreted as the sum of the stochastic idiosyncratic information shocks generating entry decisions, i.e., the integral (over the whole population of workers

$n_t(1 - h_t)$ at time t of the perceived probability that the wage is set at a lower level than the expected present discounted value of the future profits as an entrepreneur in case of entry.

$$\text{Pr(entry)}_t = \int_0^{n_t(1-h_t)} (\text{Pr}(w_t < E_{t-1,i}(\Phi_t)))_i \, di \tag{2.30}$$

Given the equilibrium equality $w_t = E_{t-1,i}(\Phi_t)$, the expression

$$\int_0^{n_t(1-h_t)} (\text{Pr}(w_t < E_{t-1,i}(\Phi_t)))_i \, di$$

is the integral of all the idiosyncratic information shocks on $E_{t-1,i}(\Phi_t)$ for any individual worker i at time t, which depends on the variance of the expectation $E_{t-1,i}(\Phi_t)$, which is induced, as indicated previously, by $var(\Psi_t)$. The rationale of this assumption is that increases in the volatility of Ψ_t force the potential entrants to update their expectations, by collecting and processing data and the higher the volatility of Ψ_t, the higher the variance of individual predictions $E_{t-1,i}(\Phi_t)$ around the "market" average $E_{t-1}(\Phi_t)$, due to increasing costs in data collecting and data processing. If there were no idiosyncratic shocks and the expectations were all identical, there would not be any individuals thinking that $\text{Pr}(w_t < E_{t-1,i}(\Phi_t))_i$ and, therefore, no entry would take place. However, since expectations are interpreted (as suggested in Lucas 1976) as a frequency distribution of predictions, when the variance of these idiosyncratic predictions increase (even though the average of the predictions may be completely unaffected), then the number of individuals i thinking that $\text{Pr}(w_t < E_{t-1,i}(\Phi_t))_i$ increases and, as a consequence, entry increases.

In other words, the integral

$$\int_0^{n_t(1-h_t)} (\text{Pr}(w_t < E_{t-1,i}(\Phi_t)))_i \, di$$

represents the portion of "optimistic" workers trusting on a successful entry. If agents' expectations were identical (i.e., if there were no hidden actions nor diverging incentives among all the agents), then there would not be any "prediction mistake" nor any macroeconomic fluctuations, because macroeconomic fluctuations are generated (like in conventional macromodels and in the DSGE literature) by stochastic shocks: we have here shocks generated by the outcome among oligopolistic firms, and not the technology shocks that generate the business cycle in the Real Business Cycle literature and in most DSGE contributions; however, without these shocks, expectations would turn out to be "true" ex post. Nevertheless, since expectations are not a point value and the stochastic shocks generate macroeconomic fluctuations, the rational agents, time after time, have to adjust their expectations to the observable variables, that include the outcomes of the stochastic shocks. Like in conventional macromodels, these shocks generate the divergence between predicted and ex post observable variables. This is the reason why in this model it is assumed that the expectation of each relevant variable is equal to its last observable value. Of course, the market expectation is interpreted as the *average* of the expectations of all the individuals.

2.5 A Digression on the Link Between the Labor Market Equilibrium, the Firm's Output and the Entry Decision

This work follows, in spirit (although not in some details of the modeling technique and in some algebraic features), Aoki and Yoshikawa's (2007) approach to macroeconomic modeling. Loosely speaking, there is a correspondence between the assumptions by Aoki and Yoshikawa (2007, ch. 2) and our assumption on how the interacting agents behave at a microeconomic level. Aoki and Yoshikawa (2007) assume that agents have binary choices. The two choices can be represented by two states (say state 0 and state 1). If we have n agents, the state of n agents may be represented as $s = (s_1, s_2, \ldots, s_n)$, where the choice by agent i is denoted by $s_i = 1$ or $s_i = 0$ and so on. A set of all the possible values of s is called "state space" S. The purpose of this assumption is to describe the dynamic process of how do agents revise their choices in time, due to incentives, externalities, costs, and unexpected news. Since we are interested in the time evolution of the states, we consider a stochastic process in discrete time (differently from Aoki and Yoshikawa, who consider jump Markov processes in continuous time). However, in our formalization of the jump Markov process, we use more variables than Aoki and Yoshikawa to introduce our formalization. We start by following the notation by Aoki and Yoshikawa, in terms of transition rates, between time $t - 1$ and t:

$$q(n_t h_t, n_t h_t + 1) = [n_t(1 - h_t)] \eta_1(h_t) \tag{2.31}$$

$$q(n_t h_t, n_t h_t - 1) = n_t h_t \eta_2(h_t) \tag{2.32}$$

Equation (2.31) represents the transition rate of an increase in the number of workers who were not entrepreneurs and decide to enter the market as entrepreneurs (with $0 < h_t < 1$).

The process we are interested in concerns the workers who become entrepreneurs and the entrepreneurs who go bankrupt. The increase or decrease in n_t is a mere consequence of the process of entry/exit of new firms and may be modeled, recalling our assumption that in each period t the number of workers employed by each firm is determined between $t - 1$ and t, when the number of firms operating next period t is known and all the firms set their quantity precommitment by setting the labor contracts.

The transition rate refers to an individual (and not to the aggregation of all the individuals) making her/his choice to enter the market. In Aoki and Yoshikawa's approach, it applies to the number $n_t(1 - h_t)$ of individuals who can make this choice (i.e., the employed people who are not entrepreneurs), and $\eta_1(h_t)$ should be a function of h_t because, according to Aoki and Yoshikawa, it would not be rational for an individual to neglect externalities; therefore, it is a decreasing function of h_t because the decision to enter the market is discouraged by a high number of existing entrepreneurs. The higher the h_t, the smaller the $\eta_1(h_t)$. In the benchmark case, where the economy reaches full employment, the workers will be remunerated exactly like the entrepreneurs, and there will be no incentive and no room for new entries. As shown below, we follow this assumption by Aoki and Yoshikawa, but we attempt to model more in detail the behavioral assumptions behind it (i.e., the theoretical reasons that induce a worker to enter the market as an entrepreneur).

The second transition rate (2.32) refers to exit and its causes,[4] which is consistent with the assumption of proportional rationing in the price determination (discussed in the previous section).

Aoki and Yoshikawa (2007) define the "master equation," or Chapman-Kolmogorov equation, as the equation describing the time

---

[4] This assumption is qualitatively different from the assumption of exogenous and constant bankruptcy rate made by Etro and Colciago (2010).

evolution of the probability distribution of states.[5] They define the *equilibrium probabilities of states* as follows:

$$\Pr(s(s_1, s_2, \ldots, s_n))_{t+1} - \Pr(s(s_1, s_2, \ldots, s_n))_t =$$
$$= \sum_{s'} q(s', s) \cdot \Pr(s', t) - \Pr(s, t) \sum_s q(s, s')$$

where the sum is taken over all states $s' \neq s$ and $q(s', s)$ is the transition rate from state s' to s. Intuitively speaking, $\Delta \Pr(\cdot)/\Delta t = $ (inflow of probability fluxes into s) $-$ (outflow of probability fluxes out of s). Here, of course, Δt is only a unit time interval.

In our case, we can define the net inflow of probability of "being entrepreneur" $\Delta^h \Pr(\cdot)t$ as follows:

$$\Delta^h \Pr(\cdot) = \sum_{j=1}^{(n-h)} q(n_t h_t, n_t h_t + 1) \cdot \Pr(\text{entry})_t -$$
$$- \sum_{j=1}^{nh} q(n_t h_t, n_t h_t - 1) \cdot \Pr(\text{exit})_t$$

In this chapter, we do not explicitly formalize a Chapman-Kolmogorov equation, but we formalize (as shown in the previous section) a difference equation showing a similar kind of information: the dynamics of the existing firms in the system $n_t h_t$, related to its level $n_{t-1} h_{t-1}$ at time $t - 1$, which depends on the probability of entry and on the probability of exit. Let us recall the definition of "shifting parameter":

$$\Psi_t = \sum_{i=0}^{\infty} [(1 + E(R_{t+i}))]^{-i} \cdot$$
$$\cdot E[n_{t+i}(W_{t+i} + h_{t+i}^e E(\Pi_{t+i}^e) + h_{t+i}^{in} E(\Pi_{t+i}^{in}))]\}$$

And let us recall that on the basis of our assumptions, we have:

$$E(r_{t+i}) = r_t$$
$$E(\iota_{t+i}) = \iota$$

---

[5] For our purposes, we only need to use it here in a simplified way, to identify the stationarity or equilibrium probabilities of states, without considering other solution tools and techniques suggested by Aoki and Yoshikawa, like the probability generating function of the Taylor expansion or the cumulant generating function.

$$E(n_{t+i}) = n_t$$
$$E(w_{t+i}) = w_t$$
$$E(h^e_{t+i}) = h^e_t$$
$$E(h^{in}_{t+i}) = h^{in}_t$$
$$E(\Pi^e_{t+i}) = \Pi^e_{t-1}$$
$$E(\Pi^{in}_{t+i}) = \Pi^{in}_{t-1}$$
$$E(\Pi^{eR}_{t+i}) = \Pi^{eR}_{t-1}$$
$$E(\Pi^{inR}_{t+i}) = \Pi^{inR}_{t-1}$$

The decision to enter the market is affected by the market size, and since changes in the earlier defined "shift parameter,"

$$\Psi_t = \sum_{i=0}^{\infty}(1+E\,(R_{t+i}))^{-i}\cdot E[n_{t+i}(W_{t+i}+h^e_{t+i}E(\Pi^e_{t+i})+h^{in}_{t+i}E(\Pi^{in}_{t+i}))]$$

$$(2.33)$$

determine parallel shifts in the aggregate demand, we assume that an increase in the variance of Ψ_t causes an increase in the probability of "optimistic" information shocks that make the potential entrant (i.e., the worker) to enter the market. This happens because the complexity of calculus to determine the agents expectations increase, and this makes the prediction "mistakes" by the individual agents more likely and more frequent, even though their expectations are *on average* correct. In other words, when the demand shifts and the variance of the elements composing the term Ψ_t increases, the process of information collecting and calculus performed by all the individuals is affected by an increase in idiosyncratic mistakes, and even though it is *still* rational (i.e. the market expectations are still, *on average*, correct), it makes the frequency of prediction mistakes (i.e., the variance of the individual expectations with respect to the correct market expectation) higher.

Another way to interpret the effects of $var(\Psi_t)$, which is relevant for the sake of our simulations is given by the fact that an increase in $var(\Psi_t)$ is assumed to increase the variance of the firms' profits: ideally speaking, the new entrant would be a worker observing that the firm he works in earns profits beyond a certain level.

For what concerns the behavior of the profits, we have:

$$\Pr(\Pi^{eR}_t < 0) = 1 - \Pr(\Pi^{eR}_t \geq 0)$$

and

$$\Pr(\Pi_t^{inR} < 0) = 1 - \Pr(\Pi_t^{inR} \geq 0)$$

When a firm Goes bankrupt, both the entrepreneur and the workers lose their jobs and become unemployed. Therefore an entrepreneur who goes bankrupt at time t, is unemployed at time $t+1$ and can only hope to be hired as a worker at time $t+2$. With this assumption, we do not need to impose any "ad hoc" bankruptcy costs.

As shown in the previous section (2.4), w_t^* behaves rather intuitively:

$$\frac{\partial w_t^*}{\partial r_{t-1}} < 0; \quad \frac{\partial w_t^*}{\partial R_{t-1}} < 0; \quad \frac{\partial w_t^*}{\partial n_{t-1}} > 0; \quad \frac{\partial w_t^*}{\partial \Pi_{t-1}^{inR}} > 0; \quad \frac{\partial w_t^*}{\partial \Pi_{t-1}^{eR}} > 0$$

Hence we may define w_t^* as the following generic function, which also includes the assumption that the workers do not suffer from money illusion:

$$w_t^* = w_t^*(\overset{-}{r_{t-1}}, \overset{+}{n_{t-1}}, \overset{+}{\Pi_{t-1}^{inR}}, \overset{+}{\Pi_{t-1}^{eR}})$$

$\Pr(\Pi^{inR} \geq 0)$ is an exogenous ex ante average value (since it represents the propensity of the oligopolists to collude), but it may be ex post subject to stochastic deviations that may be interpreted as changes in the propensity of the oligopolists to collude/conflict.

With unemployment, the oligopolistic firms set the wage w_t^*, determined by the incentive compatibility constraint explained above. If the wages, in case of unemployment, were set below the incentive-compatible level $w_t^*(\cdot)$, all the workers would have incentive to leave their jobs and start a new firm. If the economy is in full employment, the bargaining power is on the side of the workers, and the wages are set at the "zero-profit" level.

As we said, with full employment there are no extra-profits, all the entrepreneurs are incumbent and their only remuneration is given by the wages they pay to themselves. In this case, the wage is then obtained by the condition $E_{t-1}(\Pi_t^e) = 0$, or, equivalently, $E_{t-1}(\Pi_t^e) = 0$, which implies

$$W_t^{fu} = \frac{E_{t-1}(P_t) \cdot \Lambda E_{t-1}(L_{j,t}^*)^{\alpha} - \tau_R - (1+\iota)(1+r_{t-1})F_R}{E_{t-1}(L_{j,t}^*)}$$

If full employment is reached after at least one period with no new entries, then the condition is $E_{t-1}(\Pi_t^{in}) = 0$, because all the firms are incumbents after one period, i.e.,

$$W_t^{fu} = \frac{E_{t-1}(P_t) \cdot \Lambda E_{t-1}(L_{j,t}^*)^\alpha - \tau_R}{E_{t-1}(L_{j,t}^*)}$$

The wage determination has a point of discontinuity corresponding to the level of full employment:

$$W_t = \begin{cases} w_t^* & n < l \\ w_t^{fu} & n = l \end{cases} \tag{2.34}$$

Of course, the situation of full employment is subject to a number of shocks and may be interpreted as a temporary equilibrium.

Given the production function of the generic firm i, the amount of labor set by the generic firm i determines the optimal firm's output $\varphi_{i,t}$; since the expected value of $\psi_{i,t}$ is 0 and $\psi_{i,t}$ is uncorrelated with $\varphi_{j,t}$, we have:

$$L_{j,t} = \left(\frac{E_{t-1}(\varphi_{j,t})}{\Lambda} \right)^{1/\alpha}$$

Aggregating for all the firms, the overall amount of employed labor:

$$L_t^* = \sum_{i=1}^{H_t} L_{j,t} = \sum_{j=1}^{H_t} \left(\frac{E_{t-1}(\varphi_{j,t})}{\Lambda} \right)^{1/\alpha} \tag{2.35}$$

It is important to remind, in this case, the assumptions we made on the timing of consumption: the consumption takes place at the end of each period. Still, at the end of the period, the ex post profits and the firms going bankrupt are known.

For given average market expectations $E_t(\Pi_{t+1}^{eR})$ and $E_t(\Pi_{t+1}^{inR})$, when the variance of the distributions of these two variables increases, we have a higher frequency of prediction mistakes. We can summarize and simplify that by the following equation:

$$\Pr(\text{entry})_t = \beta(var(\Psi_t))$$

The entry decisions are taken just after the wage for time t (applying from t to $t + 1$) are set. The new entrants and the incumbents decide the number of workers to hire for the next period (i.e. from t to $t + 1$), on the basis of their profit expectations, because the labor contract establishes a fixed number of hours to be worked. In this way, the labor contract establishes a capacity constraint for the oligopolistic firms. The firms are binded, at time t, with contracts to their workers and to the lenders who lent them the money to cover the fixed entry cost $(1 + \iota)(1 + r_t)F_R$ and set the amount of output to produce. This means that they have a quantity precommitment for the quantity to be produced and sold from t to $t + 1$. Therefore the total number of firms (H_t in our notation) is known at time t; still at time t (although, sequentially, after the total number of firms is known), the firms determine the Cournot-Nash equilibrium in mixed strategies, specifying the output and price of each firm.

If the wage are set by the oligopolistic firms according to the incentive compatibility constraint (2.29) and if the expectations were perfectly identical for all the individuals (i.e., if no individual had any idiosyncratic informational shocks or prediction mistake), there would be no entry and $\Pr(\text{entry})_{t+1}$ would be null. This means that ex post deviations are those caused by all the possible stochastic shocks affecting the right-hand side of inequality (2.29).

As in Aoki and Yoshikawa (2007, ch. 2), the dynamics of the model are determined by the birth and death of firms and on the basis of the previous definitions; the total number of existing firms at time t is determined as follows:

$$
n_t h_t = n_{t-1} h_{t-1} + \overbrace{n_{t-1} h_{t-1} \frac{1 - h_{t-1}}{h_{t-1}} \beta(var(\Psi_t))}^{\text{Number of new entrants for time } t} -
$$

$$
- \underbrace{[1 - \Pr(\Pi^{inR} \geq 0)] n_{t-1} h_{t-1}^{in}}_{\substack{\text{Non-surviving incumbents from} \\ \text{time } t - 1}} -
$$

$$
- \underbrace{[1 - \Pr(\Pi^{eR} \geq 0)] n_{t-1} h_{t-1}^{e}}_{\substack{\text{Non-surviving new entrants from} \\ \text{time } t - 1}}
$$

Hence, given the definition of $\Pr(\Pi^{eR} \geq 0)$ and since $h_t = h_t^{in} + h_t^{e}$ and

$$
h_t^e = \frac{n_{t-1}(1 - h_{t-1})\beta(var(\Psi_t))}{n_t}
$$

and

$$h_t = n_t^{-1} \cdot \{n_{t-1}h_{t-1}\left[\Pr(\Pi^{inR} \geq 0) + (1 - h_t)h_t^{-1}\beta(var(\Psi_t))\right] - $$
$$- \xi(1 + \iota)(1 - r_{t-1})F_R(1 - h_{t-2})\beta(var(\Psi_{t-1}))\}$$

we get:

$$n_t h_t = n_{t-1}h_{t-1}\left[\Pr(\Pi^{inR} \geq 0) + \frac{1 - h_{t-1}}{h_{t-1}}\beta(var(\Psi_t))\right] - $$
$$- \xi(1 + \iota)(1 + r_{t-1})F_R n_{t-2}(1 - h_{t-2})\beta(var(\Psi_{t-1}))$$

On the basis of the previous theoretical points on the determination of the number of existing firms, we may also derive the number of incumbents at time t:

$$n_t h_t^{in} = n_{t-1}h_{t-1} \cdot \Pr(\Pi^{inR} \geq 0) - $$
$$- \xi(1 + \iota)(1 + r_{t-2})F_R n_{t-2}(1 - h_{t-2})\beta(var(\Psi_{t-1}))$$

Or, using a different notation:

$$H_t^{in} = n_{t-1}h_{t-1} \cdot \Pr(\Pi^{inR} \geq 0) - $$
$$- \xi(1 + \iota)(1 + r_{t-2})F_R n_{t-2}(1 - h_{t-2})\beta(var(\Psi_{t-1}))$$

Recalling that $H_t = n_t h_t$, $H_t^e = n_t h_t^e$, $H_t^{in} = n_t h_t^{in}$, we are now enabled to express the number of total existing firms as a function of exogenous and predetermined variables, as follows:[6]

$$H_t = H_{t-1}[\Pr(\Pi^{inR} \geq 0)] + [(n_{t-1} - H_{t-1})\beta(var(\Psi_t))] - $$
$$- \xi(1 + \iota)(1 + r_{t-1})F_R(n_{t-2} - H_{t-2})\beta(var(\Psi_{t-1})) \tag{2.36}$$

By substituting the definition of H_t into the aggregate demand and rearranging, we get the following definition of the aggregate demand:

---

[6] We may also define the overall probability of exit, for the all existing firms (both new entrants and incumbents):

$$\Pr(exit)_t = 1 - \Pr(\Pi^{inR} \geq 0) + \left[\xi(1 + \iota)(1 + r_{t-1})F^R\right]$$
$$\cdot \left[n_{t-1}h_{t-1}\frac{(1 - h_{t-1})}{h_{t-1}}\beta(var(\Psi_t))\right] \cdot \{n_{t-1}h_{t-1}[\Pr(\Pi^{inR} \geq 0) \cdot$$
$$+ h_{t-1}^{-1}(1 - h_{t-1})\beta(var(\Psi_t))] - \xi(1 + \iota)(1 + r_{t-1}) \cdot$$
$$\cdot F^R n_{t-2}(1 - h_{t-2})\beta(var(\Psi_{t-1}))\}$$

$$D(\cdot)_t = (\Omega(r_t)/P_t) \cdot [A_t + [1/(1 + R_t)] \sum_{i=0}^{\infty} [(1 + E(r_{t+i})) \cdot (1 + \iota)]^{-i} \cdot$$

$$\cdot E \left\{ (n_{t+i} W_{t+i}) + [(n_{t+i-1} - H_{t+i-1})\beta(var(\Psi_{t+i}))]\Pi_{t+i}^e + \right.$$

$$+ [H_{t-1} \cdot \Pr(\Pi^{in} \geq 0) - (1 + R_{t-2})\xi F_R \cdot$$

$$\left. \cdot (n_{t-2} - H_{t-2})\beta(var(\Psi_{t-1}))]\Pi_{t+i}^{in}] \right\} \qquad (2.37)$$

This last notation for the nominal aggregate demand may be useful for further analyses, since it puts into clear evidence the effects of the predetermined variables of the model, given the assumed valued of the (exogenous) variable Ψ.

From the above equations, we observe that entry and exit can generate distributional shocks affecting the aggregate demand. P_t, the general price level in macroeconomic terms, is interpreted as the average of the price distribution set by all the oligopolistic firs, while the inflation rate ι_t is defined, as we said, as $\frac{P_t - P_{t-1}}{P_{t-1}}$.

The aggregate demand could also be written by using the definitions of h_t^e and h_t^{in} as follows (although we are going to use the previous definition):

$$D(\cdot)_t = (\Omega(r_t)/P_t) \cdot$$

$$\cdot [A_t + [1/(1 + R_t)] \sum_{i=0}^{\infty} [(1 + E(r_{t+i})) \cdot (1 + \iota)]^{-i} \cdot$$

$$\cdot E \left\{ (n_{t+i} W_{t+i}) + [n_{t+i-1}(1 - h_{t+i-1})\beta(var(\Psi_{t+i}))]\Pi_{t+i}^e + \right.$$

$$+ [n_{t-1} h_{t-1} \cdot \Pr(\Pi^{inR} \geq 0) - (1 + R_{t-2})\xi F_R \cdot$$

$$\left. \cdot n_{t-2}(1 - h_{t-2})\beta(var(\Psi_{t-1}))]\Pi_{t+i}^{in}] \right\}$$

2.6 Interpreting the Nature of the Equilibrium in the Oligopolistic Market

The proof of the existence of a mixed strategy equilibrium with symmetric firms in an oligopolistic market, in the case of constant and increasing marginal costs, where the firms simultaneously decide both prices and quantities is due to Gertner (1985, pp. 74–98). In this work, we assume, on the contrary, that the oligopolistic firms enter a two-stage game à la Kreps and Scheinkman (1983), but with the modifications and extensions provided by Madden (1998), as explained in this section.

Dasgupta and Maskin (1986) proved the general existence of mixed strategy equilibrium in a Bertrand-Edgeworth model with a continuous demand function that is equal to zero for sufficiently high prices and with discontinuities in the payoffs of the oligopolistic firms. Allen and Hellwig (1986) extended the result to the case of a demand curve that does not intersect the horizontal axis, and Maskin (1986) proved the existence result of a mixed strategy equilibrium in an oligopolistic model where firms simultaneously choose both prices and quantities to a case where firms' symmetry is not required and with rather general costs functions. Maskin's provides his proofs for a duopolistic market, but he points out that they are valid for a finite number of oligopolistic firms (Maskin, 1986, p. 382). As Vives (2001) points out, the use of mixed strategy equilibria in economic modeling is somehow controversial, since "in a mixed-strategy equilibrium all actions in the support of the equilibrium distribution of a player are best responses to the distributions used by the rivals" (Vives, 2001, p. 45). However, Vives suggests that players choices may depend on random factors that are not relevant for the payoffs and, as Harsanyi (1973) also suggests, an interpretation of mixed strategies as pure strategies in a perturbed game: in other words, in a mixed-strategy equilibrium, each player may be using a pure strategy subject to a small random disturbance on his own payoff. This might happen, for instance, if a firm is observing the costs of its rival with a slight uncertainty.

This model is broadly consistent with the interpretation by Harsanyi, since it is assumed that the oligopolistic firms imperfectly observe the cost choices of their rivals and approximate them on the basis of conjectures: in other words, they play a perturbed game.

The mixed-strategy equilibria are interpreted as stochastic steady states by (Osborne and Rubinstein, 1994, p. 39), where each occurrence of the game takes place after n players are randomly chosen from different populations. This last interpretation is also consistent with the assumptions of this model because here the firms interacting in the market, due to entry and exit, are not the same in each occurrence of the game and since entry and exit are affected by stochastic shocks, the firms existing in each time t are chosen stochastically.

As discussed above, we have made three relevant assumptions.

1) Starting a new firm requires entrepreneurial skills (that are lost after being unemployed for at least one period) and exogenous nominal sunk costs of entry F (organizational costs and setting up costs) that the new entrant entrepreneur has to support just before entering the market.
2) Only labor is employed in the production process. Because of skill loss, only the workers can enter the market as new entrepreneurs and are therefore perceived by the incumbents as potential entrants.
3) The labor contract establishes a fixed number of working hours for each worker, i.e., hiring a worker implies hiring a fixed number of working hours for the firm. This means that labor also is a sunk cost.

As said earlier, the firms enter a two-stage game where, at stage 1 (at the end of time $t - 1$, just immediately before time t) they take the entry decision (i.e., support the cost $(1 + \iota)(1 + r_{t-1})F$) and hire the workers that will be employed for time t (and therefore commit themselves to support the labor cost).

At stage 2, the firms, having implicitly set their quantity precommitment (the number of hired workers implicitly set a maximum amount of output that can be produced next period) simultaneously decide their price and profits.

What we need for the sake of our model is the existence of a Cournot-Nash equilibrium in mixed strategies among the oligopolistic firms. The proof of the existence of such an equilibrium is provided by Madden (1998), who provides an extension of the famous Kreps and Scheinkman (1983) result to the case of a uniformly elastic demand curve (like the aggregate demand of our model). Section 2.9 recalls the relevant proofs showing the existence of a Cournot-Nash equilibrium in mixed strategies among the oligopolistic firms operating in the goods market.

For an agent-based simulation of this model, the mixed-strategy equilibrium emerging in the game among the oligopolistic firms can be justified by Harsanyi's (1973) or by Osborne and Rubinstein's (1994) interpretation, and our modeling assumptions could be easily adapted to be consistent with Maskin (1986) results.

We assume that proportional rationing applies and that the profit (payoff) function of the firm is continuous in prices. We also assume that the amount of work hired by each firm constitutes a capacity constraint, on the basis of the labor contracts set for time t, until time $t + 1$.

We want to explicitly formalize another potential source of stochastic shocks: conflict. For this purpose, we assume that the quantities decided by the firms, instead of being commodities, are "contracts," i.e., "commitments" to sell commodities to the customers. These commitments are subject to stochastic shocks. These stochastic shocks may cause some firms to go bankrupt and, in this way, the firms' failure does not imply any lack of rationality in the determination of the Nash Equilibrium among oligopolistic firms because in the Nash equilibrium in mixed strategies emerging among the oligopolistic firms, the firms' bankruptcies are not the effects of a planned choice, but are stochastic. This point also carries relevant implications for the determination of the macroeconomic equilibrium.

Given the timing assumptions of this model, both entry costs and labor costs are sunk for the new entrants. Still, for the timing assumptions of the model, all the incomes (profits, labor and unemployment subsidies) for time t are received at the end of time t: labor costs are accounted as debt of the firms toward the workers, at the beginning of time t (and this is why they are sunk), even though they are paid out to workers at the end of time t.

The amount of labor $L_{i,t}$ hired by the generic firm i at time t is decided on the basis of ex ante expectations. Let us define it as the optimal ex ante amount of labor, associated with the optimal ex ante individual firm output $E_{t-1}(\varphi_{i,t})$ at time t. All the firms, both incumbents and new entrants, have the same technology and production function. Ex ante expectations, ex ante amount of employed labor and ex ante individual firm's output, are all chosen on the basis of the ex ante demand curve at time t, which is the ex post demand for time $t - 1$, i.e., the empirically observable demand curve that has emerged after all the stochastic shocks of the model. All the firms make their choices on the basis of the equation of the aggregate demand (i.e., each firm picks up a point on the aggregate demand), and the price level is to be interpreted has the ex post weighted average of the different prices set by the various firms.

2.7 A Few Equations Summarizing the Model for the Agent-Based Simulations

The existence of a Cournot-Nash equilibrium in mixed strategies among the oligopolistic firms, for the sake of the agent-based simulations contained in the next chapter, is rendered by a sequence of decisions where the entrepreneurs first make decision plans, adapt production plans, decide to hire or fire workers, entrepreneurs produce and various stochastic shocks set the price, or, to be more precise, the price distribution.

Obviously, for the sake of the agent-based simulations of the next chapters, the equations reflect the general outcome of the behavior of individuals observing the information available to them and proceeding by credible behavior rules that do not implicitly assume infinite knowledge and infinite data processing ability.

For our purposes, the theoretical model boils down into the aggregate demand, the wage determination (from equation (2.34)), the employment dynamics.

The first relevant equation for the sake of simulations is the nominal aggregate demand (2.18):

$$D(\cdot)_t = \frac{\Omega(r_t)}{P_t}\left(A_t + \frac{1}{(1+R_t)}\sum_{i=0}^{\infty}\left(\frac{1}{(1+E(r_{t+i}))(1+\iota)}\right)^i E(Y_{t+i})\right)$$

The aggregate demand may be also rewritten in a way that specifically accounts for the distributional shocks, as in (2.20):

$$D(\cdot)_t = \frac{\Omega(r_t)}{P_t}\{A_t + ((1+r_t)(1+\iota))^{-1}\sum_{i=0}^{\infty}[(1+E(r_{t+i})(1+\iota)]^{-i}\cdot$$
$$\cdot E(n_{t+i}(W_{t+i} + h_{t+i}^e\Pi_{t+i}^e + h_{t+i}^{in}\Pi_{t+i}^{in}))\}$$

However we may use, for the sake of our simulations, the aggregate demand equivalently, rewritten as in (2.37):

$$D(\cdot)_t = (\Omega(r_t)/P_t)\cdot[A_t + [1/(1+R_t)]\sum_{i=0}^{\infty}[(1+E(r_{t+i}))\cdot(1+\iota)]^{-i}\cdot$$
$$\cdot E\left\{(n_{t+i}W_{t+i}) + [(n_{t+i-1} - H_{t+i-1})\beta(var(\Psi_{t+i}))]\Pi_{t+i}^e +\right.$$
$$+ [H_{t-1}\cdot\Pr(\Pi^{in} \geq 0) - (1+R_{t-2})\xi F_R\cdot$$
$$\left.\cdot (n_{t-2} - H_{t-2})\beta(var(\Psi_{t-1}))]\Pi_{t+i}^{in}]\right\}$$

As we indicated previously, "this last notation for the nominal aggregate demand may be useful for further analyses, since it puts into clear evidence the effects of the predetermined variables of the model, given the assumed valued of the (exogenous) variable Ψ."

From the above equations, we observe that entry and exit can generate distributional shocks affecting the aggregate demand. P_t, the general price level in macroeconomic terms, is interpreted as the average of the price distribution set by all the oligopolistic firs, while the inflation rate ι_t is defined, as we said, as $\frac{P_t - P_{t-1}}{P_{t-1}}$.

As posed previously, wages are determined by (2.34):

$$W_t = \begin{cases} w_t^* & n < l \\ w_t^{fu} & n = l \end{cases}$$

The amount of workers hired by firm j is:

$$L_{j,t} = \left(\frac{E_{t-1}(\varphi_{j,t})}{\Lambda} \right)^{1/\alpha}$$

The total amount of workers employed by all the firms is given:

$$L_t^* = \sum_{i=1}^{H_t} L_{j,t} = \sum_{j=1}^{H_t} \left(\frac{E_{t-1}(\varphi_{j,t})}{\Lambda} \right)^{1/\alpha}$$

Hence all the employed individuals (workers and entrepreneurs) are given by $L_t^* + H_t = L_t^* + H_t^e + H_t^{in}$.

The above equations are the basis of the numerical simulations contained in the next chapter.

2.8 Concluding Remarks

This chapter has introduced a new theoretical model to explain macroeconomic fluctuations. The model is employed in the next chapters for agent-based simulations reproducing an oligopolistic economy with heterogeneous agents and wage rigidity. The business cycle can be determined by the stochastic outcome of the rivalry among the oligopolistic firms operating in the market. The typical technology shocks characterizing the conventional DSGE models could be included in an extended version of this model (with capital in the production function), but since we specifically intended to focus our attention on the role of strategic interactions among oligopolists as a potential source of fluctuations, we have chosen, for our purpose, to stick to the simplified version of the model presented in this chapter.

A particular feature of our model is the fact that the process of entry/exit potentially interacts with distributional shocks among workers and entrepreneurs and (as shown in the next chapters, dedicated to numerical simulations) with the cyclical or countercyclical behavior of firms' markups.

Our microfoundation allows us to model agents who are heterogeneous in their budget constraint and have the same preferences and may change their social group in each period according to a stochastic process, interacting both with labor market and with the process of entry/exit. As shown in the next chapters, this modeling strategy allows us to reproduce macroeconomic fluctuations and formalize other kinds of shocks, like the "conflict" shocks among workers and entrepreneurs.

In this model, the price level (i.e., the average value of the price distribution determined by all the oligopolistic firms) is jointly determined by the behavior of the oligopolistic firms and by the monetary authorities whose decisions in terms of current and future expected interest rates affect the "shift parameter" Ψ_t in the aggregate demand.

This means that the effectiveness (or noneffectiveness) of monetary policy may also depend on how the decisions of the monetary authorities may affect the entry decisions of new potential firms (i.e., making "overoptimistic" a subset of workers who decide to turn into entrepreneurs). Also, the price rigidity/flexibility does not only depend on the workers' market power (like in conventional models) but also on the probability of the oligopolistic firms to collude or to choose price competition. This last point, as well as the entry decision of new firms is modeled here by stochastic variables capturing the firms' propensity to compete or collude, rendered as a Nash equilibrium in mixed strategies, stochastic by definition. The stochastic nature of the Nash equilibrium in mixed strategies can be interpreted as a generalization of the Hayekian process of price setting by firms, described in the earlier chapters of this book.

The next chapters contain agent-based simulations and empirical analyses showing how this new interpretation of the economic system is consistent with the empirical observations and how it may reproduce macroeconomic fluctuations.

2.9 Technical Specifications – Entry and Output Determination: The Existence of a Cournot-Nash Equilibrium

In the model presented here, since the labor contracts establish the amount of hours to be worked by each worker, the labor is a sunk cost and, as a consequence, there is no need to distinguish between capacity and output decision. A few assumptions guarantee the existence of the aggregate equilibrium in the goods market. These assumptions correspond to those contained in Madden (1998), showing that, with a uniformly elastic demand function, the K-S-M two-stage quantity-price game reduces to the Cournot model with any rationing mechanism between the efficient and proportional extremes and if all costs are sunk at the first stage.

Assumption D1

a) The aggregate demand function $D : R_{++} \rightarrow R_{++}$ is C^2 with $D'(p) < 0$ everywhere, $\lim_{p \to 0} D(p) = +\infty$ and $\lim_{p \to \infty} D(p) = 0$.

b) Having defined the market revenue function for firm i in terms of price as $\varkappa_t^i(p_i, \varphi^i)$, where $\varkappa^i : R_{++} \rightarrow R_{++}$, there exists $a \geq 0$ such that the market revenue function $\varkappa_t^i : R_{++} \rightarrow R_{++}$ is strictly increasing on $(0, a)$ and non-increasing on (a, ∞).

Madden also introduces the equivalent assumption, applying to the inverse demand (in his paper, Assumption 2), which we will not consider here, since it is equivalent and unnecessary.

Consistently with the preliminary assumptions made in Madden (1998), when the prices are null, there is no economic activity, no production and, as a consequence, the market revenue function of each individual firm $\varkappa(P_t, \varphi_t)$ is null.

Part (a) of *Assumption D1* ensures that the market demand curve is well-behaved, downward sloping and therefore asymptotic to the axes (like our demand function (2.18)). Part (b) says that market demand is inelastic at prices $P < a$ and elastic at $P > a$. The case $a = 0$ indicates *uniformly elastic demand*, while $a > 0$ admits *eventually inelastic demand*. In our case, we have, of course, $a = 0$; therefore, we always have a uniformly elastic demand function. As Madden points out, "a well-known special case of the uniform elastic demand specification is provided by the constant elasticity demand functions," which applies to our case. Therefore, in our case, the revenues are constant and thus non-increasing.

In the Cournot model firms choose output levels φ^i simultaneously, producing an aggregate output $D = \sum_{i=1}^{n} \varphi^i$.

Furthermore, we define the Cournot payoff functions π_i^c for the generic firm i as:

$$\pi_i^c(\varphi^1, \ldots, \varphi^h) = \begin{cases} \varkappa(p_i, \varphi^i) - c^i(\varphi^i) & c^i > 0 \\ 0 & c^i = 0 \end{cases}$$

where $\varkappa(\varphi^i)$ is the revenue of the individual firm (assumed to be null if prices are null and there is no production) and $c^i(\varphi^i)$ is the cost function. In the Kreps-Scheinkman model, the firms simultaneously choose their output levels at stage 1. Then, with sunk production costs and production levels that are common knowledge, the firms simultaneously choose the prices at stage 2. Then, with sunk production costs and production levels that are common knowledge, the firms simultaneously choose the prices at stage 2. In Kreps and Scheinkman (1983) the demand at stage 2 is rationed among the firms according to the efficient (or surplus-maximizing) rule; the following one is the demand faced by firm i applying the production vector φ^i if the announced prices for stage 2 are p:

$$\Delta_{iE}(\varphi, p) = \max \left\{ 0, \left[D(p_i) . \sum_{p_k < p_i} \varphi^k \right] \frac{\varphi^i}{\sum_{p_k = p_i} \varphi^k} \right\}$$

With this rationing rule, the firms charging less than firm i serve those consumers with the highest valuation of the good, and the term in square brackets is shared among the firms charging p_i, in proportion to their production level. At an opposite extreme is the proportional (or Beckmann 1967) rule, used by Allen and Hellwig (1986):

$$\Delta_{iP}(\varphi, p) = \max \left\{ 0, \left[1 - . \frac{\varphi^k}{\sum_{p_k < p_i} D(p_k)} \right] D(p_i) . \frac{\varphi^i}{\sum_{p_k = p_i} \varphi^k} \right\}$$

In this case, the consumers served by lower priced firms are chosen randomly; $\varphi^k / D(p_k)$ is the fraction of consumers served by k.

Then we can define assumption D2 (corresponding to assumption 3 in Madden 1998):

Assumption D2

The rationed demand function at stage 2 of the Kreps-Scheinkman game for firm i, $i = 1, \ldots, h$ is $\Delta_i : R_+^n \times R_+^n \to R_+$ and satisfies

i) $\Delta_{iE}(\varphi, p) \leq \Delta_i(\varphi, p) \leq \Delta_{ip}(\varphi, p)$, $(\varphi, p) \in R_+^n \times R_{++}^n$
ii) Δ_i only depends on these p_i for which $\varphi^i > 0$

Madden introduces the following definition (Madden 1998, p. 203):

The Kreps-Scheinkman model has the exact Cournot reduced form if for all $\varphi_i \in R_+^n$ and for all mixed strategy Nash equilibria $(\mu_1, \ldots, \mu_n)$ of the stage 2 subgame following φ_i, $\int\limits_{R_{++}^n} R(\varphi_i, p) \cdot d\mu(p) - c_i(\varphi_i) = \pi_i^c(\varphi_i)$, $i = 1, \ldots, n$.

where $R(\varphi_i, p)$ are the revenues of the generic firm i, $c_i(\varphi_i)$ its (sunk) cost, function of its output φ_i,[7] $\pi_i^c(\varphi_i)$ its profits, $(\mu_1, \ldots, \mu_n)$ a vector of mixed strategies of the stage 2 subgame following φ_i. Furthermore (Madden, 1998, p. 203),

it is obvious that proportional rationing will ensure that firms announcing the market-clearing price $p_i = F(Q), i = 1, \ldots, n$ will be a Nash equilibrium of the stage 2 Kreps-Scheinkman subgame, if Q is at an elastic point of the demand curve. No firm will lower price, since they can sell all available output at $F(Q)$. And raising price will capture a fraction of market demand, and hence the same fraction of market revenue, which falls as price is raised because of elasticity, so no firm will raise price either.

Madden defines the correspondence between $\pi_i^c(\varphi^1, \ldots, \varphi^h)$ and the "exact Cournot reduced form," meaning that if the quantities are chosen at stage 1 of the Kreps-Scheinkman game, then the second stage subgame Nash equilibrium that follows, always induce expected payoffs equal to the Cournot payoffs: this is also consistent with the interpretation of mixed strategies as beliefs, suggested by Osborne and Rubinstein (1994, p. 43). Madden (1998) theorem 2, reported

---

[7] For this variable φ_i we have kept our notation and not Madden's notation.

below, shows that, under the assumptions of our model, the two-stage K-S-M game has the "exact Cournot reduced form," which guarantees the existence of a C-N equilibrium in mixed strategies, for an arbitrary number of firms, since each action set is a convex and compact subset of an Euclidean space and each payoff function $\int_{R^n_{++}} R(\varphi_i, p) \cdot d\mu(p) - c_i(\varphi_i) = \pi_i^c(\varphi_i)$ is continuous.

Theorem 1 (Madden 1998). Suppose that assumptions D1 and D2 hold and that the quantity $D(P) = \sum \varphi^i$ is given at stage 1 of the Kreps-Scheinkman game; if demand is elastic at $D(P)$, then the expected revenue in any Nash equilibrium of the stage 2 following $D(P)$ is $\pi_i^c(\varphi^1, \ldots, \varphi^h)$. (See Theorem 1 in Madden 1998, p. 204, for the proof.) When $D(P) > 0$, Madden shows that Theorem 1 is proved by the lemmas 1 and 2.

Following Madden, we can characterize the equilibrium as follows:

Theorem 2 (Madden 1998). If assumptions D1 and D2 hold and the quantity $D(P) = \sum^i \varphi^i$ is given at stage 1 of the Kreps-Scheinkman game, if demand is elastic at $D(P)$, then the Kreps-Scheinkman model has the exact Cournot reduced form. (See theorem 2 in Madden 1998, p. 204, for the proof.)

Theorem 1 and the exact Cournot reduced form resulting from theorem 2 do not apply to the case of an inelastic demand curve.

In particular, the existence of the "exact Cournot reduced form" exactly amounts to the existence of a mixed strategy equilibrium, as Madden himself points out.

Theorem 2 shows that, under the assumptions of our model, we do have the existence conditions for a Cournot-Nash equilibrium in mixed strategies among the oligopolistic firms in the goods market.

PART TWO

Model

3 A Computable Market Model: The Structure of the Agent-Based Simulation

MATTEO MORINI AND PIETRO TERNA

3.1 A Scheme to Start

Starting from the equation based construction introduced in Chapter 2, we build now a macroeconomic simulation model of an economy, using the agent-based technique; the model is microfounded and so our explanation starts from the behavior of the agents and of the market frameworks where they behave.

Agent-based simulation is a form of explicit modeling, so let us point out, with Epstein (2008), that:

Another advantage of explicit models is the feasibility of sensitivity analysis. One can sweep a huge range of parameters over a vast range of possible scenarios to identify the most salient uncertainties, regions of robustness, and important thresholds. I don't see how to do that with an implicit mental model. It is important to note that in the policy sphere (if not in particle physics) models do not obviate the need for judgment. However, by revealing trade-offs, uncertainties, and sensitivities, models can discipline the dialogue about options and make unavoidable judgments more considered.

Most of all, with Axtell (2000):

An agent-based model consists of individual agents, commonly implemented in software as objects. Agent objects have states and rules of behavior. Running such a model simply amounts to instantiating an agent population, letting the agents interact, and monitoring what happens. That is, executing the model – spinning it forward in time – is all that is necessary in order to "solve" it. Furthermore, when a particular instantiation of an agent-based model, call it A, produces result R, one has established a sufficiency theorem, that is, the formal statement R if A (Newell and Simon, 1972, p. 13).

There are, ostensibly, several advantages of agent-based computational modeling over conventional mathematical theorizing. First, as described above, it is easy to limit agent rationality in agent-based computational models. Second, even if one wishes to use completely rational agents, it is a trivial matter to make agents heterogeneous in agent-based models. One simply instantiates a population having some distribution of initial states, e.g., preferences. That is, there is no need to appeal to representative agents. Third, since the model is "solved" merely by executing it, there results an entire dynamical history of the process under study. That is, one need not focus exclusively on the equilibria, should they exist, for the dynamics are an inescapable part of running the agent model. Finally, in most social processes either physical space or social networks matter. These are difficult to account for mathematically except in highly stylized ways. However, in agent-based models it is usually quite easy to have the agent interactions mediated by space or networks or both.

However, the agent-based modeling methodology has one significant disadvantage *vis-a-vis* mathematical modeling. Despite the fact that each run of such a model yields a sufficiency theorem, a single run does not provide any information on the robustness of such theorems. That is, given that agent model A yields result R, how much change in A is necessary in order for R to no longer obtain? In mathematical economics such questions are often formally resolvable via inspection, simple differentiation, the implicit function theorem, comparative statics, and so on. The only way to treat this problem in agent computing is through multiple runs, systematically varying initial conditions or parameters in order to assess the robustness of results.

In our case, the search for the R if A cases via simulation is:

- based on the articulated model framework of Chapter 2;
- required by the absence of closed-form solutions for the algebraic version for the model;[1]
- calculated via a well-defined simulation tool, open source, so explorable by scholar, and grounded on the starting root of the simulation packages, i.e., the Santa Fe Institute package Swarm, emerging in the mid-1990s.

3.1.1 SLAPP – Swarm-Like Agent Protocol in Python

We use SLAPP (Swarm-Like Agent Protocol in Python) that you can find online at:

---

[1] A problem has a closed-form solution if it possible to solve it via mathematical operations.

- https://terna.github.io/SLAPP/ and
- https://github.com/terna/SLAPP.

Boero et al. (2015) also describes SLAPP.
The code of the agent-based model of this book is at:

- https://terna.github.io/oligopoly/ and
- https://github.com/terna/oligopoly.

The code has a reference handbook, whose title is *Oligopoly: the Making of the Simulation Model*,[2] in compliance with the AEA Data Availability Policy.[3]

Appendix C explains how to run the code, with some documented exception for the different cases of Chapter 4.

3.1.2 The Structure of the Simulation Model

The structure of the simulation model is well represented via the sequence of the 12 items of Figure 3.1.

Following the circular sequence of the events, we can identify both those related (i) to a conventional simple market aggregate clearing mechanism (SMAC) or (ii) to an atomistic simplified Hayekian market (ASHAM) interpretation of the price formation.

In SMAC, the aggregate production in quantity at time t is compared with the aggregate demand in value always at time t, to fix a clearing price, as in Section 3.8 (or, which is the same, in item 8 of Figure 3.1), under the hypothesis that the unique good of the economy is a perishable one, so we have no warehouses and stocks.

In ASHAM, the interaction among sellers (the entrepreneurs) and buyers (the workers and the entrepreneurs) is built via an atomistic market where each agent meets her/his counterpart: this is the activity described in Section 3.7 (or, which is the same, in item 7 of Figure 3.1).

We work here in the perspective of a simplified Hayekian market; a suggested reading about Hayek is a quite recent paper of Bowles et al. (2017), with coauthors Alan Kirman and Rajiv Sethi.

---

[2] https://github.com/terna/oligopoly/blob/master/Oligopoly.pdf.

[3] https://www.aeaweb.org/journals/policies/data-availability-policy.

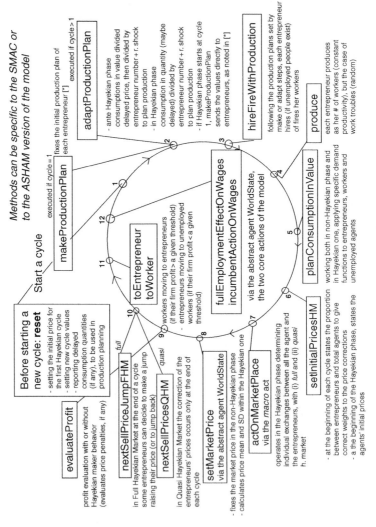

Figure 3.1 The outline of the simulation model with its 12 items

Quoting from the introduction:

Friedrich A. Hayek (1899-1992) is known for his vision of the market economy as an information processing system characterized by spontaneous order, the emergence of coherence through the independent actions of large numbers of individuals each with limited and local knowledge, coordinated by prices that arise from decentralized processes of competition.

From the article, we report the Hayek quotation:

[The market is] a system of the utilization of knowledge which nobody can possess as a whole, which [. . .] leads people to aim at the needs of people whom they do not know, make use of facilities about which they have no direct information; all this condensed in abstract signals [. . .T]hat our whole modern wealth and production could arise only thanks to this mechanism is, I believe, the basis not only of my economics but also much of my political views (Hayek, 1994, p. 69).

The simplified version – proposed here – is that of considering decentralized elementary processes of price adaptation in exchanges.

The price adaptation is continuous on the side of the buyers.

About the sellers – as in Sections 3.7 (or item 7 in Figure 3.1), 3.10.1 (or item 10-*full* in Figure 3.1), or 3.10.2 (or item 10-*quasi* in Figure 3.1) – we have the *full* paradigm with continuous price adaptation or the *quasi* paradigm with the seller prices adapting only at the beginning of each period (cycle of the simulation).

We refer to Appendix A for a deep explanation of the interacting market mechanism.

An immediate warning: in Appendix A and in this chapter (Figures 3.2, 3.3, 3.4, and 3.5), seemingly we have offer curves. Actually, they are more complicated objects, as on the x-axis we do not have quantities, but agents: at the price reported in the y-axis the agent can sell all the quantity she owns (a unitary quantity in the simple examples reported in Appendix A and in the quoted figures; any quantity in the ASHAM case). Specifically, in ASHAM each seller has a true horizontal offer curve: at a given price, she sells any quantity. We do not call it supply curve on purpose. The prices reported in the figures are reservation prices for the buyers, while for the sellers they are closer to sell prices like those exposed in a mall. Correct and descriptive names for both the curves of these figures are: buyers' price curve; sellers' price curve.

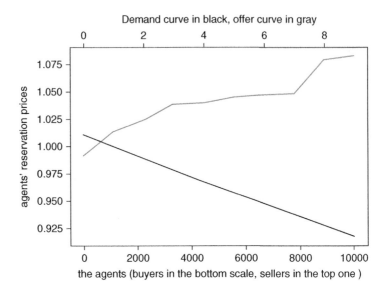

Figure 3.2 Case i: buyers' price curve with 10,000 agents, ε_B in $[-0.09, 0.01)$; sellers' price curve with 10 agents, ε_S in $[-0.01, 0.09)$

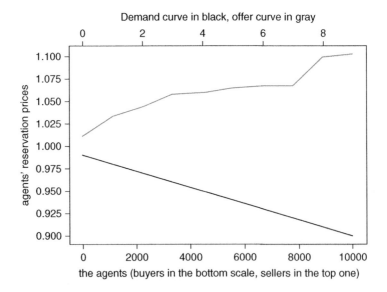

Figure 3.3 Case ii: buyers' price curve with 10,000 agents, ε_B in $[-0.11, -0.01)$; sellers' price curve with 10 agents, ε_S in $[0.01, 0.11)$

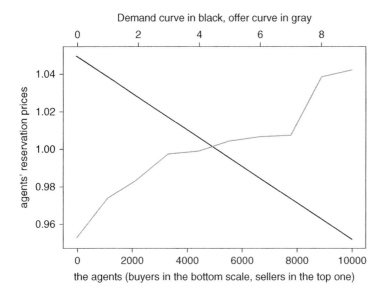

Figure 3.4 Case iii: (a) buyers' price curve with 10,000 agents, ε_B in $[-0.05, 0.05)$; sellers' price curve with 10 agents, ε_S in $[-0.05, 0.05)$

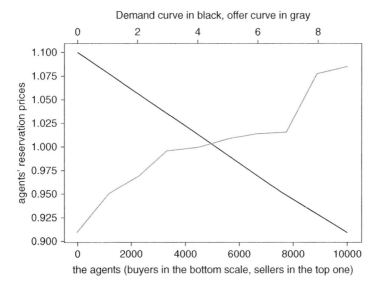

Figure 3.5 Case iii: (b) buyers' price curve with 10,000 agents, ε_B in $[-0.10, 0.10)$; sellers' price curve with 10 agents, ε_S in $[-0.10, 0.10)$

The following sections help us understand the items of Figure 3.1; to deepen how the different items are linked among them, it is possible to have a look to the reference handbook: *The Oligopoly Project: The Making of the Simulation Model.*[4]

The sequence of the items of the figure are also related to the explanation in Section C.1.

3.1.3 What Is a Cycle and What Are Sub-Steps?

How the time operates: each cycle of 12 steps, as described in Figure 3.1, is equivalent to a step ahead of the time counter t.

The number of cycles of the simulation is reported in the variable nCycle, as in Appendix B.

In ASHAM, the item 7 as in Section 3.7 is subdivided in sub-steps.

As explained in n the reference handbook The *Oligopoly Project: The Making of the Simulation Model*, the sequence of the events is managed by a schedule mechanism, defining steps and sub-steps.

Firms produce a unique kind of good.

3.1.4 Item 1: Reset Action

We refer to item 1 in Figure 3.1.

Before starting a new cycle, we have to run a reset action. The reset action acts once in each simulation cycle, because in our case is related only to common variables of the simulation. The agent executing the cleaning operation is that with the identifier (the variable *number*) equal to 1. If no agent has that identifier, all will be acting, with not useful repetitions of the same task.[5]

3.2 Item 2: *makeProductionPlan* or *adaptProductionPlan*

3.2.1 makeProductionPlan

We refer to item 2 in Figure 3.1.

---

[4] Online at https://github.com/terna/oligopoly/blob/master/
Oligopoly.pdf.

[5] For technical details, look at the section "The Scheduling Mechanism at the Level of the Model" in the reference handbook *Oligopoly: The Making of the Simulation Model.*

The method (or command) makeProductionPlan, acting uniquely at time $t = 1$, sent to the entrepreneurs, orders them to guess their production for the current first period. The production plan for entrepreneur i at time $t = 1$, $\widehat{P}_t^i$, is determined in a random way, using a Poisson distribution, with ν as a mean.

Controlling the ρ value (as rho in Appendix B), we calculate ν (used uniquely in the first Item) as:

$$\nu = \rho \frac{(N_{workers} + N_{entrepreneurs})}{N_{entrepreneurs}} \tag{3.1}$$

In this way, being the productivity set to 1 (laborProductivity, as in Appendix B), about a ρ ratio of the agents is employed and productive in the beginning.

We have also the wage level set to 1 (wage, as in Appendix B).

3.2.2 adaptProductionPlan

We again refer to item 2 in Figure 3.1.

This function or method has to work both if we use:

- a SMAC to fix the price of each period, comparing the production in quantity, as realized, with the aggregate the demand function in value, or
- an ASHAM, using a person to person system of exchanges, as described in Appendix A. (Appendix A will contain a quite synthetic presentation of https://terna.github.io/microHayekianMarket/.)

We have two working situations.

1) Whether we are in a SMAC period, i.e., in a *warming up* phase of the run of the model non initially ASHAM[6], or in a whole

---

[6] A possible way to start the *Oligopoly* model in ASHAM way is that of *warming up* the model with the price setting system employed by SMAC, i.e., comparing the total offer in quantity and the total demand in value and calculating a clearing price.

If ASHAM has to start at $t = k$, after $k - 1$ cycles of *warming*, the last price is used in cycle k, considering it to be the *previous cycle price* that both the entrepreneurs (as producers) and the entrepreneurs and the workers (as consumers) remember and use in their first time step, starting to act in a decentralize market, in the ASHAM perspective.

SMAC situation, the method `adaptProductionPlan`, sent to `entrepreneurs`, orders to the ith firm to set its production plan, for the current period, to their (equal, being i here not relevant) fraction of the total demand of the previous period, in value, corrected with a random uniform relative correction in the interval $-\varepsilon$ to $+\varepsilon$, or `randomComponentOfPlannedProduction` as in Appendix B.

This method works at time $t > 1$. If $t = 1$ the method of Section 3.2.1, i.e., `makeProductionPlan`, is acting.

Being $\widehat{P}_t^i$ the planned production of firm i, we have:

- if $u_t^i \geq 0$

$$\widehat{P}_t^i = \frac{D_{t-1}}{N_{entrepreneurs}}(1 + u_t^i) \qquad (3.2)$$

- if $u_t^i < 0$

$$\widehat{P}_t^i = \frac{D_{t-1}}{N_{entrepreneurs}}/(1 + |u_t^i|) \qquad (3.3)$$

with $u_t^i \sim \mathcal{U}(-\varepsilon, \varepsilon)$

2) Whether we are in a whole ASHAM experiment or in a mixed one, starting SMAC e moving to ASHAM, being k (that can be $k = 1$) the starting time of the ASHAM run, with $t \geq k$, the methods is operating in the direction of the atomistic simplified Hayekian market. In Appendix B, k is `startHayekianMarket`.

The entrepreneurs evaluate expected production in each period by dividing the total consumptions of the previous period, measured in quantity (prices are too heterogeneous in an ASHAM situation), by the number of entrepreneurs.

With:

- $\varphi_{i,t}$ as individual firm production in t;
- $C_{n_s,t-1}$ as one of the buying actions, measured in quantity, of the consumer s at time $t - 1$;
- N_E as the entrepreneur number;
- u_t as a random addendum (drawn from a uniform distribution to have super-fat tails) representing the difficulty of having correct information about all the buy actions made into the economic system;
- Q and $1 - Q$ as the weights to be attributed to the consumption at time $t - 1$ and $t - 2$, with $0 \leq Q \leq 1$;

We have:

$$\varphi_{i,t} = Q\frac{\sum_s \sum_{n_s} C_{n_s,t-1}}{N_E} + (1-Q)\frac{\sum_s \sum_{n_s} C_{n_s,t-2}}{N_E} + u_t \quad (3.4)$$

The calculations of Eq. (3.4) are a part of the reset actions of Section 3.1.4.

3.3 Item 3: *hireFireWithProduction*

We refer to item 3 in Figure 3.1.

The method `hireFireWithProduction` orders to the `entrepreneurs` to hire or fire comparing their actual labor force with that required for the production plan $\widehat{P}_t^i$, considering the labor productivity π; we have the required labor force (L_t^i is the current one, before the new calculation):

$$\widehat{L}_t^i = \widehat{P}_t^i / \pi \quad (3.5)$$

Effects:

1 if $\widehat{L}_t^i = L_t^i$, nothing has to be done;
2 if $\widehat{L}_t^i > L_t^i$, the entrepreneur is hiring with the limit of the number of unemployed workers;
3 if $\widehat{L}_t^i < L_t^i$, the entrepreneur is firing the workers in excess.

3.4 Item 4: *produce*

We refer to item 4 in Figure 3.1.

The method (or command) `produce` sent to the `entrepreneurs` orders them – in a deterministic way, in each unit of time or cycle – to produce proportionally to their labor force, obtaining profit Π_t^i, where i identifies the firm and t the time.

L_t^i is the number of workers of firm i at time t. We add 1 to L_t^i, to account for the entrepreneur herself as a worker. π is the `laborProductivity`, with its value set to 1, not changing with t. P_t^i is the production of the firm i at time t.

$$P_t^i = \pi(L_t^i + 1) \quad (3.6)$$

The production is corrected for work troubles measured by ψ (Section 3.4.1) calculating the corrected value Pc_t^i with:

$$Pc_t^i = P_t^i(1 - \psi_{i,t}) \quad (3.7)$$

The production (corrected or not) of the firm i is added to the total production of the time step.

3.4.1 Item 4, Continuation: workTroubles

We again refer to item 4 in Figure 3.1.

The method `workTroubles` refers to the `entrepreneurs`. For each entrepreneur i, at time t, we generate a shock $\psi_{i,t} > 0$ due to work troubles, with probability p_ψ (set for all the entrepreneurs via the `schedule.xls` file)[7] and value uniformly distributed between $V_\psi/2$ and V_ψ. The shock reduces the production of firm i in a relative way, as in:

$$Pc_t^i = P_t^i(1 - \psi_{i,t}) \tag{3.8}$$

where Pc means *corrected production*.

If the global logical value `wageCutForWorkTroubles` is *true*, also wages are cut in the same proportion. With w indicating the constant basic wage level, cw_t^i is the corrected value at time t and for firm i; the correction is superimposed to the other possible corrections (due to full employment or to artificial barrier creation).

$$cw_t^i = w(1 - \psi_{i,t}) \tag{3.9}$$

The firm variable `hasTroubles` takes note – via $\psi_{i,t}$ assuming a value > 0, being 0 otherwise – if the firm has work problems in the current time step and the worker variable `workTroubles` reports the information for all the workers of that specific firm.

3.5 Item 5: *planConsumptionInValue*

We refer to item 5 in Figure 3.1.

The method `planConsumptionInValue` orders both to the `workers` or to the `entrepreneurs`, to plan the consumptions in value for the current cycle and its sub-steps (as defined in Section 3.1.3).

Consumption behavior of the agent i at time t is defined as:

$$C_{i,t} = a_k + b_k Y_{i,t} + u_{i,t} \tag{3.10}$$

---

[7] SLAPP displays – in its text output – a dictionary of method probabilities, if at least one method is linked to a probability.

with $u_{i,t}$ from $u \sim \mathcal{N}(0, sd)$.[8]

The individual i can be:

1 an entrepreneur, with $Y_{i,t} = profit_{i,t-1} + wage$;
2 an employed worker, with $Y_{i,t} = wage$ and the special[9] case $Y_{i,t} = wc_t^i$, with wc_t^i defined in Eq. (3.9);
3 an unemployed workers,[10] with $Y_{i,t} = socialWelfareCompensation$.

The a_k and b_k values are set via the parameters of the model. We use socialWelfareCompensation as in Appendix B.

Finally, a quota of the unspent consumption capability coming from the past, is added to the result. The quota, with a value in the interval $[0, 1]$, has value q^{res}, and it is applied to reUseUnspentConsumptionCapability as in Appendix B, giving:

$$C_{i,t}^+ = C_{i,t} + q^{res} \cdot unspentConsumptionCapability \qquad (3.11)$$

Referring to the *planned consumption in value in a time step*, the method updates that value only until the starting point of ASHAM, so in SMAC phase, if any.

In the ASHAM phase, in each sub-step of a cycle (look at Section 3.1.3) we establish a max quantity of consumptions, via a quota introduced interactively in the starting session of the simulation (variable consumptionQuota, as in Appendix B). This action mimics the behavior of the households within each time period.

When ASHAM operates, the consumption total amount comes from summing up all the consumption actions generated by this (item 5) method.

3.6 Item 6: *setInitialPricesHM*

We refer to item 6 in Figure 3.1.

The method (or command) setInitialPricesHM, sent to all, operates only in the ASHAM phase of each run.

The method performs several actions.

---

[8] With *sd* value reported by the parameter *consumptionRandomComponentSD*.
[9] Activated if the *common* value *wageCutForWorkTroubles* is *true*.
[10] In this case, if the random component exceeds the consumption coming from social welfare compensation, we can have negative consumption; in case, consumption is set to 0.

1) In each cycle, while the ASHAM is working, the method calculates the ratio $Z = \frac{\text{number of sellers}}{\text{number of buyers}}$ between sellers and buyers as requested in adopting the ASHAM paradigm: the modification of the prices is continuous, both on the side of the buyers (all the agents) and of the side of the sellers (the entrepreneurs); the frequencies of the modifications belong to two highly different scales and as a consequence the amplitude of the price corrections are very different.

2) In the first step of the ASHAM phase, the method states the initial common price: being at time k, we use as starting point the price at time $k - 1$ or, if $k > 2$, at $k - 2$. The double lagged price correction is justified because we are considering the production decisions at time t as based on the decisions of consumption at $t - 1$, related to the income at time $t - 1$; these decisions are made before the determination of the prices at $t - 1$ (in the SMAC scheme emerges only when comparing the demand and the predetermined offer). If we want to evaluate the consumption in quantity, without the effect of a too limited or too abundant offer, we have to use $t - 2$ prices. This construction is eliminated with ASHAM interaction of buyers and sellers in a dispersed way.

   If $k = 1$, we use the SMAC structure market, calculating the price as the equilibrium price that would have been created at $t = 1$ in the SMAC execution, but avoiding the random shocks of item 8 in Section 3.8.

3) Calculation of the individual starting prices. The parameters in use here are `initShock` and `initShift`. Here we calculate both the individual `buyPrice` and the individual `sellPrice`, because each agent can act both as entrepreneur-seller and as buyer.

   • We add random corrections to both the types of initial prices; so, we will start the first cycle of the simulation with two initial distributions of values for the buyers and for the sellers. Let `initShock` be the variable containing the relative value ι as range of the correction of the individual starting prices in a random uniform way, with the internal variable `initShift`, having value v, reasonably[11] in the interval $[-1, 1]$, e.g., 0.10, shifting the range of the whole correction.

---

[11] With very different effects.

Our goal here is that of initializing (i) buyer prices mostly *below/above* the starting price and (ii) seller prices mostly *above/below* the starting price, to induce more or less intensively the necessity of individual price corrections from the beginning of the exchanges.[12]

With $p_{S,i}$ as initial sell price of agent i, $p_{B,i}$ as initial buy price of agent i and p_H as starting ASHAM price, we have the following equations:

- if $\varepsilon_{S,i} \geq 0$

$$p_{S,i} = p_H(1 + \varepsilon_{S,i}) \tag{3.12}$$

- if $\varepsilon_{S,i} < 0$

$$p_{S,i} = p_H/(1 + |\varepsilon_{S,i}|) \tag{3.13}$$

with $\varepsilon_{S,i} \sim \mathcal{U}(-v\,\iota, (1-v)\,\iota)$. Also,

- if $\varepsilon_{B,i} \geq 0$

$$p_{B,i} = p_H(1 + \varepsilon_{B,i}) \tag{3.14}$$

- if $\varepsilon_{B,i} < 0$

$$p_{B,i} = p_H/(1 + |\varepsilon_{B,i}|) \tag{3.15}$$

with $\varepsilon_{B,i} \sim \mathcal{U}(-(1-v)\,\iota, v\,\iota)$.

i) If we adopt $v = 0.10$ and $\iota = 0.10$, we only have a quite small overlapping of the initial price correction (correction are never too rational, with someone moving in the wrong direction). The ε corrections will be uniformly distributed between -0.01 and 0.09 for the sellers and between -0.09 and 0.01 for the buyers.

Considering the individual prices as reservation prices, we have a buyers' price and sellers' price curves crossing on the left side of their graphic representation, as in Figure 3.2.

ii) If we want not overlapping curves, we can use $v < 0$, e.g., $v = -0.1$, with $\iota = 0.10$. The ε corrections will be uniformly

---

[12] At creation time, for each agent *sellPrice* is set to 1,000 and *buyPrice* to $-1,000$, as implausible values, not operational.

   In any case, the sellers (entrepreneur) cannot operate into the ASHAM until their starting price is defined; this information is reported setting to (True) the agent's variable *sellPriceDefined*.

distributed between 0.01 and 0.11 for the sellers and between −0.11 and −0.01 for the buyers, as in Figure 3.3.

iii) We can also choose to start in a balancing situation, with $v = 0.5$ and, e.g., $\iota = 0.10|0.20$. ε corrections will be uniformly distributed

(a) between −0.05 and 0.05 for the sellers and between −0.05 and 0.05 for the buyers, as in Figure 3.4 for $\iota = 0.10$,

or (b) between −0.10 and 0.10 for the sellers and between −0.10 and 0.10 for the buyers, as in Figure 3.5 for $\iota = 0.20$, *doubling the y scale.*

We generate symmetric effect both for positive and negative rates of change, using the so-called rational discount rule, with a simple structure such as:

- if the rate of change $i \geq 0$, x_c (i.e., x after the correction) is

$$x_c = x(1 + i) \tag{3.16}$$

- if the rate of change $i < 0$, x_c (i.e., x after the correction) is

$$x_c = x/(1 + i) \tag{3.17}$$

3.7 Item 7: *actOnMarketPlace*

We refer to item 7 in Figure 3.1.

The method operates only in the ASHAM phase of each run.

Both the `entrepreneurs` and the `workers` are *buyers*, while the *sellers* are uniquely the `entrepreneurs`.

The following is the sequence of the actions.

- The method is repeating its action several times in each cycle, for each sub-step (about sub-steps in cycles, look at the Section 3.1.3).

  Technically, sub-steps are included in a macro and the number of repetitions for each buyer in each cycle (the number of buy attempts) is regulated by the number of repetitions into the macro.[13] In each repetition, the program shuffles the agents. Each agent has in memory the effect of the action done in the previous repetition within a cycle.

---

[13] See https://github.com/terna/oligopoly/blob/master/Oligopoly.pdf for the reference handbook *The Oligopoly Project: The Making of the Simulation Model.*

The number of sub-steps is incremented to cope with the phenomenon of the idle agents reported in Section A.5 of Appendix A.

- Search for sellers. In the first sub-step of each multiple call of the method in each cycle, and for each buyer, a seller is chosen from a temporary list of sellers having still unsold products.
- Sold products are recorded in each sub-step and reset to 0 when a new cycle starts.

The deal between a buyer and a seller is based on the confrontation of the prices. Considering the buy price of agent i and the sell price of agent j, if $p_{B,i} \geqslant p_{S,j}$ the agents exchange, at the seller price, the minimum quantity between (i) the buying capacity of the buyer at that price, i.e., its maximum spending value in each step of a cycle at that price,[14] and (ii) the actual production residual quantity of the seller.

The revenue of the seller (one of the entrepreneurs) is accounted for profit calculations.

- Prices: what price in each action for each agent?
  - The best is *their* price, i.e., the price at which they have concluded a deal (the last one, if more than a deal were made in a same time interval)[15] or that of the last bid (if buyers) or ask (if sellers) they made without concluding a deal. This price is corrected with the rules below.
  - To generate symmetric effect both for positive and negative rates of change, we apply a symmetric rational calculation, as described in Section 3.5. Missing this device, or trick, the cumulative effect of negative and positive corrections would always be negative.[16]
  - The continuous process of correction of the individual prices, applied to the transactions within each cycle, works in the following way.
    1) We modify the buy price (a random correction) if the last agent negotiation, also if unsuccessful, was on the buy side.

---

[14] As stated in Section 3.5, in each step of a cycle, we establish a maximum quantity of consumptions, via a quota introduced interactively in the starting session of the program.

[15] The event is possible if the agents buy or sell only fractions of their buying or selling quantities, thus repeating their actions.

[16] $x(1 - i)(1 + 1) = x(1 - i^2) < x.$

2) The same is true for the sell price, but here only in case of hParadigm (as in Appendix B) set to `full` (see Section 3.1 and Section 3.6); if this is the case, the sellers' price correction is limited by the factor Z reporting the value of `ratioSellersBuyers`, to account for the different (extremely higher) number of corrections they made in a cycle.

Consider now price correction as running shocks calculated with a shift upon or below the 0; the values are different for buyers and sellers with `runningShockB`, `runningShiftB` and `runningShockS`, `runningShiftS` (as in Appendix B). Let `runningShock` B or S be the internal variable containing the relative value $\tilde{\iota}$ (e.g., 0.05) as the range of the correction or the individual running prices in a random uniform way (but shifted, with the internal variable `runningShift` B or S containing the value of $\tilde{v}$ defined in the interval $[0, 0.5]$, e.g., 0.10, having in case a quite low effect below, for the sellers, and above, for the buyers, the 0), with $p_{B,i}$ as buy price of agent i and $p_{S,i}$ as sell price of agent i.

The equations are the same as 3.12, 3.13, 3.14, and 3.15, with $\tilde{v}_B$ or $\tilde{v}_S$ substituting v and $\tilde{\iota}_B$ or $\tilde{\iota}_S$ substituting ι. Remember Z, the ratio of sellers to buyers.

- After the starting cycle of the ASHAM phase, the agents use two *status* variables (technically: `statusB` and `statusS`), initialized to 0 and reporting their short-term history both as buyers (workers or entrepreneurs) and as sellers (entrepreneurs).

  Conventions:

  – `self.statusB`
    o 0 means never used;
    o 1 if previous action was a successful buy attempt;
    o −1 if previous action was an unsuccessful buy attempt.
  – `self.statusS`
    o 0 means never used;
    o 1 if previous action was a successful sell attempt;
    o −1 if previous action was an unsuccessful sell attempt.
  – *Buyer* case:
    o if the last transaction succeeded ($statusB = 1$) and $\varepsilon_{Bdown,i} \geq 0$:

$$p_{B,i_t} = p_{B,i_{t-1}}(1 + \varepsilon_{Bdown,i}) \tag{3.18}$$

o if the last transaction succeeded (*statusB* = 1) and $\varepsilon_{B^{down},i} < 0$:

$$p_{B,i_t} = p_{B,i_{t-1}}/(1 + |\varepsilon_{B^{down},i}|) \qquad (3.19)$$

with $\varepsilon_{B^{down},i} \sim \mathcal{U}(-(1 - \tilde{v}_B)\,\tilde{\iota}_B, \tilde{v}_B\,\tilde{\iota}_B)$, so mostly negative (the agent tries to decrease its reservation price);

o if the last transaction failed (*statusB* = 1) and $\varepsilon_{B^{up},i} \geq 0$:

$$p_{B,i_t} = p_{B,i_{t-1}}(1 + \varepsilon_{B^{up},i}) \qquad (3.20)$$

o if the last transaction failed (*statusB* = −1) and $\varepsilon_{B^{up},i} < 0$:

$$p_{B,i_t} = p_{B,i_{t-1}}/(1 + |\varepsilon_{B^{up},i}|) \qquad (3.21)$$

with $\varepsilon_{B^{up},i} \sim \mathcal{U}(-\tilde{v}_B\,\tilde{\iota}_B, (1 - \tilde{v}_B)\,\tilde{\iota}_B)$, so mostly positive (the agent tries to increase its reservation price).

– *Seller* case:[17]

o if the last transaction succeeded (*statusS* = 1) and $\varepsilon_{S^{up},i} \geq 0$:

$$p_{S,i_t} = p_{S,i_{t-1}}(1 + Z\varepsilon_{S^{up},i}) \qquad (3.22)$$

o if the last transaction succeeded (*statusS* = 1) and $\varepsilon_{S^{up},i} < 0$:

$$p_{S,i_t} = p_{S,i_{t-1}}/(1 + Z|\varepsilon_{S^{up},i}|) \qquad (3.23)$$

with $\varepsilon_{S^{up},i} \sim \mathcal{U}(-\tilde{v}_S\,\tilde{\iota}_S, (1-\tilde{v}_S)\,\tilde{\iota}_S)$, so mostly positive (the agent tries to increase its reservation price);

o if the last transaction failed (*statusS* = −1) and $\varepsilon_{S^{down},i} \geq 0$:

$$p_{S,i_t} = p_{S,i_{t-1}}(1 + Z\varepsilon_{S^{down},i}) \qquad (3.24)$$

o if the last transaction failed (*statusS* = −1) and $\varepsilon_{S^{down},i} < 0$:

$$p_{S,i_t} = p_{S,i_{t-1}}/(1 + Z|\varepsilon_{S^{down},i}|) \qquad (3.25)$$

with $\varepsilon_{S^{down},i} \sim \mathcal{U}(-(1 - \tilde{v}_S)\,\tilde{\iota}_S, \tilde{v}_S\,\tilde{\iota}_S)$, so mostly negative (the agent tries to decrease its reservation price).

– The rational calculation introduced in Section 3.6 is applied here to the couples of eqs.: (3.18) or (3.19); (3.20) or (3.21); (3.22) or (3.23); (3.24) or (3.25).

---

[17] Operating in case of *hParadigm* (as in Appendix B) set to *full*; if set to *quasi* the correction is made once per cycle; if the parameter is set to a value, which is neither *full* nor *quasi*, we have a side effect, because no corrections will happen on sell prices. In the case of the *quasi* scheme, in the first cycle the *full* scheme is anyway operating, see Section 3.10.2.

- The method *actOnMarketPlace* also has a tool to generate an optional report about residual consumption in value
and unsold production in quantity, at the beginning of
each *sub-step* in a cycle. To obtain the report, the variable
checkResConsUnsoldProd (as in Appendix B) has to be *true*.
The report is printed in the regular output flow of the model.

3.8 Item 8: *setMarketPrice*

We refer to item 8 in Figure 3.1.

The method setMarketPrice orders to the abstract agent
WorldState to evaluate the market clearing prices in a SMAC situation or simply to record the mean and the standard deviation of the
prices in each cycle of an ASHAM.

In agent-based model, usually the agents are mimicking an actual
subject existing in the reality; in this case, we have an abstract agent
making computations both (i) relevant from a theoretical economic
point of view or (ii) simply accounting statistical data.

Considering (ii) in the SMAC case, the method evaluates the market
clearing price, considering each agent behavior plus *an external shock,
potentially large*.

We introduce a shock Ξ uniformly distributed between $-L$
and $+L$, where L is a rate on base 1, e.g., 0.10, defined as
maxDemandRelativeRandomShock in Appendix B. To keep the
effect as symmetric, we have the following equations determining the
learing price:

if the shock Ξ is (≥ 0):

$$p_t = \frac{D_t(1 + \Xi)}{O_t} \tag{3.26}$$

if the shock Ξ is (< 0):

$$p_t = \frac{D_t/(1 + \Xi)}{O_t} \tag{3.27}$$

with p_t clearing market price at time t; D_t demand in value[18] at time
t; O_t offer in quantity[19] at time t.

---

[18] Generated by the agent *entrepreneurs* and *workers* as in Section 3.5.
[19] Generated by the agent *entrepreneurs* as in Section 3.4.

3.9 Item 9: *evaluateProfit*

We refer to item 9 in Figure 3.1.

The method orders to the `entrepreneurs` to calculate their profits, using P_t^i, the production, and L_t^i, the labor force, plus 1 to account for the entrepreneur herself.

The use of P_t^i, the actual production of the entrepreneurs, accounts both for the production plan decided with `adaptProductionPlan`, Section 3.2, and for the limits in hiring, if any, in `hireFireWithProduction`, Section 3.3. The sum of all the actual productions of each entrepreneur is used, as in Section 3.8, in `setMarketPrice`.

p_t is the `price`, coming from the analysis of Section 3.7 for ASHAM, or 3.8 for SMAC.

w is the `wage` per employee and time unit, set to 1.0 in these research and not changing with t, but the case of the important events of:

- wage rise due both to full employment (Section 3.12.1), and
- to the creation of barriers against new entrants (Section 3.12.2).

C are extra costs for new entrant firms. They are calibrated to assure the effectiveness of the action described in Section 3.12.2, but in a non rigid way, thanks to the movements in prices.

If the variable `wageCutForWorkTroubles` (as in Appendix B) is set to *True*, the costs determination takes in account the reduction of the wages (but the wage of the entrepreneur, not changing).

Considering the presence of work troubles (see Section 3.4.1), the determination of the clearing price, as at page 96, can signal an increase in the equilibrium price, due to the lacking production.

The (relative) shock $\psi_{i,t} > 0$ due to work troubles is defined in Section 3.4.1.

Within the SMAC paradigm, in the presence of work troubles the firm has to accept a reduction of its price, to compensate its customers for having undermined the confidence in the implicit commitment of producing a given quantity (the production plan, specified in Section 3.2.1). The penalty value, as a relative measure, is reported in `penaltyValue` (as in Appendix B) and here shortly as pv. Locally, pv_t^i, for the firm i at time t, is set to pv if $\psi_{i,t} > 0$; otherwise ($\psi_{i,t} = 0$) is set to 0.

Eqs. (3.28) and (3.29) are used in the SMAC context, while Eqs. (3.30) and (3.31) work in the ASHAM one.

The profit evaluation in SMAC, if `wageCutForWorkTroubles` is set to *True*, is:

$$\Pi_t^i = p_t(1 - pv_t^1)P_t^i - (w - \psi_{i,t})(L_t^i - 1) - 1w - C \qquad (3.28)$$

being $1w$ the wage of the entrepreneur.

If `wageCutForWorkTroubles` is set to *False*, the result is:

$$\Pi_t^i = p_t(1 - pv_t^i)P_t^i - wL_t^i - C \qquad (3.29)$$

In ASHAM we have, with REV_t^i reporting the revenue of firm i at time t, and `wageCutForWorkTroubles` set to *True*:

$$\Pi_t^i = REV_t^i - (w - \psi_{i,t})(L_t^i - 1) - 1w - C \qquad (3.30)$$

being $1w$ the wage of the entrepreneur.

If `wageCutForWorkTroubles` is set to *False*, the result is:

$$\Pi_t^i = REV_t^i - wL_t^i - C \qquad (3.31)$$

The experiments run in April 2017 (with V5 of this method) for the final version for the *Italian Economic Journal* have the penalty value pv_t^i set to 0.

The new entrant firms have extra costs C to be supported, retrieved in XC variables, but only for k periods, as stated in `commonVar.py` and activated by method `toEntrepreneur`.

3.10 Item 10: *nextSellPriceJumpFHM* and *nextSellPricesQHM*

The methods `nextSellPriceJumpFHM` and `nextSellPricesQHM` are related to ASHAM and work in two different perspectives: the first method, in the *full* ASHAM case, with the sellers – as the buyers – changing continuously their prices and sometimes adjusting them in an extraordinary way (with a jump); the second one, in the *quasi* ASHAM case, where the sellers change their prices only once in each time period, in the beginning.

3.10.1 Item 10–full: nextSellPriceJumpFHM

We refer to item 10-*full* in Figure 3.1.

The method `nextSellPriceJumpFHM` operates only in the ASHAM context. It works modifying the sell price of a specific *entrepreneur-seller* with jump-up corrections of her reservation prices. The method operates with a given probability. The settings are the `jump` size and the `pJump` probability (as in Appendix B).

`jump` is a relative value, so $p^J = p(1 + jump)$.

The probability of jumping operates as a switch, moving the agent to be a jumper and vice versa.

If a worker of a jumping-up entrepreneur moves to be an entrepreneur herself, she starts as a jumper.

In the *full*-case (as described in Section 3.7), with the use of `jump`, an entrepreneur making a jump continues anyway to modify her price within the `actOnMaketPlaceMethod` in each sub-step (as defined in Section 3.1.3).

3.10.2 Item 10–quasi: nextSellPricesQHM

We refer to item 10-*quasi* in Figure 3.1.

The method `nextSellPricesQHM` operates in the ASHAM context and specifically in the *quasi* case (as described in Section 3.7).

In this case, with the price correction switch `hParadigm` set to `quasi`, the correction of the entrepreneurs' prices occurs only at the end of each cycle.[20]

We have several possible choices. To select an option we use the variable `quasiHchoice` (as in Appendix B) with possible values: `unsold`, `profit`, and `randomUp`.

i) Case `quasiHchoice` set to `unsold`. We compare $\frac{sold\ production}{production}$, as sold-ratio, with two thresholds:
 * `soldThreshold1`[21] and
 * `soldThreshold2`[22], both in Appendix B;
 * if the result is less or equal than `soldThreshold1`, a random correction is applied, dividing the price by

---

[20] In this case, it could be important to start with a well-balanced initial situation, as in solution (iii) in Section 3.6.

[21] E.g., 0.90.

[22] E.g., 0.99.

$1 + |u_1|$, with u_1 drawn from a flat distribution $u_1 \sim \mathcal{U}(decreasing\,Rate\,Range, 0)$;[23]

- if the result is greater or equal than `soldThreshold2`, a random correction is applied, multiplying the price by $1 + u_2$ with u_2 drawn from a flat distribution $u_2 \sim \mathcal{U}(0, increasing\,Rate\,Range)$;[24]

- between the `soldThreshold1` and `soldThreshold2` values, no corrections occur;

- if `entrepreneursMindIfPlannedProductionFalls` is *True* and (Section 3.2.2) the planned production is falling more than a given threshold,[25] the entrepreneurs (individually) reduce their prices, with the same mechanism above; this condition supersede the confrontation of the sold-ratio with the two thresholds.

ii) Case `quasiHchoice` set to `randomUp`. The logical scheme is the same of the jump in Section 3.10.1 for the *full* implementation, but here the huge difference is that we have no corrections within the specific cycle, with the jumped or un-jumped price kept constant.

We use the same parameters of Section 3.10.1, so the `jump` size with the `pSize` probability (as in Appendix B).

`jump` is a relative value, so $p^J = p(1 + jump)$.

The probability of jumping operates as a switch, moving the agent to be a jumper and vice versa. If a worker of a jumping up entrepreneur moves to be an entrepreneur herself, she starts as a jumper.

In the *quasi*-case (as described in Section 3.7), with the use of `jump`, an entrepreneur making a jump will keep unchanged the price for a whole cycle (or more, if the opposite action is not turning up).

iii) Case `quasiHchoice` set to `profit`. The entrepreneur decides to raise or to lower her price if the profit is negative. `priceSwitchIfProfitFalls` is a switch with values *"raise"* or *"lower."* To summarize the actual difficulty of knowing the demand elasticity, the actual choice between raising or lowering the price is a random one, with 60% of probability

---

[23] E.g., *decreasing Rate Range* $= -0.10$.

[24] E.g., *increasing Rate Range* $= 0.01$.

[25] *thresholdToDecreaseThePriceIfTotalPlannedPFalls*, e.g., 0.05 (Appendix B).

to the first choice ("raise") and 40% to the other one if `priceSwitchIfProfitFalls` is set to "raise"; vice versa, if it set to "lower." The correction is made with probability `pJump`[26] defined as above and size `jump`, again as above (both in Appendix B), calculating:

$$p^P = p(1 + jump)$$

if the switch is on *"raise"* or

$$p^P = p/(1 + jump)$$

if it is on *"lower."*

This action works from $t = 1$.

We have also the parameter `profitStrategyReverseAfterN` (in Appendix B). The effects are:

1) as default, if positive, it determines the time for a reverse action, lowering the price if raised and vice versa. In the while, no other actions on price are allowed;

2) if the parameter `profitStrategyReverseAfterN` is greater than the length of the run, the reverse action will never took place and so a unique price correction is possible;

3) if the parameter is 0, no reverse actions are possible and the *raise* or *lower* actions can be repeated if the profit is negative.

If a worker of a profit-jumping up entrepreneur moves to be an entrepreneur herself, she starts with her `profitStrategyReverse AfterN` counter set to the value of her former company.

Being here, the price corrections for the entrepreneurs uniquely at the end of each period, the *full* ASHAM paradigm (as described in Section 3.7) anyway operates in the first period Hayekian period. The goal of this exception is that of avoiding that the sellers would be using the initial random prices for the full length of the first cycle. As we indicated previously, it is important here to start with a well balancing structure of the buyers' price and sellers' price curves.

---

[26] If *pJump* is set to -1 the random number generation is avoided (for retro-compatibility problems).

3.11 Item 11: *toEntrepreneur* and *toWorker*

We refer to item 11 in Figure 3.1.

Changes of status are related both:

- to the workers moving to be entrepreneurs, in case of success of the firm where they are employed, and
- entrepreneurs moving to be workers (employed or unemployed), in case of failure of their activity.

3.11.1 *Item 11:* toEntrepreneur

We always refer to item 11 in Figure 3.1.

With this method, the agent, being a worker, decides to become an entrepreneur at time t, if her employer has a relative profit (reported to the total of the costs) greater or equal a given *threshold* at time $t - 1$. The threshold is defined by the parameter thresholdToEntrepreneur, as in Appendix B.

In the real world, the decision is a quite rare one, so we have to set a higher level threshold in absoluteBarrierToBecome Entrepreneur, defined in Appendix B. This parameter represents a *potential max number of new entrepreneurs* in each cycle.

Internally, it works in the following way: given an absolute value as number of workers that actually become entrepreneurs, we transform that value in a probability, dividing it by the total number of the agents, used as an adaptive scale factor.

The agent changes its internal type, and starts counting the k periods of extra costs (to k is assigned the value extraCostsDuration, in the measure stated in newEntrantExtraCosts, as defined in Appendix B).

3.11.2 *Item 11:* toWorker

We always refer to item 11 in Figure 3.1.

With the method (or command) toWorker, an entrepreneur moves to be an unemployed worker if her relative profit (reported to the total of the costs) at time t is greater or equal a given *threshold* in t as in Appendix B, parameter thresholdToWorker. The agent changes its internal type.

3.12 Item 12: *On wages: fullEmploymentEffect* and *incumbentAction*

We refer to item 12-*fullEmploymentEffectOnWages* and *incumbentActionOnWages* in Figure 3.1.

As in Section 3.8, we use here an abstract agent. As stated there, in agent-based models, the agents are usually mimicking an actual subject existing in the reality; in this case, we have an abstract agent making computations both (i) relevant from an theoretical economic point of view or (ii) simply accounting statistical data.

3.12.1 Item 12: fullEmploymentEffectOnWages

We refer to item 12, *fullEmploymentEffectOnWages*, in Figure 3.1.

The method, sent to the `WorldState` abstract agent, orders it to modify wages accordingly to full employment situation, in a reversible way.

Sequence: (i) at the beginning of each cycle, the wage level is reset to its base value; (ii) within the cycle, a wage raise due to the full employment effect on wages can happen; (iii) in the same cycle, we can have more than one wage raise (the other one due to the action described in Section 3.12.2), with cumulative effects.

With U_t as the unemployment rate at time t, ζ as the unemployment threshold (`fullEmploymentThreshold` in Appendix B) to recognize the *full employment* situation, s as the proportional increase step (reversible) of the wage level (`wageStepInFullEmployment` in Appendix B), and w_t as the wage level at time t (being w_0 the initial level), we have:

$$\begin{cases} w_t = w_0(1 + s) \text{ if } U_t \leq \zeta \\ w_t = w_0 \text{ if } U_t > \zeta \end{cases} \tag{3.32}$$

3.12.2 Item 12: incumbentActionOnWages

We refer to item 12-*incumbentActionOnWages* in Figure 3.1.

The method, sent to the `WorldState` abstract agent, orders it to modify wages for one period, accordingly to the attempt of creating an entry barrier when new firms are observed into the market.

As a consequence, wage measure contains a variable addendum, set to 0 as regular value and modified temporary by this method.

Sequence: (i) at the beginning of each cycle, the wage level is reset to its base value; (ii) within the cycle, a wage raise due to incumbent action on wages can happen; (iii) in the same cycle, we can have more than one wage raise (the other one due to the action described in Section 3.12.1), with cumulative effects.

The current number of entrepreneurs H_t^E is calculated at the end (so the superscript E) of a cycle, and the previous values H_i^B are extracted from the structural data frame, containing the data at the beginning of each period. In H_i^B, the superscript B indicates the beginning of the cycle i. Pay attention: $H_i^B = H_{i-1}^E$.

Consistently, $\frac{H_t^E}{H_t^B} - 1$ measures the relative increment/decrement of the number of the entrepreneurs in cycle t.

The wage level has two components, mutually exclusive:

1) the effects of full employment on wages, as in Section 3.12.1;
2) the effect described in this section, about the actions of the incumbent oligopolists, which are strategically increasing wages to create an artificial barrier against new entrants; the new entrepreneurs suffer temporary extra costs, so for them the wage increment can generate so relevant losses to produce their bankruptcy.

   We have here two levels: K as the (relative) threshold of entrepreneur presence to determine the reaction on wages and k as the relative increment of wages (temporaryRelativeWage IncrementAsBarrier in Appendix B).

   K is the maxAcceptableOligopolistRelativeIncrement parameter in Appendix B.

   k is the (temporaryRelativeWageIncrementAsBarrier parameter in Appendix B.

   How can we measure the increment in the number of the entrepreneurs?

I) If we compare H_t^E and H_t^B, we have a simple direct measure,
II) but if we have a continuous series of small increments – all with $\frac{H_t}{H_t^B} - 1 \leq K$, so under the threshold – the overall effect is invisible.

If cumulativelyMeasuringNewEntrantNumber, as in Appendix B, is set to *True*, we use the second measure.

In case I:

$$\begin{cases} w_t = w_0(1+k) \text{ if } \dfrac{H_t^E}{H_t^B} - 1 > K \\[3mm] w_t = w_0 \text{ if } \dfrac{H_t^E}{H_t^B} - 1 \le K \end{cases} \qquad (3.33)$$

In case II:

First of all, we define the *reference level*, or R^L, as a dynamic value, calculating, at any time t:[27]

$$\begin{cases} R_t^L = H_t^B \text{ if } \dfrac{H_{t-1}^E}{R_{t-1}^L} - 1 > K \\[3mm] R_t^L = R_{t-1}^L \text{ otherwise} \end{cases} \qquad (3.34)$$

remembering that in $t = 1$ (starting time), $R_0^L = H_1^B$ and $H_0^B = H_0^E = H_1^B$.

As a consequence, always in case II:

$$\begin{cases} w_t = w_0(1+k) \text{ if } \dfrac{H_t^E}{R_t^L} - 1 > K \\[3mm] w_t = w_0 \text{ if } \dfrac{H_t^E}{R_t^L} - 1 \le K \end{cases} \qquad (3.35)$$

[27] We could consider to have the first condition in the form:
$R_t^L = H_t^B$ if $H_t^B - H_{t-1}^B \le 0$ or $\dfrac{H_{t-1}^E}{R_{t-1}^L} - 1 > K$.

4 | *The Results of the Simulation Agent-Based Model, in SMAC and ASHAM Modes*

MATTEO MORINI AND PIETRO TERNA

4.1 Initial Results, Cases 0a (*g* in Figure 4.17) and 0b (*h* in Figure 4.17)

Appendix C contains all the information to run the model experiments of this chapter.[1]

Regarding the space of the parameters, as reported in Appendix B, it is easy to observe that while their number is large (52), the majority of them are quite rarely modified. So we still have branches of the model to be explored. The value of `startHayekianMarket`, in pure SMAC (see Section 3.2.2 for a mixed mode reference), has to be greater than the number of cycle; so, if missing, it is set by default to "51" and not to "-" in the Table B.4. In this way, we can run those SMAC experiments with the last version of the *oligopoly* project.

We analyze the simulation results considering both the dynamic of the time series of the main economic variables of the model and their correlation structure.

These are cases of the last two rows of Table 4.25.

The first results of our model, in its early stage, are those we published in the Mazzoli et al. (2017) paper. The model was in its SMAC mode. SMAC and ASHAM modes are technically introduced in Section 3.1.2.[2][3]

---

[1] The sets of the parameters of the two experiments are reported in Tables B.3 and B.4 of Appendix B. Each case requires the input of a few parameters in an interactive way. We report them in Table C.1 of Appendix C.

[2] Concerning the SMAC and ASHAM acrostics, see Appendix B and, for explanations, Section 3.1.2. Synthetically, (i) in SMAC, the aggregate production in quantity at time t is compared with the aggregate demand in value always at time t, to fix a clearing price under the hypothesis that the unique good of the economy is a perishable one, so we have no warehouses and stocks; (ii) in ASHAM, the interaction among sellers (the entrepreneurs) and buyers (the workers and the entrepreneurs) is built via an atomistic market

Table 4.1 *Legends*

unempl	Unemployment, measured *at the end* of each period
totalProfit	Total profits of the entrepreneurs, measured *at the end* of each period
totalProd	Total production of the entrepreneurs/firms, measured *at the end* of each period
plannedP	Total planned production of the entrepreneurs/firms, *at the beginning* of each period
cQ	Total consumptions in quantity, measured *at the end* of each period
hPSd	*Standard deviation* of the prices in ASHAM, related to each period
price	Price *at the end* of each period, in SMAC the mean the prices of the transactions, in ASHAM
wage	Wage level, *at the end* of each period
entrepreneurs	Number of entrepreneurs, *at the beginning* of each period
workers (right)	Number of workers, *at the beginning* of each period (on the right scale)

The legends of all the time series figures of the chapter are defined in Table 4.1 (the same legends are employed in the correlation tables). For continuity reasons, we report here the results of Mazzoli et al. (2017). The two models have the numbers *0a* and *0b* in Tables B.3 and B.4.

Figures 4.1[4] and 4.2 show the results of the case *0a*, while Figures 4.3 and 4.4 are related to the case *0b*, always with runs of 50 cycles.

where each agent meets her/his counterpart, modifying their reservation prices as they succeed or fail in making an exchange.

[3] To run this specific model example, use the Oligopoly code version at https://github.com/terna/oligopoly/releases/tag/V5 or at https://github.com/terna/oligopoly/releases/tag/V5bP2_fd, running the project with SLAPP 2.0 as at https://github.com/terna/SLAPP2 . and controlling that the parameters are those of rows 1 and 2 of Tables B.3 and B.4. NB In this case, using a SMAC specific version of the *oligopoly* project, the parameter *startHayekianMarket* is not used, while in the Table B.4 is anyway "51" by default.

[4] The legends are in Table 4.1.

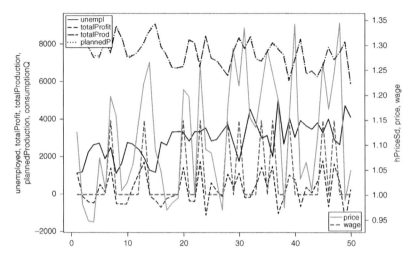

Figure 4.1 Case *0a* from the 2017 paper, macro-variable series with new entrant firms

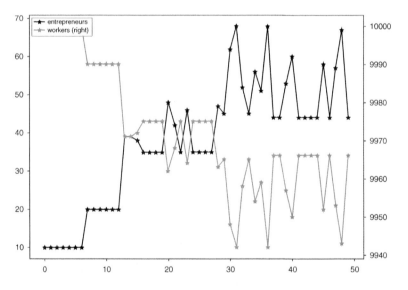

Figure 4.2 Case *0a* from the 2017 paper, agent series with new entrant firms

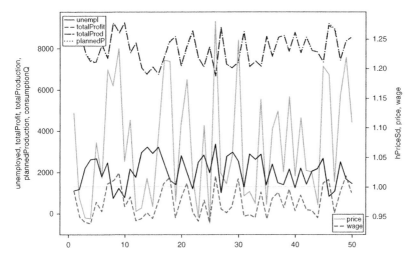

Figure 4.3 Case *0b* from the 2017 paper, macro-variable series without new entrant firms

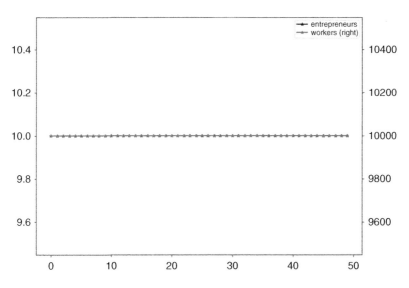

Figure 4.4 Case *0b* from the 2017 paper, agent series without new entrant firms

Table 4.2 *Case* 0a *from the 2017 paper, correlations with new entrant firms*

	unempl	totalProfit	totalProd	plannedP	price	wage
unempl	1.00	−0.18	−0.57	−0.56	−0.02	−0.02
totalProfit	−0.18	1.00	−0.36	−0.37	0.53	0.77
totalProd	−0.57	−0.36	1.00	1.00	0.02	−0.25
plannedP	−0.56	−0.37	1.00	1.00	0.02	−0.25
price	−0.02	0.53	0.02	0.02	1.00	0.46
wage	−0.02	0.77	−0.25	−0.25	0.46	1.00

In case *0b* we stopped the possibility of new entrant firms acting on the variable `absoluteBarrierToBecomeEntrepreneur`, as in Appendix B, reducing the maximum possible number of new entrants from 20 to 0.[5]

The main result of this starting experiment is that of showing an emergent business cycle from the proposed system of rules. If we compare Figures 4.1 and 4.3, it is easy to notice that the second one displays series smoother than the first one, due to the simplification of the environment (no new entrant firms). Indeed, the most of the complexity of these artificial economic worlds is coming from the presence of the new entrant oligopolists, generating wage movements, while without the entry possibility, we also have no exit (no firms in bankruptcy).

Figures 4.2 and 4.4 show the dynamic of the entrepreneur number.

We observe in Tables 4.2 that *profits* are positively related to *prices*, negatively to *total production* or *planned production* (high production reduces prices), negatively to *unemployment* (low unemployment increases demand and prices), positively to *wages*: here we have a complicated loop, as high profits are attracting more firms and so incumbent oligopolists increase wages to create a barrier.

That described is a clear countercyclical markup phenomenon (negative correlation between profits and production).

The negative link of *profits* with *total production* or *planned production* is stronger in Tables 4.3 and 4.4, calculating the partial

---

[5] The sets of the parameters of the experiment are reported in Tables B.3 and B.4 of Appendix B. Each case requires the input of a few parameters in an interactive way. We report them in Table C.1 of Appendix C.

Table 4.3 *Case 0a from the 2017 paper, partial correlations (excluding plannedProduction) with new entrant firms*

	unempl	totalProfit	totalProd	price	wage
unempl	1.00	−0.63	−0.76	0.39	0.30
totalProfit	−0.63	1.00	−0.65	0.52	0.68
totalProd	−0.76	−0.65	1.00	0.45	0.24
price	0.39	0.52	0.45	1.00	−0.05
wage	0.30	0.68	0.24	−0.05	1.00

Table 4.4 *Case 0a from the 2017 paper, partial correlations (excluding totalProduction) with new entrant firms*

	unempl	totalProfit	plannedP	price	wage
unempl	1.00	−0.63	−0.76	0.40	0.30
totalProfit	−0.63	1.00	−0.66	0.53	0.68
plannedP	−0.76	−0.66	1.00	0.47	0.25
price	0.40	0.53	0.47	1.00	−0.06
wage	0.30	0.68	0.25	−0.06	1.00

correlations[6] excluding alternatively the two variables related to the production, because too much is correlated in the absolute majority of the cases.

The phenomenon completely disappears in Tables 4.5, where the simulation does not allow the entry of new firms. In this case, partial correlation does not add other useful information. The hint is that the key element of our simulation engine is properly the entry/exit mechanism about firms. Without being countercyclical, it is very significant the effects of the prices on profits.

In Table 4.5, the NaN (Not a Number) results are due to the wage level, never moving in this case. This is also an interesting side effect resulting from the no-entry situation.

---

[6] Partial correlation measures the degree of association between two variables, removing the effect of a set of controlling variables.
  The calculations are made via the *readingCsvOutput_par_corr_BWter.ipynb* code that you can find in the https://github.com/terna/oligopoly repository; that code employs a routine written by Fabian

Table 4.5 *Case* 0b *from the 2017 paper, correlations without new entrant firms*

	unempl	totalProfit	totalProd	plannedP	price	wage
unempl	1.00	−0.02	−1.00	−1.00	0.05	nan
totalProfit	−0.02	1.00	0.02	0.02	0.99	nan
totalProd	−1.00	0.02	1.00	1.00	−0.05	nan
plannedP	−1.00	0.02	1.00	1.00	−0.05	nan
price	0.05	0.99	−0.05	−0.05	1.00	nan
wage	nan	nan	nan	nan	nan	nan

4.2 Synopsis of SMAC Experiments, from Atomistic to Oligopolistic Markets

Both the negative markup phenomenon and the market structure emerging in the previous section are worthy, of further investigations. Most of all, to prepare the ASHAM version of the model, it was necessary to explore different market dimensions and their related behavior. Doing the exploration, some regularities – which are quite complex, anyway – have been arising.

We found a changing continuum from an *atomistic market* to an *oligopolistic* one; this process intersect that of the emergence of the *countercyclical markup* phenomenon.[7]

4.2.1 Case 1 (a in Figure 4.17): 100 Entrepreneurs and 100,000 Workers

We introduce, as a first case, a significant number of entrepreneurs, to characterize the offer side of the market with a relevant quantity of

Pedregosa-Izquierdo, online at https://gist.github.com/fabianp/9396204419c7b638d38f.
[7] An *atomistic* market, in our definition, is composed of a multitude of firms reacting to quantity stimuli; having, in our model, a linear cost structure, the profits are related to the prices, which firms took as (i) exogenous plus individually specific shocks in the SMAC case and (ii) strictly individually specific in the ASHAM case: two realistic frameworks. A The atomistic competition is referred to, as in Loury (1979), being it is often taken as synonymous with perfect competition, which is not our case.

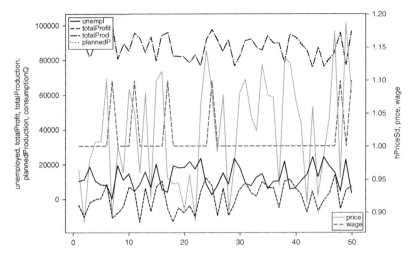

Figure 4.5 Case *1*, 100 entrepreneurs and 100,000 workers, macro-variable series

agents. The goal is that of building a dispersed market. This is case 1 in Table 4.25.[8]

Figure 4.5[9] reports the time series of the run, and Figure 4.6 reports the entry/exit dynamic.[10]

In Figure 4.5 we have a cyclical behavior of the economy, with a stable long-term trend. Prices are cyclical too, with relevant movements. Profits alternate with losses. We have a few episodes of wage jumps, due to situations of low unemployment level.

In Figure 4.6 we see that the number of entrepreneurs is lightly decreasing, with a final recovery due to new entrant entrepreneurs, in the presence of extra profits coming from the increasing prices.

In Table 4.6 we have the first *side result*: in italic, we signal the lack of the countercyclical markup and the strong importance of

---

[8] The sets of the parameters of the experiment are reported in Tables B.3 and B.4 of Appendix B. Each case requires the input of a few parameters in an interactive way. We report them in Table C.1 of Appendix C.

[9] The legends appear in Table 4.1.

[10] The scale on the right of figure 4.6 – and of the other similar figures – has to be read adding 1e5, i.e., 100,000, to the values reported.

Table 4.6 *Case* 1, *100 entrepreneurs and 100,000 workers, correlations*

	unempl	totalProfit	totalProd	plannedP	price	wage
unempl	1.00	−0.00	−1.00	−1.00	0.06	−0.54
totalProfit	−0.00	1.00	−0.02	−0.02	0.93	−0.05
totalProd	−1.00	−0.02	1.00	1.00	−0.07	0.54
plannedP	−1.00	−0.02	1.00	1.00	−0.07	0.55
price	0.06	0.93	−0.07	−0.07	1.00	−0.09
wage	−0.54	−0.05	0.54	0.55	−0.09	1.00

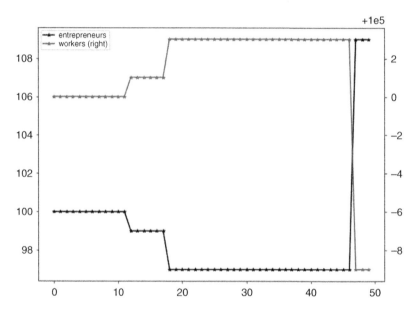

Figure 4.6 Case *1*, 100 entrepreneurs and 100,000 workers, agent series

the price dynamics on profits. Both the stability of the – medium, not small – number of firms and the strong role of the prices on profits seem to identify a situation nearly close to an *atomistic market*.

A control calculation about partial correlations also shows elements of countercyclical markup in this case, as shown in Tables 4.7 and 4.8.

Table 4.7 *Case* 1, *partial correlations* (*excluding plannedProduction*)

	unempl	totalProfit	totalProd	price	wage
unempl	1.00	−0.53	−1.00	0.46	0.00
totalProfit	−0.53	1.00	−0.53	0.95	0.02
totalProd	−1.00	−0.53	1.00	0.45	0.03
price	0.46	0.95	0.45	1.00	−0.04
wage	0.00	0.02	0.03	−0.04	1.00

Table 4.8 *Case* 1, *partial correlations* (*excluding totalProduction*)

	unempl	totalProfit	plannedP	price	wage
unempl	1.00	−0.54	−1.00	0.45	0.05
totalProfit	−0.54	1.00	−0.54	0.95	0.04
plannedP	−1.00	−0.54	1.00	0.45	0.07
price	0.45	0.95	0.45	1.00	−0.06
wage	0.05	0.04	0.07	−0.06	1.00

4.2.2 Case 2 (b in Figure 4.17): 1,000 Entrepreneurs and 100,000 Workers

This is a control experiment (case 2 in Table 4.25) about the number of entrepreneurs: with 1,000 entrepreneurs and 100,000 workers, the role of prices in profit is strongly confirmed.[11]

Figure 4.7[12] reports the time series of the run, and Figure 4.8 reports the entry/exit dynamic (see the note in the previous section about the right scale).

We see a long-term decreasing trend and increasing unemployment (wages never move). The large number of firms discourages new entries, but we have frequent oscillations in the number of entrepreneurs. Prices are highly relevant; the *countercyclical markup* emerges.

---

[11] The sets of the parameters of the experiment are reported in Tables B.3 and B.4 of Appendix B. Each case requires the input of a few parameters in an interactive way. We report them in Table C.1 of Appendix C.

[12] The legends appear in Table 4.1.

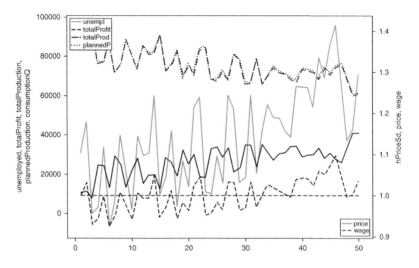

Figure 4.7 Case 2, 1,000 entrepreneurs and 100,000 workers, macro-variable series

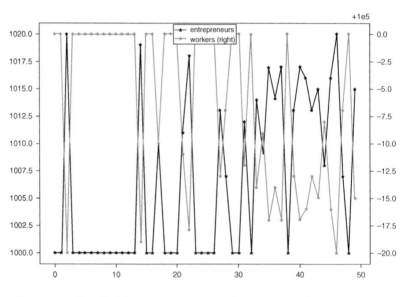

Figure 4.8 Case 2, 1,000 entrepreneurs and 100,000 workers, agent series

Table 4.9 *Case 2, 1,000 entrepreneurs and 100,000 workers, correlations*

	unempl	totalProfit	totalProd	plannedP	price	wage
unempl	1.00	0.36	−1.00	−1.00	0.43	nan
totalProfit	0.36	1.00	−0.34	−0.34	0.99	nan
totalProd	−1.00	−0.34	1.00	1.00	−0.41	nan
plannedP	−1.00	−0.34	1.00	1.00	−0.41	nan
price	0.43	0.99	−0.41	−0.41	1.00	nan
wage	nan	nan	nan	nan	nan	nan

Table 4.10 *Case 2, partial correlations (excluding plannedProduction)*

	unempl	totalProfit	totalProd	price	wage
unempl	1.00	−0.64	−1.00	0.67	−0.02
totalProfit	−0.64	1.00	−0.62	0.99	−0.00
totalProd	−1.00	−0.62	1.00	0.64	−0.02
price	0.67	0.99	0.64	1.00	−0.36
wage	−0.02	−0.00	−0.02	−0.36	1.00

Due to the absolutely strong role of the prices (in correlations) and to the number of entrepreneurs, this is a clear case of atomistic market.

See Section 4.2.8 for a detailed analysis of this case, also comparatively.

4.2.3 Case 3 (c in Figure 4.17): 10 Entrepreneurs and 100,000 Workers

Figure 4.9[13] reports the time series of the run, and Figure 4.10 reports the entry/exit dynamic (see the note in Section 4.2.1 about the right scale).[14]

In this case, the time series are quite articulated, with a cyclical behavior and a very short period. Wages are jumping both in

---

[13] The legends are in Table 4.1.

[14] The sets of the parameters of the experiment are reported in Tables B.3 and B.4 of Appendix B. Each case requires the input of a few parameters in an interactive way. We report them in Table C.1 of Appendix C.

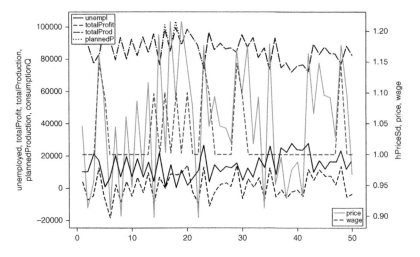

Figure 4.9 Case 3, 10 entrepreneurs and 100,000 workers, macro-variable series

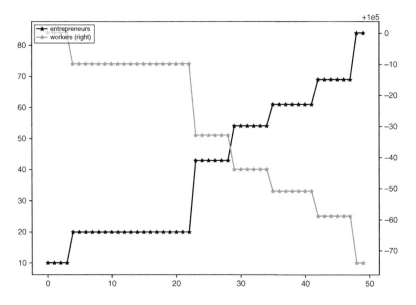

Figure 4.10 Case 3, 10 entrepreneurs and 100,000 workers, agent series

Table 4.11 *Case 2, partial correlations (excluding totalProduction)*

	unempl	totalProfit	plannedP	price	wage
unempl	1.00	−0.65	−1.00	0.67	0.01
totalProfit	−0.65	1.00	−0.62	0.99	−0.01
plannedP	−1.00	−0.62	1.00	0.64	−0.02
price	0.67	0.99	0.64	1.00	−0.10
wage	0.01	−0.01	−0.02	−0.10	1.00

Table 4.12 *Case 3, 10 entrepreneurs and 100,000 workers, correlations*

	unempl	totalProfit	totalProd	plannedP	price	wage
unempl	1.00	0.37	−1.00	−1.00	0.22	−0.22
totalProfit	0.37	1.00	−0.37	−0.35	0.83	0.24
totalProd	−1.00	−0.37	1.00	1.00	−0.21	0.22
plannedP	−1.00	−0.35	1.00	1.00	−0.21	0.23
price	0.22	0.83	−0.21	−0.21	1.00	0.30
wage	−0.22	0.24	0.22	0.23	0.30	1.00

Table 4.13 *Case 4, 20 entrepreneurs and 100,000 workers, correlations*

	unempl	totalProfit	totalProd	plannedP	price	wage
unempl	1.00	0.57	−1.00	−0.98	0.47	−0.08
totalProfit	0.57	1.00	−0.59	−0.59	0.86	0.28
totalProd	−1.00	−0.59	1.00	0.98	−0.47	0.07
plannedP	−0.98	−0.59	0.98	1.00	−0.48	0.11
price	0.47	0.86	−0.47	−0.48	1.00	0.18
wage	−0.08	0.28	0.07	0.11	0.18	1.00

the presence of artificial barriers against new entrant (+15% for one period) and following situations of very low unemployment (+10% for one period).

The countercyclical markup is there (Table 4.12), but not so relevant, as emphasized by the absence in partial correlations.

In Figure 4.10 we see that the number of entrepreneurs is significantly increasing, due to the entry process. In simplified terms, the presence of too few entrepreneurs at the starting point, with a high pressure generated by the market, produces a relevant entry phenomenon. The affect of the prices on the profits is relevant. In Table 4.25, this case is reported as moving toward an *atomistic market*, with countercyclical markup.

4.2.4 Case 4 (d in Figure 4.17): 20 Entrepreneurs and 100,000 workers

Figure 4.11[15] reports the time series of the run and Figure 4.12 reports the entry/exit dynamic (see the note in Section 4.2.1 about the right scale).[16]

We have here a cyclical behavior with periods of different length – not always uniform – and a lightly decreasing trend of the production, with a symmetric increase of the unemployment.

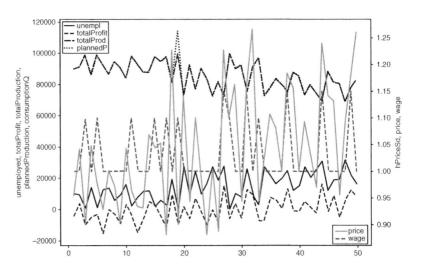

Figure 4.11 Case 4, 20 entrepreneurs and 100,000 workers, macro-variable series

---

[15] The legends are in Table 4.1.
[16] The sets of the parameters of the experiment are reported in Tables B.3 and B.4 of Appendix B. Each case requires the input of a few parameters in an interactive way. We report them in Table C.1 of Appendix C.

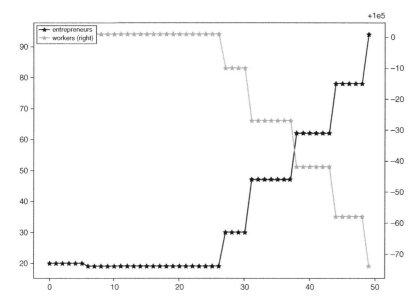

Figure 4.12 Case 4, 20 entrepreneurs and 100,000 workers, agent series

We note also strong movements in prices and in wages. As in Section 4.2.3, we underline that wages are jumping both in the presence of artificial barriers against new entrant (+15% for one period) or following situations of very low unemployment (+10% for one period).

In Figure 4.12 we see that the number of entrepreneurs is significantly increasing, due to the entry process. Again, in simplistic terms, this is the effect of too few entrepreneurs at the starting point in the presence of a high pressure of the market. As in Section 4.2.3, the role of the prices is relevant. In Table 4.25, this case is also reported as moving toward an *atomistic market* with countercyclical markup. This markup in mainly due to the relationship profit/total production, as we can see in Tables 4.14 and 4.15; the circumstance is summarized in Table 4.24.

4.2.4.1 Analyzing the Correlations
In Figure 4.12, we clearly have two periods: for t in the intervals 1–25 and 26–50.

Table 4.14 *Case 4, partial correlations (excluding plannedProduction)*

	unempl	totalProfit	totalProd	price	wage
unempl	1.00	−0.31	−1.00	0.20	0.07
totalProfit	−0.31	1.00	−0.35	0.82	0.35
totalProd	−1.00	−0.35	1.00	0.21	0.10
price	0.20	0.82	0.21	1.00	−0.16
wage	0.07	0.35	0.10	−0.16	1.00

Table 4.15 *Case 4, partial correlations (excluding totalProduction)*

	unempl	totalProfit	plannedP	price	wage
unempl	1.00	−0.03	−0.96	−0.01	0.13
totalProfit	−0.03	1.00	−0.16	0.80	0.36
plannedP	−0.96	−0.16	1.00	0.02	0.23
price	−0.01	0.80	0.02	1.00	−0.14
wage	0.13	0.36	0.23	−0.14	1.00

Table 4.16 *Case 4, 20 entrepreneurs and 100,000 workers, correlations, t in 1–25*

	unempl	totalProfit	totalProd	plannedP	price	wage
unempl	1.00	0.45	−0.99	−0.95	0.55	−0.68
totalProfit	0.45	1.00	−0.50	−0.49	0.86	−0.21
totalProd	−0.99	−0.50	1.00	0.95	−0.57	0.67
plannedP	−0.95	−0.49	0.95	1.00	−0.57	0.69
price	0.55	0.86	−0.57	−0.57	1.00	−0.33
wage	−0.68	−0.21	0.67	0.69	−0.33	1.00

Exploring the sub-periods, the expected result is that of different correlations about profits in the first and in the second interval; the results in Table 4.16 and Table 4.17 show a relevant difference of the effect of the wages, as underlined in Section 4.2.8 and, specifically for this case, in Section 4.2.8.1.

Table 4.17 *Case 4, 20 entrepreneurs and 100,000 workers, correlations,* t *in 26–50*

	unempl	totalProfit	totalProd	plannedP	price	wage
unempl	1.00	0.51	−1.00	−1.00	0.17	0.19
totalProfit	*0.51*	1.00	*−0.50*	*−0.51*	*0.82*	*0.53*
totalProd	−1.00	−0.50	1.00	1.00	−0.17	−0.18
plannedP	−1.00	−0.51	1.00	1.00	−0.17	−0.18
price	0.17	0.82	−0.17	−0.17	1.00	0.39
wage	0.19	0.53	−0.18	−0.18	0.39	1.00

Table 4.18 *Case 5, 50 entrepreneurs and 100,000 workers, correlations*

	unempl	totalProfit	totalProd	plannedP	price	wage
unempl	1.00	0.20	−1.00	−0.97	0.19	−0.64
totalProfit	0.20	1.00	*−0.23*	*−0.25*	*0.91*	0.00
totalProd	−1.00	−0.23	1.00	0.98	−0.22	0.64
plannedP	−0.97	−0.25	0.98	1.00	−0.25	0.64
price	0.19	0.91	−0.22	−0.25	1.00	−0.05
wage	−0.64	0.00	0.64	0.64	−0.05	1.00

4.2.5 Case 5 (e in Figure 4.17): 50 Entrepreneurs and 100,000 Workers

Figure 4.13[17] reports the time series of the run and Figure 4.14 reports the entry/exit dynamic (see the note in Section 4.2.1 about the right scale).[18]

In Table 4.18, we have the time series correlations.

Again, a great pressure of the market with a relevant growth of the entrepreneurs, to a large atomistic market. The *countercyclical*

---

[17] The legends are in Table 4.1.
[18] The sets of the parameters of the experiment are reported in Tables B.3 and B.4 of Appendix B. Each case requires the input of a few parameters in an interactive way. We report them in Table C.1 of Appendix C.

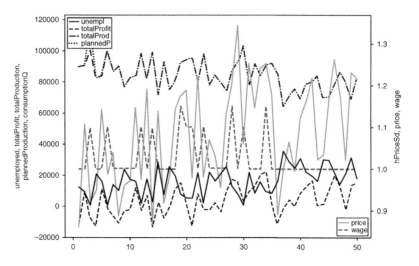

Figure 4.13 Case 5, 20 entrepreneurs and 100,000 workers, macro-variable series

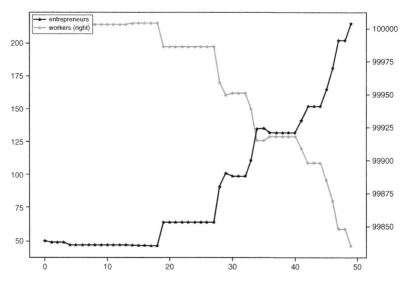

Figure 4.14 Case 5, 20 entrepreneurs and 100,000 workers, agent series

markup exists, but it is quite limited and disappears in the partial correlation view, excluding total production; the role of prices is highly relevant.

Table 4.19 *Case 5, partial correlations (excluding plannedProduction)*

	unempl	totalProfit	totalProd	price	wage
unempl	1.00	−0.24	−1.00	0.01	0.05
totalProfit	−0.24	1.00	−0.26	0.88	0.22
totalProd	−1.00	−0.26	1.00	0.02	0.10
price	0.01	0.88	0.02	1.00	−0.14
wage	0.05	0.22	0.10	−0.14	1.00

Table 4.20 *Case 5, partial correlations (excluding totalProduction)*

	unempl	totalProfit	plannedP	price	wage
unempl	1.00	−0.00	−0.96	−0.09	−0.07
totalProfit	−0.00	1.00	−0.05	0.90	0.20
plannedP	−0.96	−0.05	1.00	−0.07	0.12
price	−0.09	0.90	−0.07	1.00	−0.13
wage	−0.07	0.20	0.12	−0.13	1.00

In Section 4.2.8 we see that the case, probably due to the large change in the supply side dimension, has high standard deviations both in profits and in production. The overall view of this case classifies it as a special, separated realization in our simulated experiments.

4.2.6 Case 6 (f in Figure 4.17): 50 entrepreneurs and 10,000 workers

Figure 4.15[19] reports the time series of the run, and Figure 4.16 reports the entry/exit dynamic (see the note in Section 4.2.1 about the right scale). In Table 4.21, we have the time series correlations.[20]

Without too much market pressure, the number of the entrepreneurs is quite stable and less than medium in our cases.

---

[19] The legends are at in Table 4.1.
[20] The sets of the parameters of the experiment are reported in Tables B.3 and B.4 of Appendix B. Each case requires the input of a few parameters in an interactive way. We report them in Table C.1 of Appendix C.

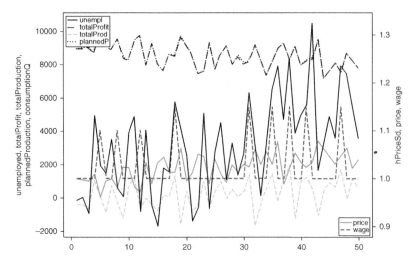

Figure 4.15 Case 6, 50 entrepreneurs and 10,000 workers, macro-variable series

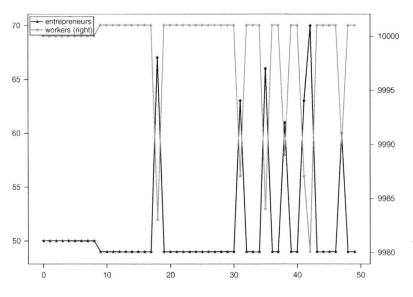

Figure 4.16 Case 6, 50 entrepreneurs and 10,000 workers, agent series

Table 4.21 *Case 6, 50 entrepreneurs and 10,000 workers, correlations*

	unempl	totalProfit	totalProd	plannedP	price	wage
unempl	1.00	−0.09	−0.53	−0.54	0.38	−0.17
totalProfit	−0.09	1.00	−0.44	−0.42	0.65	0.46
totalProd	−0.53	−0.44	1.00	1.00	−0.25	0.01
plannedP	−0.54	−0.42	1.00	1.00	−0.24	0.03
price	0.38	0.65	−0.25	−0.24	1.00	0.34
wage	−0.17	0.46	0.01	0.03	0.34	1.00

Table 4.22 *Case 6, partial correlations (excluding plannedProduction)*

	unempl	totalProfit	totalProd	price	wage
unempl	1.00	−0.80	−0.81	0.80	−0.00
totalProfit	−0.80	1.00	−0.80	0.84	0.24
totalProd	−0.81	−0.80	1.00	0.66	0.15
price	0.80	0.84	0.66	1.00	0.03
wage	−0.00	0.24	0.15	0.03	1.00

See Section 4.24 for a detailed analysis of this case (also comparatively), but immediately we can note the presence of the countercyclical markup in Table 4.21 and an even stronger presence in Tables 4.22 and 4.23.

4.2.7 Summarizing Countercyclical Markup Presence in Cases 0a to 6

Table 4.24 summarizes the countercyclical markup presence in the different cases.

4.2.8 Synopsis of Cases from 0a to 6, in the SMAC Economy

Table 4.25 resumes our focus on of (i) the size of the market as number of entrepreneurs, (ii) the entry/exit phenomenon, (iii) the prices, (iv) the dynamic of the unemployment, and (v) the wage level, on the types of the emerging markets and on the countercyclical markup (if any).

Table 4.23 *Case 6, partial correlations (excluding totalProduction)*

	unempl	totalProfit	plannedP	price	wage
unempl	1.00	−0.80	−0.82	0.80	0.02
totalProfit	−0.80	1.00	−0.80	0.84	0.27
plannedP	−0.82	−0.80	1.00	0.67	0.18
price	0.80	0.84	0.67	1.00	0.01
wage	0.02	0.27	0.18	0.01	1.00

Table 4.24 *Countercyclical markup presence*

Case	Countercyclical markup in correlation tables	in partial correlation tables
1, Sec. 4.2.1	no	but present in partial corr., both excluding plannedProduction and totalProduction
2, Sec. 4.2.2	yes	also in partial corr., both excluding plannedProduction and totalProduction
3, Sec. 4.2.3	yes	not in partial corr.
4, Sec. 4.2.4	yes	lighter in partial corr., excluding plannedProduction, absent excluding totalProduction
5, Sec. 4.2.5	yes, light	light also in partial corr., excluding plannedProduction, absent excluding totalProduction
6, Sec. 4.2.6	yes	also in partial corr. (stronger), both excluding plannedProduction and totalProduction
0a, Sec. 4.1	yes	also in partial corr. (stronger), both excluding plannedProduction and totalProduction
0b, Sec. 4.1	no	neither in partial corr.

The table goes, by rows, from cases of *atomistic* markets to cases of *oligopolistic* ones. How do we explain the movement from one extreme to the other? Let us summarize.

Table 4.25 *Moving from atomistic markets to oligopolistic ones*

Section or reference	agents in the model at $t = 1$	number of entrepreneurs	entry/exit	data by firm	ρ profit unempl. wage price prod.	type of market	*id* in Figure 4.17
4.2.1 case 1	100 entrepreneurs 100,000 workers	medium to medium	the number of entrepreneurs is nearly constant[a]	production m. 883.55 std 83.49 profit m. 6.03 std 78.94	-0.00 -0.05 0.93 -0.02	an atomistic market without countercyclical markup	a
4.2.2 case 2	1,000 entrepreneurs 100,000 workers	very large to very large	the number of entrepreneurs is nearly constant[b]	production m. 74.48 std 8.99 profit m. 9.32 std 9.71	0.36 *nan* 0.99 -0.34	rather close to an atomistic market, with countercyclical markup	b
4.2.3 case 3	10 entrepreneurs 100,000 workers	small to medium	the number of entrepreneurs is increasing, until ≈ 80	production m. 2133.24 std 1540.38 profit m. 33.92 std 255.46	0.37 0.24 0.83 -0.37	moving toward an atomistic market, with countercyclical markup	c

Table 4.25 *(cont.)*

Section or reference	agents in the model at $t=1$	number of entrepreneurs	entry/exit	data by firm	ρ profit unempl. wage price prod.	type of market	*id* in Figure 4.17
4.2.4 case 4	20 entrepreneurs 100,000 workers	small to medium	the number of entrepreneurs is increasing, until ≈ 90	production m. 2333.96 std 1535.31 profit m. −1.85 std 262.99	0.57 0.28[c] 0.86[d] −0.59	moving toward an atomistic market with countercyclical markup	d
4.2.5 case 5	50 entrepreneurs 100,000 workers	greater than small to nearly large	the final number of entrepreneurs is $> 200^e$	production m. 918.08 std 553.89 profit m. 39.85 std 118.53	0.20 0.00 0.91 −0.23	an atomistic market with a light countercyclical markup	e
4.2.6 case 6	50 entrepreneurs 10,000 workers	less than medium to less than medium	the number of entrepreneurs is oscillating between 50 and 70	production m. 165.69 std 19.71 profit m. 3.73 std 20.56	−0.09 0.46 0.65 −0.44	moving toward an oligopolistic market with countercyclical markup	f

paper[f] case 0a, infos in Section 4.1	Entry freedom; 10 entrepreneurs, 10,000 workers	increasing until ≈ 70 with up and down (mean ≈ 50)	small to less than medium	production m. 197.71 std 135.34 profit m. −6.30 std 32.63	−0.18 0.77 0.53 −0.36	oligopolistic market with countercyclical markup	g
paper[g]. case 0b, infos in Section 4.1	Entry stopped; 10 entrepreneurs, 10,000 workers	the number of entrepreneurs is constant	small to small	production m. 794.43 std 85.49 profit m. 54.32 std 75.98	−0.02 nan 0.99 0.02	oligopolistic market without counter cyclical markup	h

[a] But a final jump to 109.
[b] With frequent limited swings.
[c] See also Section 4.2.4.
[d] See also Section 4.2.4.
[e] We can limit the entrepreneur growth, by increasing the *max new entrant number in a time step* value – currently 20; the internal name is *absoluteBarrierToBecomeEntrepreneur*.
[f] Mazzoli et al. (2017).
[g] Mazzoli et al. (2017)

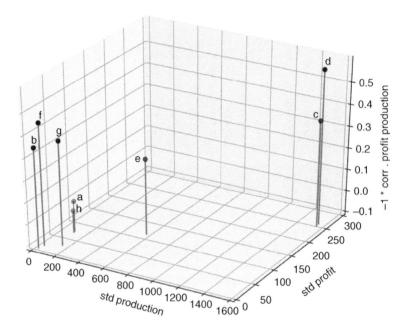

Figure 4.17 A scatter plot from Table 4.25 (SMAC cases), considering the
standard deviations of production and profit vs. the correlation
profit-production (countercyclical markup); the droplines are intended to
facilitate the observer in reading the coordinates of each point; the z values
are multiplied by -1 to improve the readability of the plot

- Both the first case (atomistic)[21] and the last one (oligopolistic) are
  characterized by:
  - a static number of entrepreneurs, medium in the first case and
    small in the last one;
  - no entry/exit dynamic;
  - absence of correlation among unemployment, wage level, produc-
    tion ad profits;
  - high correlation between price and the profit determination;
  - in both the cases, we observe the complete absence of
    countercyclical markup (see also Table 4.24);
  - in Figure 4.17 they form a mini-cluster (cases *a* and *h* with low
    standard deviations of production and profit values).

---

[21] *Atomistic* is used here, as in the note in Section 4.2.1.

- Analysis of the atomistic cases:
  - the case of Section 4.2.1 shows limited changes in the number of entrepreneurs, slightly decreasing (but the small final jump), with the profits uniquely related to prices and no countercyclical markup;
  - the case of Section 4.2.2 shows again limited changes in the number of entrepreneurs, but with an up and down walk (Figure 4.8); the profits are strongly related to prices, with the presence of a negative correlation with the production (countercyclical markup) and a positive correlation with the unemployment (consistent with the negative correlation with the production); the wage level never moves;[22]
  - the case of Section 4.2.3 is characterized by a continuous increment of the number of entrepreneurs, so it is classified as *small to medium*, with a final dimension that includes it into the atomistic market set; prices are relevant, but less than in the previous cases; we have also the presence of an evident countercyclical markup; the correlation with the unemployment is consistent with the production; the limited positive effect of wage level on profits is probably indirect, due to expansion phases;[23]
  - the case of Section 4.2.4 is similar to the previous one (Section 4.2.3) as continuous growth of the number of firms, *small to medium*, with a final situation as atomistic market; prices are relevant as in the case of Section 4.2.3; we again have a highly evident countercyclical markup; the correlation with the unemployment is consistent with the production; as above, the (limited) positive effect of wage level on profits is probably indirect, due to expansion phases.

The key point is: why does such an evident countercyclical markup emerge? The case shows a double dynamic of firms, as reported in Figure 4.12: until $t = 25$ and after that sub-period. Splitting in two time segments the correlation analysis, as in Section 4.2.4.1, the unique difference we see is the correlation of

---

[22] Why is the countercyclical markup emerging in this case and not in the previous one? In both cases, we have limited movements in the number of the entrepreneurs, but only in this second case do we have a considerably high frequency in the up and down sequence.

[23] Why the countercyclical markup? We emphasize the large positive movement in the number of entrepreneurs.

wage level on profits, negative in the first sub-period (wages were increasing for full employment conditions in a static situation of the firms, with negative profits) and positive in the second one (wage increasing mainly for the role of entry barrier, in a dynamic situation with positive profits). In both the sub-periods we have the same presence of the countercyclical markup.

• The figures related to the two cases coming from Mazzoli et al. (2017) are in Section 4.1. As an example, the data of Figure 4.2 are used in Table 4.25, row 7.

4.2.8.1 Introducing Clusters

The construction of the scatter plot reported in Figure 4.17 is based upon the standard deviations measured for production and profits, as a way to measure variability in a comparable way. The standard deviation looks only to the dispersion of the data, not being influenced by their mean value; in some way, it is scale independent.

The individual data of each firm are elaborated to obtain mean and standard deviations about production and profits. The results are very close, by the dimensionality, to those obtained via the same program using the aggregated time series. The differences are due to the changes in the number of entrepreneurs in each period, so the calculations based on the time series use data that are not always homogeneous.

We resume now the considerations about markets and *countercyclical markup*, considering the clusters of Figure 4.17. The letters identifying the different cases are those of the last column of Table 4.25.

• If the number of entrepreneurs does not evolve, as in cases *a* and *h* of Table 4.25 and Figure 4.17, showing low variability in production and profits, the *countercyclical markup* does not appear.

  In both the cases, the prices play a central role in profits determination; when missing the *countercyclical markup*, the correlation of the profits with the unemployment also cannot be found; wages are quite stable or absolutely stable, so no correlation arises.

  – In case *a*, the number of entrepreneurs is endogenously stable, in an atomistic market where the low unitary profits, with limited variability: (i) puts the potential new entrants off and, at the same time, (ii) avoids firms to go in bankruptcy.

  – In case *h*, the number of entrepreneurs is exogenously constant, being the new entrants stopped by a rule; on the contrary, profits (look at the level in Table 4.25, last row) are attractively relevant; due to the number of firms, the market is clearly oligopolistic.

• In the cases *b*, *f*, and *g* of Table 4.25 and Figure 4.17, showing a medium level of *countercyclical markup*, the standard deviations of production and profits are low and nearly close, but the conditions are quite different, considering that in the three cases the number of entrepreneurs is stable or slowly moving.

In these cases, the prices play very different roles in profits determination, due to different market pressures; the correlation of the profits with the unemployment is consistent with that of the production only in case *b* and irrelevant in case *f* and *g*; wages are stable in case *b*, so without correlation with profits, while in cases *f* and *g* they are positively related to profits, via the demand growth that they generate.

– In case *b*, the action made by such a large number of entrepreneurs (1,000, giving an atomistic market) causes a set of very close results, with low profits, low production (correctly, about 1/10 of case *a*), and low standard deviations.

The variability in the number of entrepreneurs (Figure 4.8) is mainly due to a small number of new entrants and to limited bankruptcies. It can be justified, considering (i) that in a large number of firms, some bypassing the profit threshold, thus attracting new entrepreneurs, surely can be found, and (ii) that with limited profits, also a group having negative results surely exists.

The large presence of entrepreneurs survives, but in a stable endogenous situation; in either case, the micro-variability justifies the emergence of the *countercyclical markup*.

– In case *f*, where we have 10,000 workers and 50 entrepreneurs, there is a limited pressure of the market on the firms: we have a moderated dynamic of the number of the entrepreneurs, being this market is nearly stable, as in case *a* above. The profits are limited, with a low standard deviation; the standard deviation of the production is very low.

This is an atomistic market shifting toward an oligopolistic one. The variability of the number of firms is consistent with the presence of the *countercyclical markup*.

– In case *g*, having initially 10 firms and 10,000 workers, the pressure of the market is more significant. The profit mean level is negative (losses), but the production shows a greater variability if compared with the previous case; the relevance of prices is also greater than in case *f*. We have the presence of the *countercyclical markup* in an oligopoly.

- In cases *c* and *d* of Table 4.25 and Figure 4.17, the number of the entrepreneurs is increasing, due to the high pressure of the market; in both cases, the *countercyclical markup* is evident. The standard deviations of production and profits are relevant, and this characteristic is certainly related to the dynamic of the supply side.

  In these cases, the prices play an important role in profits determination, due to the market pressure; the correlation of the profits with unemployment is always consistent with that of production. Wages are positively related to profits, via the demand growth that they generate.

  – In case *c*, having initially only 10 entrepreneurs and 100,000 workers, the pressure of the market is quite high; wages move frequently, as they are used as an entry barrier.

  – In case *d*, the initial number of entrepreneurs is 20, but the pressure of the market is anyway high, with a lot of new entries (Figure 4.12) and a highly significant *countercyclical markup*.

- Case *e*, starting with 50 entrepreneurs and increasing until a level of 200, is quite atypical, with a light *countercyclical markup* and high variance of profits and production, mainly a high effect of prices. We underline the difference with case *b*, looking at the standard deviations.

4.3 A Qualitative Analysis of ASHAM Experiments

In this part of the chapter we explore the complicated, but more realistic, world of the ASHAM construction. SMAC and ASHAM modes are technically introduced in Section 3.1.2. The ASHAM case uses Appendix A as a source of ideas. We repeat here the same warning provided in Section 3.1.2: in Appendix A and in Chapter 3 (Figures 3.2, 3.3, 3.4, and 3.5), seemingly we have offer curves. Actually, they are more complicated objects, as on the x-axis we do not have quantities, but agents: at the price reported in the y-axis, the agent can sell all the quantity she owns (a unitary quantity, in the simple examples reported in Appendix A and in the quoted figures; any quantity, in the ASHAM case). Specifically, in ASHAM each seller has a true horizontal offer curve: at a given price, she sells any quantity. We do not call it "supply curve" on purpose. The prices reported in the figures are reservation prices for the buyers, while for the sellers they are close to fixed sell prices like those exposed in a mall. Correct and descriptive names for both the curves of these figures are *buyers' price curve* and *sellers' price curve*.

We do not reproduce the same synoptic analysis that we built for SMAC, where *the market structures* and the *countercyclical markup* phenomenon have been emerging. We now follow a fine grained-qualitative search for realistic way of behaving in price formation, keeping in mind the strong hypothesis in Chapter 2 about price heterogeneity among firms.

Doing that with the ASHAM scheme, we are outside the too mechanistic perspective of the SMAC construction, built on a too simple and abstract process of price formation.

We have four different implementations of the ASHAM world:

- in Section 4.4, the *full* ASHAM, introduced in Section 3.1.2, as a paradigm with continuous price adaptation, on both the side of the sellers (firms-entrepreneurs) and of the buyers (workers and entrepreneurs, as consumers); the price adaptation is related to price changes, if any, in each sub-step of each cycle, or time step, as explained in Section 3.7; within this paradigm, we have also the option of random corrections pushing up the prices (as actions of the sellers, related to information shocks);
- in Section 4.5, the *quasi* ASHAM with the *unsold* option; the *quasi* specification is introduced in Section 3.1.2, as a paradigm with the seller prices adapting only at the beginning of each period (cycle of the simulation); the *unsold* option is introduced in Section 3.10.2 as a behavior of the entrepreneurs modifying their prices at the end of a period for the next one, if they have unsold production;
- in Section 4.6, the *quasi* ASHAM, with the *randomUp* option; as above, the *quasi* specification is introduced in Section 3.1.2, as a paradigm with the seller prices adapting only at the beginning of each period (cycle of the simulation); the *random up* option is introduced in Section 3.10.2 as a behavior of the entrepreneurs increasing their prices at the end of a period for the next one, in a seemingly random way, that we can imagine to be related to information shocks, as indicated previously;

- in Section 4.7, the *quasi* ASHAM, with the *profit* option; as above, the *quasi* specification is introduced in Section 3.1.2, as a paradigm with the seller prices adapting only at the beginning of each period (cycle of the simulation); the *profit* option is introduced in Section 3.10.2 as a behavior of the entrepreneurs *increasing* or *decreasing* their prices at the end of a period for the next one, trying to recover a falling profit. To summarize the actual difficulty of knowing the demand elasticity, the actual choice between raising or lowering the price is a random one, with 60% of probability to the first choice ("raise") and 40% to the other one, if priceSwitchIfProfitFalls is set to "raise" and vice versa if it set to "lower."

4.4 *Full* ASHAM

4.4.1 *Case 7: 10 Entrepreneurs and 10,000 Workers, in a* Stable *Economy, with an* Increasing Number of Firms

We start the exploration of our peculiar *ASHAM economics* with a simple case on the edge of stability, with micro-movements within the data series. The sets of the parameters of the experiment are reported in Tables B.3 and B.4 of Appendix B. Table B.2 reports all the definitions and the links to the sections where the variables are introduced and explained, in Chapter 3. Each case requires the input of a few parameters in an interactive way: we report them in Table C.1 of Appendix C.

- The case starts with:
  - 10 entrepreneurs and 10,000 workers;
  - an initial distribution of the prices of the agents based on a choice of the parameters of Section 3.6 (related to the Item 6 of the model outline of Figure 3.1, and specifically to the function setInitialPricesHM), with the purpose of generating an initial situation like that of Figure 3.3, with two not overlapping distributions of the reservation prices.[24]
  We specify such kind of situation with the parameter initShift set to −0.15 and the parameter initShock set to 0.10.

---

[24] The *max* price a buyer could pay and the *min* one a seller could accept. For sellers, these prices are close to sell prices like those exposed in a mall.

- The second relevant choice is that of having the parameter `runningShockB`, for the buyers, set to 0.2 and `runningShockS`, for the sellers, to 0.05. In this way, both the buyers and the sellers quickly adapt their prices to make deals.

  Following Section A.4.1.3 of Appendix A, the *winners* are the sellers, acting with a slow pace of price correction, as they would *cherry-pick* the best buyers (those with the higher reservation price). In this way, they avoid contributing to the fall of the prices. This behavior is consistent with the usual description of the sell prices as *sticky*, where *sticky* is a general economics term that, when applied to the sell prices, means that the firms are reluctant to change their prices also in the presence of modifications in input cost or demand quantities.[25]

  The *cherry-picking* process is not related always to the same buyers, because with the sequence of sub-steps within each time step, as explained in Section 3.7, we are adopting the solution of the Section A.5.2 of Appendix A: due to the continuous price corrections, the buy action are quite uncertain and in the about 50% of the cases the agents fail to buy, but as we repeat the buy-sell session several times in each cycle or time step, the failing agents are never the same. In each sub-step, (i) the buyers meet different sellers, generating the price information diffusion process via successful deals, and (ii) the agents actually buying change continuously.

- Considering the Q parameter of Section 3.2.2, the entrepreneurs, to plan their productions, weight 50% the consumption sat time $t - 1$ and 50% those at time $t - 2$, introducing some delays in production adaptation.

Given the initial construction of the prices, we have the expectation of (i) a moderate positive level of the profits with (ii) the possibility of a lack of consumption (high prices) and (iii) of a rising unemployment (low production, as a consequence of the consumption level): a recessive perspective, in short. We can control it via the level of welfare compensations (with the parameter `socialWelfareCompensation` set to 0.7, in the presence of a wage

---

[25] The whole set of the parameters of the experiment is reported in Tables B.3 and B.4 of Appendix B. Each case requires the input of a few parameters in an interactive way. We report them in Table C.1 of Appendix C.

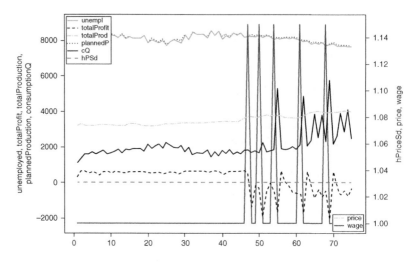

Figure 4.18 Case 7, 10 entrepreneurs and 10,000 workers, macro-variable series. The plannedP line is superimposed to the totalProd line

level of 1), forcing the theoretical construction of Chapter 2 toward the possibility of a deficit spending policy, but uniquely with the goal of generating a stable situation. We can also justify in a stronger way the level of the parameter, with the consideration of section 4.6.1.

Regardless, the economic picture that we draw, in Figures 4.18[26] and 4.19, is interestingly micro-moving and changing: from cycle 46, following some slightly random effect in production planning, one or more entrepreneurs have profits greater than the threshold (0.08); the event suggests to some of their workers to become themselves entrepreneurs. The reaction of the incumbent oligopolists is that described in Section 3.12.2 (item 12 in Figure 3.1), generating the spikes in the wage series, the related drops in the profit series, and the temporary unemployment effects. The relevant level of welfare compensation sustains the demand in the mini-crisis periods, avoiding too large reductions in planned production and production.

The final structure of the market is that of a large oligopolistic one.

Looking at the correlation tables, the countercyclical markup effect emerges if we split the analysis in two parts. Indeed, analyzing the

---

[26] The legends are in Table 4.1.

Table 4.26 *Case 7, 10 entrepreneurs and 10,000 workers, correlations (t = 1–75 series)*

	unempl	total Profit	total Prod	plannedP	cQ	hPSd	price	wage
unempl	1.00	−0.75	−0.59	−0.58	−0.59	0.27	0.57	−0.05
totalProfit	−0.75	1.00	0.38	0.35	0.39	−0.45	−0.70	−0.16
totalProd	−0.59	0.38	1.00	0.99	0.99	0.02	−0.53	−0.07
plannedP	−0.58	0.35	0.99	1.00	0.98	0.02	−0.52	−0.05
cQ	−0.59	0.39	0.99	0.98	1.00	−0.11	−0.53	−0.07
hPSd	0.27	−0.45	0.02	0.02	−0.11	1.00	0.43	0.11
price	0.57	−0.70	−0.53	−0.52	−0.53	0.43	1.00	0.24
wage	−0.05	−0.16	−0.07	−0.05	−0.07	0.11	0.24	1.00

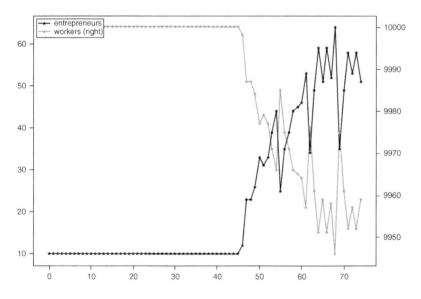

Figure 4.19 Case 7, 10 entrepreneurs and 10,000 workers, agent series

75 periods as a whole, as in Table 4.26, the correlation coefficients of the profits with the production and the planned production are both positive and the same if we look at the partial correlations in Tables 4.27 and 4.28, but with a slightly negative effect in the second case.

Table 4.27 *Case 7, partial correlations (excluding plannedProduction)*
(t = 1–75 series)

	unempl	totalProfit	totalProd	cQ	hPSd	price	wage
unempl	1.00	−0.57	−0.15	0.12	0.13	−0.15	−0.29
totalProfit	−0.57	1.00	0.31	−0.32	−0.35	−0.03	−0.13
totalProd	−0.15	0.31	1.00	1.00	0.97	−0.76	−0.10
cQ	0.12	−0.32	1.00	1.00	−0.97	0.75	0.10
hPSd	0.13	−0.35	0.97	−0.97	1.00	0.78	0.10
price	−0.15	−0.03	−0.76	0.75	0.78	1.00	0.03
wage	−0.29	−0.13	−0.10	0.10	0.10	0.03	1.00

Table 4.28 *Case 7, partial correlations (excluding totalProduction)*
(t = 1–75 series)

	unempl	totalProfit	plannedP	cQ	hPSd	price	wage
unempl	1.00	−0.66	−0.21	0.10	0.10	−0.12	−0.28
totalProfit	−0.66	1.00	*−0.18*	0.12	−0.04	−0.46	−0.17
plannedP	−0.21	−0.18	1.00	0.98	0.68	−0.36	0.01
cQ	0.10	0.12	0.98	1.00	−0.65	0.28	−0.02
hPSd	0.10	−0.04	0.68	−0.65	1.00	0.40	−0.01
price	−0.12	−0.46	−0.36	0.28	0.40	1.00	0.16
wage	−0.28	−0.17	0.01	−0.02	−0.01	0.16	1.00

Splitting the series in the intervals [1, 45] and [46, 75], we have the same picture in the first part, while in the second, the countercyclical markup emerges, with the negative correlation between profits and planned production, as in Table 4.29.

4.4.1.1 Case 7b: 10 entrepreneurs and 10,000 workers, in a *declining* economy with a *stable number of firms*

This is a control case, related to the previous one. We reduce here the socialWelfareCompensation, now set to 0.4, from 0.7 (always in the presence of a wage level of 1).[27]

---

[27] The whole set of the parameters of the experiment is reported in Tables B.3 and B.4 of Appendix B. Each case requires the input of a few parameters in an interactive way. We report them in Table C.1 of Appendix C.

Table 4.29 *Case 7, partial correlations (excluding totalProduction)* *(t = 46–75 series)*

	unempl	totalProfit	plannedP	cQ	hPSd	price	wage
unempl	1.00	−0.63	−0.15	0.10	0.15	0.00	−0.17
totalProfit	−0.63	1.00	−0.30	0.23	−0.31	−0.01	0.02
plannedP	−0.15	−0.30	1.00	0.98	0.07	−0.14	0.17
cQ	0.10	0.23	0.98	1.00	−0.14	−0.00	−0.17
hPSd	0.15	−0.31	0.07	−0.14	1.00	0.10	0.05
price	0.00	−0.01	−0.14	−0.00	0.10	1.00	−0.07
wage	−0.17	0.02	0.17	−0.17	0.05	−0.07	1.00

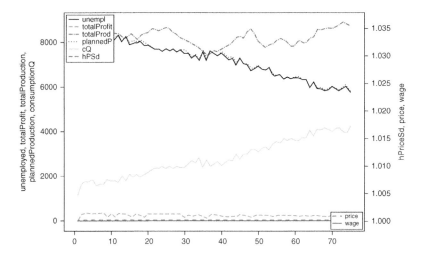

Figure 4.20 Case *7b*, 10 entrepreneurs and 10,000 workers, macro-variable series. The wage line is superimposed to the hPSd line. The plannedP line is superimposed to the totalProd line

Figure 4.20[28] confirms that, missing the consumption support of the welfare compensation or subsidies, the economy generated by the experiment is always declining, with an absolutely stable number of entrepreneurs.

---

[28] The legends are in Table 4.1.

Table 4.30 *Case 8, 10 entrepreneurs and 10,000 workers, correlations*

	unempl	total Profit	total Prod	plannedP	cQ	hPSd	price	wage
unempl	1.00	−0.63	−0.56	−0.55	−0.55	0.13	0.26	−0.18
totalProfit	−0.63	1.00	0.06	0.05	0.06	−0.17	−0.30	0.03
totalProd	−0.56	0.06	1.00	1.00	0.98	−0.04	−0.38	0.24
plannedP	−0.55	0.05	1.00	1.00	0.97	−0.05	−0.38	0.25
cQ	−0.55	0.06	0.98	0.97	1.00	−0.01	−0.37	0.20
hPSd	0.13	−0.17	−0.04	−0.05	−0.01	1.00	−0.23	−0.08
price	0.26	−0.30	−0.38	−0.38	−0.37	−0.23	1.00	0.21
wage	−0.18	0.03	0.24	0.25	0.20	−0.08	0.21	1.00

4.4.2 Case 8: 10 Entrepreneurs and 10,000 Workers, in a Stable *Economy, with* Firm Dynamic

The experiment generates a highly dynamic economy, as an effect of the significant changes compared with to the previous case:[29]

- we activate the `reUseUnspentConsumptionCapability` parameter of Section 3.5, set to 0.5 to improve the demand side;
- we introduce the `jump` set to 0.10 and `pJump` set to 0.05, referring to Section 3.10.1, to have the entrepreneurs trying to increase profits with price spot movements;
- we modify the `Q` parameter of Section 3.2.2, having the entrepreneurs weighting 25% the consumptions at time $t - 1$ and 75% those at time $t - 2$, introducing more delays in production adaptation than in the case of Section 4.4.1;
- the threshold to become entrepreneurs is here 0.10;
- the `absoluteBarrierToBecomeEntrepreneur` is set to 10;
- about `socialWelfareCompensation`, we have the same value (0.7) of Section 4.4.1; we can justify the level of the parameter with the consideration of Section 4.6.1.

Considering Section C.2 of Appendix C, we have no more backward compatibility problems, so, from now on, we always use

---

[29] The whole set of the parameters of the experiment is reported in Tables B.3 and B.4 of Appendix B. Each case requires the input of a few parameters in an interactive way. We report them in Table C.1 of Appendix C.

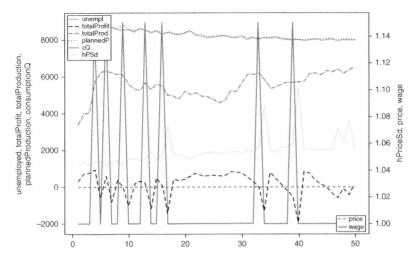

Figure 4.21 Case 8, 10 entrepreneurs and 10,000 workers, macro-variable series. The plannedP line is superimposed to the totalProd line

the `schedule6.xls` collection of actions, as explained in that section.

The Figure 4.21[30] and 4.22 report the description of a stable economy, but internally particularly dynamic, with a relevant process of entry of new firms in the market, moving from a strict oligopoly to an open market, although not an atomistic one.

The countercyclical markup emerges at the level of partial correlations, in Tables 4.31 and 4.32.

4.4.2.1 Case 8b: 10 Entrepreneurs and 10,000 Workers, in a *Stable Economy*, without *Firm Dynamic*

We refer to Figure 4.23:[31] missing the weight of the *social policy* parameter `socialWelfareCompensation`, here set to 0.4 as in Section 4.4.1.1; the difference between this case and that one is originated by the presence of the `reUseUnspentConsumptionCapability` parameter[32] (of Section 3.5), set to 0.5, effectively reinforcing the

---

[30] The legends are in Table 4.1.
[31] The legends are in Table 4.1.
[32] The whole set of the parameters of the experiment is reported in Tables B.3 and B.4 of Appendix B.

Table 4.31 *Case 8, partial correlations (excluding plannedProduction)*

	unempl	totalProfit	totalProd	cQ	hPSd	price	wage
unempl	1.00	−0.73	−0.18	−0.03	−0.07	−0.25	0.03
totalProfit	−0.73	1.00	−0.21	0.04	−0.25	−0.44	0.12
totalProd	−0.18	−0.21	1.00	0.95	−0.22	−0.29	0.27
cQ	−0.03	0.04	0.95	1.00	0.17	0.14	−0.19
hPSd	−0.07	−0.25	−0.22	0.17	1.00	−0.36	0.08
price	−0.25	−0.44	−0.29	0.14	−0.36	1.00	0.37
wage	0.03	0.12	0.27	−0.19	0.08	0.37	1.00

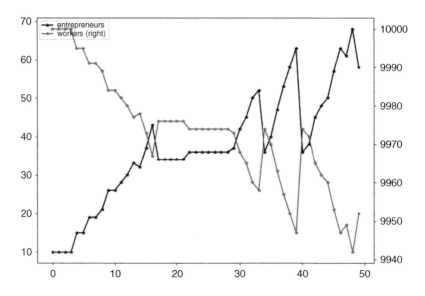

Figure 4.22 Case 8, 10 entrepreneurs and 10,000 workers, agent series

demand side. The number of the firms is always stable, maintaining the initial oligopolistic structure.

A significant countercyclical markup emerges here, in Tables 4.33 and 4.34, not in the 4.35 one, so mainly referred to the actual production and not to the planned production. The novelty here is the presence of the countercyclical markup without an entry/exit process, but due the opposite movements of profits and production levels.

Table 4.32 *Case 8, partial correlations (excluding totalProduction)*

	unempl	totalProfit	plannedP	cQ	hPSd	price	wage
unempl	1.00	−0.74	−0.21	−0.01	−0.09	−0.25	0.04
totalProfit	−0.74	1.00	−0.28	0.09	−0.27	−0.45	0.15
plannedP	−0.21	−0.28	1.00	0.95	−0.26	−0.30	0.32
cQ	−0.01	0.09	0.95	1.00	0.21	0.14	−0.24
hPSd	−0.09	−0.27	−0.26	0.21	1.00	−0.37	0.11
price	−0.25	−0.45	−0.30	0.14	−0.37	1.00	0.38
wage	0.04	0.15	0.32	−0.24	0.11	0.38	1.00

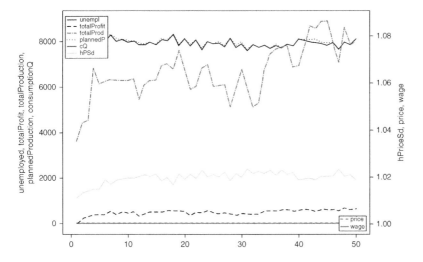

Figure 4.23 Case *8b*, 10 entrepreneurs and 10,000 workers, macro-variable series. The wage line is superimposed to the hPSd line. The plannedP line is superimposed to the totalProd line

4.5 *Quasi* ASHAM, with the *Unsold* Option

4.5.1 *Case 9: 10 Entrepreneurs and 10,000 Workers, in a Nearly Stable Economy, with a* Final Tight Oligopolistic Structure

The second step in the exploration of the *ASHAM economics*, using the *quasi* paradigm with the *unsold* option,[33] introduces a case that collapses in a tight oligopolistic market.

---

[33] Remember that the *quasi* specification is introduced in Section 3.1.2, as a paradigm with the seller prices adapting only at the beginning of each period

Table 4.33 *Case 8b, 10 entrepreneurs and 10,000 workers, correlations*

	unempl	total Profit	total Prod	plannedP	cQ	hPSd	price	wage
unempl	1.00	0.54	−0.99	−1.00	−0.97	0.03	0.39	nan
totalProfit	0.54	1.00	−0.49	−0.54	−0.40	−0.07	0.86	nan
totalProd	−0.99	−0.49	1.00	0.99	0.99	−0.04	−0.41	nan
plannedP	−1.00	−0.54	0.99	1.00	0.97	−0.03	−0.39	nan
cQ	−0.97	−0.40	0.99	0.97	1.00	−0.06	−0.37	nan
hPSd	0.03	−0.07	−0.04	−0.03	−0.06	1.00	0.00	nan
price	0.39	0.86	−0.41	−0.39	−0.37	0.00	1.00	nan
wage	nan	nan	nan	nan	nan	nan	nan	nan

Table 4.34 *Case 8b, partial correlations (excluding plannedProduction)*

	unempl	totalProfit	totalProd	cQ	hPSd	price	wage
unempl	1.00	1.00	0.63	−1.00	0.32	−1.00	0.00
totalProfit	1.00	1.00	−0.65	1.00	−0.32	1.00	−0.04
totalProd	0.63	−0.65	1.00	0.68	−0.13	0.64	−0.00
cQ	−1.00	1.00	0.68	1.00	0.32	−1.00	−0.20
hPSd	0.32	−0.32	−0.13	0.32	1.00	0.32	0.00
price	−1.00	1.00	0.64	−1.00	0.32	1.00	−0.01
wage	0.00	−0.04	−0.00	−0.20	0.00	−0.01	1.00

Table 4.35 *Case 8b, partial correlations (excluding totalProduction)*

	unempl	totalProfit	plannedP	cQ	hPSd	price	wage
unempl	1.00	0.53	−0.92	−0.53	0.01	−0.53	0.04
totalProfit	0.53	1.00	0.15	1.00	−0.29	1.00	0.12
plannedP	−0.92	0.15	1.00	−0.15	−0.12	−0.15	−0.21
cQ	−0.53	1.00	−0.15	1.00	0.28	−1.00	0.02
hPSd	0.01	−0.29	−0.12	0.28	1.00	0.29	0.02
price	−0.53	1.00	−0.15	−1.00	0.29	1.00	0.36
wage	0.04	0.12	−0.21	0.02	0.02	0.36	1.00

(cycle of the simulation); the *unsold* option is introduced in Section 3.10.2 as a behavior of the entrepreneurs modifying their prices at the end of a period for the next one, as they have unsold production.

As in the previous cases, the sets of the parameters of the experiment are reported in Tables B.3 and B.4 of Appendix B. Table B.2 reports all the definitions and the links to the sections where the parameters are introduced and explained in Chapter 3. Each case requires the input of a few parameters in an interactive way: we report them in Table C.1 of Appendix C.

The key parameters that characterize the experiment are:

- the parameter hParadigm, as *Hayekian market sell price modification*, is set to *quasi* and the sub-parameter quasiHchoice set to *unsold*;
- the entrepreneursMindIfPlannedProductionFalls choice is set *True*; as explained in Section 3.10.2, this condition operates when the individual planned production falls below the threshold (here 0.05 as a relative value) thresholdToDecreaseThePrice IfTotalPlannedPFalls;
- the main critical parameters for the *quasi unsold* framework are the levels of soldThreshold1 and soldThreshold2 (here set to 0.9 and 0.99); as explained in Section 3.10.2, the entrepreneur lowers the price if the sold quantity falls below the first threshold and raises it if the sold quantity exceeds the second one; the price movements are regulated by the parameters decreasingRateRange and increasingRateRange, set to −0.1 and 0.01;
- with initShift set to 1.1 and initShock set to 0.1, we start with a simple situation of crossed initial distribution of the prices of the agents, like those of two cases sub (iii) in Section 3.6; this initial construction is related to the necessity of *warming up* the market in the presence of tiny price corrections on the side of the buyers;
- the parameter runningShockS, set to 0.05, is in either case irrelevant here, as the sellers modify their prices once per period with the *unsold* option; the corrections (here, *tiny*) of the buyers' prices, as in Section 3.7, are regulated by the parameter runningShockB, set to 0.0008 facing a problem opposite to that of Section 3.6: each buyer is acting in each sub-step of each cycle, so one hundred times for time step, making many corrections, while the sellers have a unique correction at the beginning of each cycle. The side of the market with more corrections moves in the direction of the prices of the other side. The solution is that of reducing the pace of the corrections of the side acting more frequently;

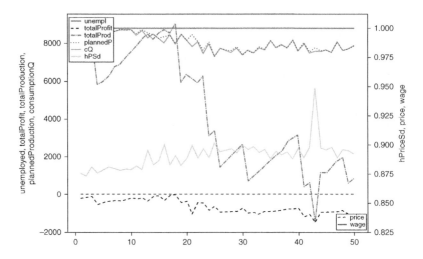

Figure 4.24 Case 9, 10 entrepreneurs and 10,000 workers, macro-variable series. The plannedP line is superimposed to the totalProd line, but the value at pos. 21 on the x-axis

- the `socialWelfareCompensation` parameter is again set to 0.7 (wage level: 1) and its effect is verified in Section 4.5.1.1; we can justify the level of the parameter with the consideration of Section 4.6.1;
- the Q parameter of Section 3.2.2, having the entrepreneurs weighting 25% the consumptions at time $t-1$ and 75% those at time $t-2$, having some delays in production adaptation.

In Figure 4.24[34] we have a highly dynamic world, lightly declining, with the prices also dropping. The Figure 4.25[35] shows a continuously decreasing movement in the number of entrepreneurs, from 10 to 4, with a tight oligopolistic market at the end.

The interpretation, consistent with the mechanism of the simulation, is that the entrepreneurs are lowering their prices in the presence of falling consumptions, due to the rising unemployment; the fall in profits is producing bankruptcies and firm disappears, with a final very reduced number of oligopolistic operators.

---

[34] The legends are in Table 4.1.
[35] The scale on the right of this figure has to be read adding 1e4, i.e., 10,000, to the values reported there.

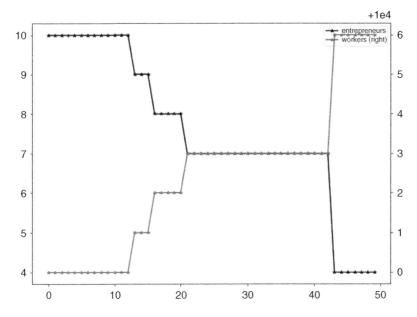

Figure 4.25 Case 9, 10 entrepreneurs and 10,000 workers, agent series

As firms disappear, the survivors improve their market shares. As a consequence, the countercyclical markup, as we can see in Tables 4.37 and 4.38, is strongly present in partial correlation values; the total correlations, without the elimination of the indirect effects, are of opposite signs (Table 4.36).

4.5.1.1 Case 9b: 10 Entrepreneurs and 10,000 Workers, in a *Declining* Economy, with a *Final Tight Oligopolistic Structure*

The parameters used here are the same of Section 4.5.1,[36] for case 9.

The unique difference is the level of the `socialWelfareCompen sation` parameter, now set to 0.4.

---

[36] The whole set of the parameters of the experiment is reported in Tables B.3 and B.4 of Appendix B. The Table B.2 reports all the definitions and the links to the sections where the parameters are introduced and explained, in Chapter 3. Each case requires the input of a few parameters in an interactive way: we report them in Table C.1 of Appendix C.

Table 4.36 *Case 9, 10 entrepreneurs and 10,000 workers, correlations*

	unempl	total Profit	total Prod	plannedP	cQ	hPSd	price	wage
unempl	1.00	−0.67	−0.69	−0.67	−0.74	0.28	−0.59	nan
totalProfit	−0.67	1.00	0.70	0.68	0.72	−0.41	0.95	nan
totalProd	−0.69	0.70	1.00	1.00	0.98	−0.08	0.76	nan
plannedP	−0.67	0.68	1.00	1.00	0.97	−0.07	0.76	nan
cQ	−0.74	0.72	0.98	0.97	1.00	−0.10	0.72	nan
hPSd	0.28	−0.41	−0.08	−0.07	−0.10	1.00	−0.34	nan
price	−0.59	0.95	0.76	0.76	0.72	−0.34	1.00	nan
wage	nan	nan	nan	nan	nan	nan	nan	nan

Table 4.37 *Case 9, partial correlations (excluding plannedProduction)*

	unempl	totalProfit	totalProd	cQ	hPSd	price	wage
unempl	1.00	−0.30	−0.18	0.08	0.16	0.27	0.00
totalProfit	−0.30	1.00	−0.90	0.89	−0.18	0.98	−0.00
totalProd	−0.18	−0.90	1.00	0.99	−0.08	0.92	−0.02
cQ	0.08	0.89	0.99	1.00	0.13	−0.90	−0.16
hPSd	0.16	−0.18	−0.08	0.13	1.00	0.10	0.00
price	0.27	0.98	0.92	−0.90	0.10	1.00	−0.01
wage	0.00	−0.00	−0.02	−0.16	0.00	−0.01	1.00

Table 4.38 *Case 9, partial correlations (excluding totalProduction)*

	unempl	totalProfit	plannedP	cQ	hPSd	price	wage
unempl	1.00	0.30	0.34	−0.36	0.32	−0.30	−0.00
totalProfit	0.30	1.00	−0.99	0.99	−0.56	1.00	−0.00
plannedP	0.34	−0.99	1.00	1.00	−0.54	0.99	−0.04
cQ	−0.36	0.99	1.00	1.00	0.55	−0.99	0.03
hPSd	0.32	−0.56	−0.54	0.55	1.00	0.54	0.00
price	−0.30	1.00	0.99	−0.99	0.54	1.00	0.00
wage	−0.00	−0.00	−0.04	0.03	0.00	0.00	1.00

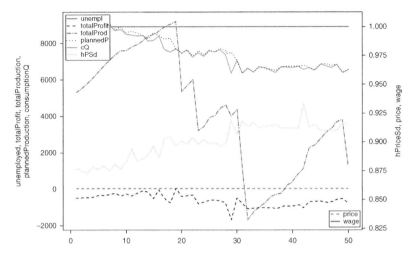

Figure 4.26 Case *9b*, 10 entrepreneurs and 10,000 workers, macro-variable series. The plannedP line is superimposed to the totalProd line, but the value at pos. 28 on the x-axis

Within a declining economy, as that of Figure 4.26,[37] Figure 4.27[38] reports the same movements of the entrepreneurs toward a limited circle of oligopolistic firms.

The countercyclical markup is absolutely relevant in the partial correlation (Tables 4.40 and 4.41); the total correlations, without the elimination of the indirect effects, are of opposite sign (Table 4.39).

4.6 *Quasi* ASHAM, with the *randomUp* Option

The third step in the exploration of the *ASHAM economics*, using the *quasi* paradigm with the *randomUp* option,[39] introduces a case that generates a stable economy with a stable oligopolistic structure.

---

[37] The legends are in Table 4.1.
[38] The scale on the right of this figure has to be read adding 1e4, i.e., 10,000, to the values reported there.
[39] Recall that the *quasi* specification is introduced in Section 3.1.2, as a paradigm with the seller prices adapting only at the beginning of each period (cycle of the simulation); the *randomUp* option is introduced in Section 3.10.2 as a behavior of the entrepreneurs increasing their prices at the end of a period for the next one, in a seemingly random way, that we can imagine to be related to information shocks.

Table 4.39 *Case 9b, 10 entrepreneurs and 10,000 workers, correlations*

	unempl	total Profit	total Prod	plannedP	cQ	hPSd	price	wage
unempl	1.00	−0.72	−0.93	−0.93	−0.97	0.45	−0.72	nan
totalProfit	−0.72	1.00	0.64	0.63	0.72	−0.65	0.80	nan
totalProd	−0.93	0.64	1.00	1.00	0.97	−0.51	0.82	nan
plannedP	−0.93	0.63	1.00	1.00	0.97	−0.50	0.82	nan
cQ	−0.97	0.72	0.97	0.97	1.00	−0.50	0.77	nan
hPSd	0.45	−0.65	−0.51	−0.50	−0.50	1.00	−0.66	nan
price	−0.72	0.80	0.82	0.82	0.77	−0.66	1.00	nan
wage	nan	nan	nan	nan	nan	nan	nan	nan

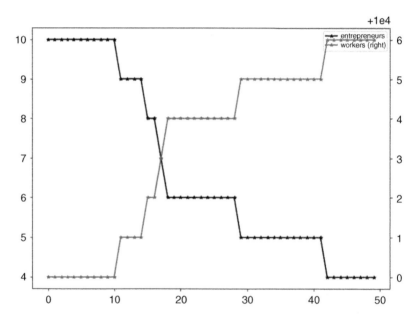

Figure 4.27 Case *9b*, 10 entrepreneurs and 10,000 workers, agent series

4.6.1 *Case 10: 10 Entrepreneurs and 10,000 Workers, in a Stable Economy, with Information Shocks and a Stable Oligopolistic Structure*

As in the previous cases, the sets of the parameters of the experiment are reported in Tables B.3 and B.4 of Appendix B. Table B.2 reports all

Table 4.40 *Case 9b, partial correlations (excluding plannedProduction)*

	unempl	totalProfit	totalProd	cQ	hPSd	price	wage
unempl	1.00	−0.31	−0.24	−0.04	−0.28	0.29	0.00
totalProfit	−0.31	1.00	−0.96	0.91	−0.59	0.96	0.02
totalProd	−0.24	−0.96	1.00	0.96	−0.53	0.96	−0.01
cQ	−0.04	0.91	0.96	1.00	0.48	−0.89	0.01
hPSd	−0.28	−0.59	−0.53	0.48	1.00	0.45	0.17
price	0.29	0.96	0.96	−0.89	0.45	1.00	0.14
wage	0.00	0.02	−0.01	0.01	0.17	0.14	1.00

Table 4.41 *Case 9b, partial correlations (excluding totalProduction)*

	unempl	totalProfit	plannedP	cQ	hPSd	price	wage
unempl	1.00	0.06	0.09	−0.19	−0.07	−0.07	−0.00
totalProfit	0.06	1.00	−0.99	0.99	−0.71	0.99	0.07
plannedP	0.09	−0.99	1.00	0.99	−0.69	0.99	0.03
cQ	−0.19	0.99	0.99	1.00	0.67	−0.98	0.05
hPSd	−0.07	−0.71	−0.69	0.67	1.00	0.66	0.15
price	−0.07	0.99	0.99	−0.98	0.66	1.00	−0.05
wage	−0.00	0.07	0.03	0.05	0.15	−0.05	1.00

the definitions and the links to the sections where the parameters are introduced and explained in Chapter 3. Each case requires the input of a few parameters in an interactive way: we report them in Table C.1 of Appendix C.

The key parameters that characterize the experiment are:

- the parameter `socialWelfareCompensation` set to 0.4 and the parameter `reUseUnspentConsumptionCapability` set to 1; explication:
  - the higher level of the parameter `socialWelfareCompensation` in the previous experiments, where we set it to 0.7, can be justified as we were simulating the presence of (family group) income transfers into the disposable income of the unemployed workers (besides subsidies);
  - with the same purposes, the transfers can be simulated also with the parameter `reUseUnspentConsumptionCapability`; we

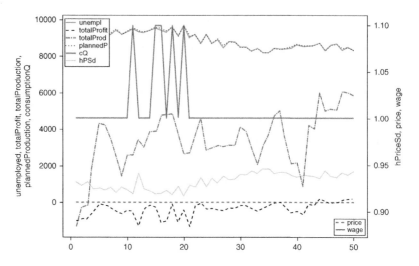

Figure 4.28 Case *10*, 10 entrepreneurs and 10,000 workers, macro-variable series. The plannedP line is superimposed to the totalProd line

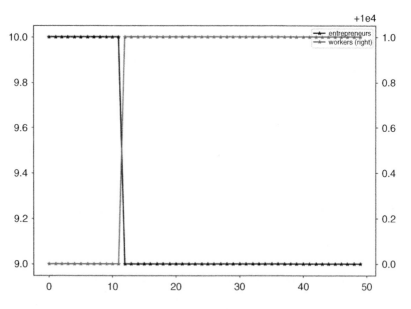

Figure 4.29 Case *10*, 10 entrepreneurs and 10,000 workers, agent series

do that in a limited way, with the 0.5 level of the cases 8, 8b, 9, 9b (it is 0 in 7, 7b); in a significant way, with the 1 level of the case 10;

– in both the situations, we refer to a specific observation: in the ASHAM construction, the employed workers always have a fraction of their consumption capability not used: we can imagine that it is (i) partially used by the subjects themselves in successive time steps and (ii) partially transferred to other (family group) persons.

- with `initShift` 1.8 and `initShock` 0.1, we start with a relevant situation of crossed initial distribution of the prices of the agents, like those of the two cases in sub (iii) in Section 3.6; this initial construction is related to the necessity of *warming up* the market in the presence of *spot* random corrections of the prices on the side of the sellers, so not converging *per se* to closer price distributions;
- the `quasiHchoice` parameter is set to *randomUp*;
- the `runningShockS` parameter is irrelevant here, as the sellers move their prices, with the *randomUp* option of Section 3.10.2, only once per time period;
- the corrections (here, *limited*) of the buyers' prices are regulated by the parameter `runningShockB`, set to 0.01; it is small, but higher than in the case 9 (Section 4.5.1), to react to the jump of the sellers; we have always to take in mind (i) that each buyer is acting in each sub-step of each cycle, so one hundred times for time step, making many corrections, while the sellers have a unique correction at the beginning of each cycle, but also (ii) that, with the jump, the sellers' corrections can be quite relevant;
- the parameters `jump` and `pJump` are set to 0.2 and 0.1, i.e., a random jump with a relative increment of the 20% with probability 0.1, as description of the behavior of the entrepreneurs increasing their prices (or decreasing them, if previously increased) at the end of a period for the next one, in a seemingly random way, that we can imagine to be related to information shocks;
- the Q parameter of Section 3.2.2, having the entrepreneurs weighting 25% the consumptions at time $t-1$ and 75% those at time $t-2$, having some delays in production adaptation.

Table 4.42 *Case* 10, *10 entrepreneurs and 10,000 workers, correlations*

	unempl	total Profit	total Prod	plannedP	cQ	hPSd	price	wage
unempl	1.00	0.30	−0.95	−0.95	−0.95	0.25	0.17	−0.57
totalProfit	0.30	1.00	−0.38	−0.41	−0.38	0.30	0.63	−0.07
totalProd	−0.95	−0.38	1.00	1.00	1.00	−0.23	−0.18	0.54
plannedP	−0.95	−0.41	1.00	1.00	1.00	−0.21	−0.17	0.55
cQ	−0.95	−0.38	1.00	1.00	1.00	−0.23	−0.18	0.54
hPSd	0.25	0.30	−0.23	−0.21	−0.23	1.00	0.29	−0.13
price	0.17	0.63	−0.18	−0.17	−0.18	0.29	1.00	0.07
wage	−0.57	−0.07	0.54	0.55	0.54	−0.13	0.07	1.00

In Figure 4.28[40] we have a quite stable economy: the prices are continuously changing in a cyclical irregular way, but are always quite low and so are the profits; the unemployment is very low and, as a consequence, in five cases we have a wage positive movement, following the method described in Section 3.12.1 (or by item 12 in Figure 3.1).

The Figure 4.29[41] depicts a unique limited negative movement of the number of the entrepreneurs.

The countercyclical markup is evident in Table 4.42 and confirmed in Table 4.44, considering the planned production alone; it is absent in Table 4.43.

4.7 *Quasi* ASHAM, with the *Profit* Option

The fourth step in the exploration of the *ASHAM economics*, using the *quasi* paradigm with the *profit* option,[42] introduces a case

---

[40] The legends are in Table 4.1.

[41] The scale on the right of this figure has to be read adding 1e4, i.e., 10,000, to the values reported there.

[42] A reminder: the *quasi* specification is introduced in Section 3.1.2, as a paradigm with the seller prices adapting only at the beginning of each period (cycle of the simulation); the *profit* option is introduced in Section 3.10.2 as a behavior of the entrepreneurs *increasing* or *decreasing* their prices at the end of a period for the next one, trying to increase a falling profit. To summarize the actual difficulty of knowing the demand elasticity, the actual choice between raising or lowering the price is a random one, with 60% of probability to the

Table 4.43 *Case* 10, *partial correlations (excluding plannedProduction)*

	unempl	totalProfit	totalProd	cQ	hPSd	price	wage
unempl	1.00	−0.31	0.01	−0.01	0.13	0.21	−0.19
totalProfit	−0.31	1.00	−0.01	0.02	0.13	0.60	0.01
totalProd	0.01	−0.01	1.00	1.00	−0.13	0.10	−0.14
cQ	−0.01	0.02	1.00	1.00	0.13	−0.09	0.14
hPSd	0.13	0.13	−0.13	0.13	1.00	0.14	−0.06
price	0.21	0.60	0.10	−0.09	0.14	1.00	0.17
wage	−0.19	0.01	−0.14	0.14	−0.06	0.17	1.00

Table 4.44 *Case* 10, *partial correlations (excluding totalProduction)*

	unempl	totalProfit	plannedP	cQ	hPSd	price	wage
unempl	1.00	−0.41	−0.28	0.07	0.21	0.30	−0.12
totalProfit	−0.41	1.00	−0.61	0.52	0.31	0.68	0.15
plannedP	−0.28	−0.61	1.00	0.97	0.35	0.40	0.22
cQ	0.07	0.52	0.97	1.00	−0.33	−0.35	−0.22
hPSd	0.21	0.31	0.35	−0.33	1.00	−0.03	−0.12
price	0.30	0.68	0.40	−0.35	−0.03	1.00	0.05
wage	−0.12	0.15	0.22	−0.22	−0.12	0.05	1.00

that generates again a stable economy with a stable oligopolistic structure.

4.7.1 Case 11: 10 Entrepreneurs and 10,000 Workers, in a Stable Economy, with a Stable Oligopolistic Market

As in the previous cases, the sets of the parameters of the experiment are reported in Tables B.3 and B.4 of Appendix B. Table B.2 reports all the definitions and the links to the sections where the parameters are introduced and explained, in Chapter 3. Each case requires the input of a few parameters in an interactive way: we report them in Table C.1 of Appendix C.

first choice ("raise") and 40% to the other one if *priceSwitchIfProfitFalls* is set to "raise" and vice versa, if it set to "lower."

The key parameters that characterize the experiment are:

- the parameter `socialWelfareCompensation` set to 0.7 and the parameter `reUseUnspentConsumptionCapability` set to 0.75 (a novelty, to compensate the uncertainty that the entrepreneurs are expected to generate in the economic system via the behavior designed for this experiment);
- `jump` and `pJump`, with the option *profit*, are both related to the reactions to the falls of profit, are set to 0.05 and 0.20;
- the entrepreneur decides to raise or to lower her price if the profit is negative. `priceSwitchIfProfitFalls`, as in Appendix B, is a switch with values *"raise"* or *"lower"*; to summarize the actual difficulty of knowing the demand elasticity, the actual choice between raising or lowering the price is a random one, with 60% of probability to the first choice ("raise") and 40% to the other one if `priceSwitchIfProfitFalls` is set to "raise"; vice versa, if it set to "lower"; in the experiment, `priceSwitchIfProfitFalls` is set to "raise";
- `profitStrategyReverseAfterN` is set to 5; in Section 3.10.2 we have the analysis of the actions of these two new parameters;
- `quasiHchoice` is set to *profit*;
- the Q parameter of Section 3.2.2, having the entrepreneurs weighting 25% the consumptions at time $t-1$ and 75% those at time $t-2$, having some delays in production adaptation.

The Table 4.30[43] shows a stable system, with regular prices and low (negative in mean)[44] profits. In Figure 4.31[45] we have a unique case of movement in the number of the entrepreneurs (an entrepreneur moving to be an unemployed worker).

The countercyclical markup is slightly present in total correlations (Table 4.45), but well acting if we analyze both the cases of partial correlation, in Tables 4.46 and 4.47; in the second, with a perfect correlation.

---

[43] The legends are in Table 4.1.

[44] How do firms survive? Alternating periods of positive and negative results.

[45] The scale on the right of this figure has to be read adding 1e4, i.e., 10,000, to the values reported there.

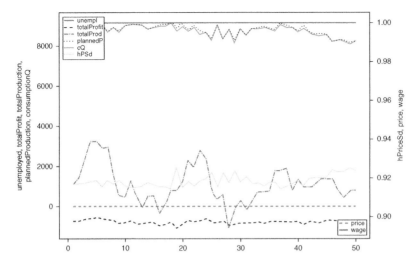

Figure 4.30 Case *11*, 10 entrepreneurs and 10,000 workers, macro-variable series. The plannedP line is superimposed to the totalProd line, but the value at pos. 19 on the x-axis

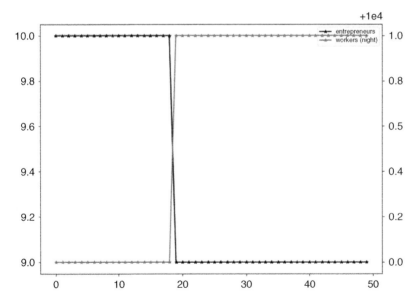

Figure 4.31 Case *11*, 10 entrepreneurs and 10,000 workers, agent series

Table 4.45 *Case 11, 10 entrepreneurs and 10,000 workers, correlations*

	unempl	total Profit	total Prod	plannedP	cQ	hPSd	price	wage
unempl	1.00	0.04	−0.90	−0.89	−0.93	0.33	−0.08	nan
totalProfit	0.04	1.00	−0.17	−0.24	−0.13	0.54	0.77	nan
totalProd	−0.90	−0.17	1.00	0.98	0.99	−0.40	0.03	nan
plannedP	−0.89	−0.24	0.98	1.00	0.97	−0.40	0.06	nan
cQ	−0.93	−0.13	0.99	0.97	1.00	−0.40	0.04	nan
hPSd	0.33	0.54	−0.40	−0.40	−0.40	1.00	0.55	nan
price	−0.08	0.77	0.03	0.06	0.04	0.55	1.00	nan
wage	nan	nan	nan	nan	nan	nan	nan	nan

Table 4.46 *Case 11, partial correlations (excluding plannedProduction)*

	unempl	totalProfit	totalProd	cQ	hPSd	price	wage
unempl	1.00	0.30	0.64	−0.75	−0.06	−0.29	−0.05
totalProfit	0.30	1.00	−0.65	0.61	0.10	0.79	0.00
totalProd	0.64	−0.65	1.00	0.99	0.04	0.55	−0.04
cQ	−0.75	0.61	0.99	1.00	−0.08	−0.51	0.03
hPSd	−0.06	0.10	0.04	−0.08	1.00	0.30	0.00
price	−0.29	0.79	0.55	−0.51	0.30	1.00	−0.00
wage	−0.05	0.00	−0.04	0.03	0.00	−0.00	1.00

Table 4.47 *Case 11, partial correlations (excluding totalProduction)*

	unempl	totalProfit	plannedP	cQ	hPSd	price	wage
unempl	1.00	0.07	0.07	−0.10	0.03	−0.07	0.01
totalProfit	0.07	1.00	−1.00	1.00	−0.78	1.00	0.03
plannedP	0.07	−1.00	1.00	1.00	−0.78	1.00	−0.01
cQ	−0.10	1.00	1.00	1.00	0.78	−1.00	0.00
hPSd	0.03	−0.78	−0.78	0.78	1.00	0.79	0.01
price	−0.07	1.00	1.00	−1.00	0.79	1.00	0.01
wage	0.01	0.03	−0.01	0.00	0.01	0.01	1.00

4.8 Synopsis of Cases from 7 to 11, in the ASHAM Economy

Table 4.48 summarizes the experiments use to explore the *ASHAM economics*, looking at the results in the perspective both of emergence of the countercyclical markup and of the changes in the structure of the market.

Let us briefly comment:

- the emergence of the countercyclical markup is here nearly a constant, but in the case of the always declining economy, confirming the relevance of the ASHAM construction as a realistic representation of an economic system;
- the case 8, with the households/workers acting in a wise way, recovering or transferring to other people their unspent consumption capability, in presence of social welfare compensations quite high, produces a movement of the structure of the market toward its openness.
- the dynamic of the market structure in cases 9 and 9b shows an important novelty, with the emergence of tight oligopolistic structures in stable or declining economies, if the entrepreneurs pay attention to the price corrections in presence/absence of unsold products.

4.9 Random Values On and Off, a Test in the ASHAM Environment

The *Oligopoly* simulation project, built for the SLAPP shell, allows us to specify experiment with the random values used to generate some of its internal values.

We run again the case 8 of Section 4.4.2, with name *8modPars*, modifying three of the random values in the middle of the simulation: when $t = 26$, we stop them with 0 as maximum value.

We use the *special action* feature of SLAPP, described in its Reference Handbook[46] (use the index to find it). This feature can be programmed in different ways.

If the file observerActions.txt (the file is in the main folder of the simulation project; see Section C.1 in Appendix C) contains

---

[46] Online at https://terna.github.io/SLAPP/.

Table 4.48 *The ASHAM cases in short*

Case	Key points	Effects	Level of the countercyclical markup
7, Sec. 4.4.1 *full*	a stable economy with price to sellers' level and with entries in the second part	countercyclical markup emerges in par. corr. with planned prod., in the second part *final structure: large oligopoly*	low
7b, Sec. 4.4.1.1 *full*	always declining economy	no countercyclical markup *final structure: stable oligopoly*	none
8, Sec. 4.4.2 *full*	a stable economy with a relevant firm dynamic	countercyclical markup emerges in partial corr. *final structure: going to open m.*	low
8b, Sec. 4.4.2.1 *full*	a stable economy without firm dynamic	countercyclical markup emerges in total and par. corr. *final structure: stable oligopoly*	high
9, Sec. 4.5.1 *quasi unsold*	a nearly stable economy generating a tight oligopolistic market	countercyclical markup emerges in partial corr. *final structure: tight oligopoly*	very high

9b, Sec. 4.5.1.1 *quasi unsold*	a declining economy generating a tight oligopolistic market	countercyclical markup emerges in partial corr. *final structure: tight oligopoly*	very high
10, Sec. 4.6.1 *quasi randomUp*	a stable economy with a stable oligopolistic market	countercyclical markup emerges in total and partial corr. *final structure: stable oligopoly*	high
11, Sec. 4.7.1 *quasi profit*	a stable economy with a stable oligopolistic market	countercyclical markup emerges in partial corr. both with production and planned production *final structure: stable oligopoly*	high or very high

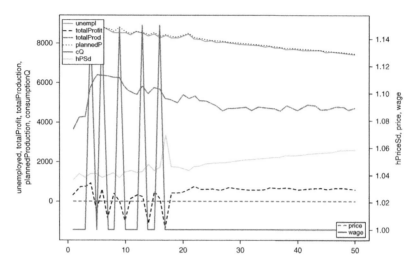

Figure 4.32 Case *8modPars*, 10 entrepreneurs and 10,000 workers, macro-variable series. The plannedP line is superimposed to the totalProd line

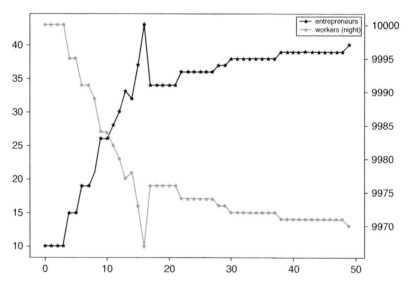

Figure 4.33 Case *8modPars*, 10 entrepreneurs and 10,000 workers, agent series

the item `specialAction`, the simulator looks for a file with name `modPars.txt`, reporting the internal names of the variables used as parameters in the model; each name followed by a new value.[47]

The program automatically produces the following output and then waits for our reply ("26" in this case):

```
The special action has to be activated at cycle ...
-1 if never
```

In this example, the file `modPars.txt` contains:

```
consumptionRandomComponentSD            0
randomComponentOfPlannedProduction   0
maxDemandRelativeRandomShock            0
```

Comparing the new Figures 4.32 and 4.33 with the original Figures 4.21 and 4.22, we can verify that the trends are the same, but the original representations are interestingly more dynamic.

---

[47] In the oligopoly folder, we have an example of *modPars.txt* file and also a file named *observerActions with specialAction.txt* that we can rename as *observerActions.txt*; the original *observerActions.txt* can be saved with another name or simply deleted; the recovery is from the files *observerActions no pause.txt* or *observerActions with pause.txt*.

5 | *The Model Facing Empirical Data*

SIMONE LOMBARDINI

In this chapter we compare the implications of our theoretical model and simulations with the empirical data. In particular, we look at the number of new firms and failed ones over the business cycle. For this purpose, we consider two time series of the number of births/deaths in the industrial sector provided by the Bureau of Labor Statistics.[1] These data refer to the US economy. We have a quarterly time series, starting from March 1993.

In Figure 5.1, the hyphened line is normally far below the continuous one. This is consistent with the fact that US GDP has generally grown over the period examined, except for quarters in the heavy recession beginning in 2008. It is possible to see that when the *dot-com* bubble broke out, the number of enterprises born was equal to that of the failed. The worst situation took place from the end of 2007 until 2009, when the number of failed businesses was higher than that of newborn businesses.

It is possible to recognize three cycles since 1993: the first one goes from 1993 to 2001, the second one from 2001 to 2007, and then a small cycle from 2009 to 2014, where the economic growth is more unstable. Around June 2013, the number of failed enterprises nearly reached that of newborn businesses.

Figure 5.2 shows the ratio between newborn and failed enterprises. The dashed line at level 1 allows us to identify the economic cycles. When the continuous line is above the dashed one, the US economy is growing, and thus the number of enterprises born is far bigger then the dead. The three previously defined business cycles are clearly

---

[1] Entrepreneurship and the U.S. Economy, Business Employment Dynamics, Bureau of Labor Statistics, April 28, 2016. Chart 5: https://www.bls.gov/bdm/entrepreneurship/bdm_chart5.htm.

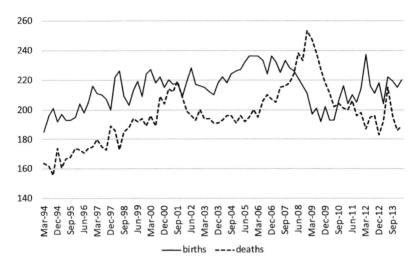

Figure 5.1 Births and deaths of enterprises (x 1,000)

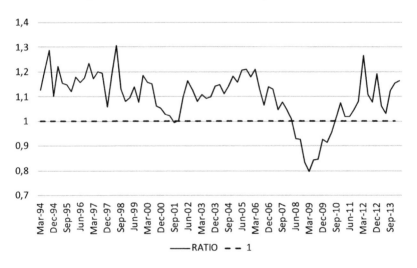

Figure 5.2 Ratio births/deaths enterprises

shown in this graph: the economic crash in 2001 (*dot-com* bubble), with the ratio equal to 1, and the second economic break, worse than the first one, with the continuous line, with a value for the ratio far below 1.

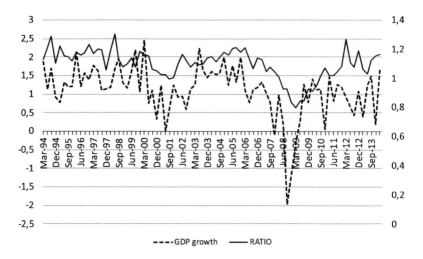

Figure 5.3 Birth/deaths enterprise ratio versus GDP rate of change

We now introduce the data on GDP growth.[2] Comparing the births-deaths enterprise index (ratio between newborn firms and failed firms, with the GDP dynamics), Figure 5.3 suggests a co-movement between the two series. The three economic cycles, identified for the enterprise index, are also clear for the US GDP, with a first drop in 2000 to 2001 and a second heavier shrink in 2008.

Figure 5.4 shows the markup index. The data comes from the Census of Bureau of Statistics for US economy. The quarterly data considered here refer to the same period of analysis of the GDP and of the enterprise index. The Bureau of Statistics reports the *all-Worker Labor Share* and the *proprietors' total income share* related to the GDP.[3] Assuming the *proprietors'* share of the GDP as a proxy for the markup, the figure shows its movements. From 1993 to 1999, the markup was growing; then it stopped and decreased until 2001. Just before the break of the recession, the markup dropped, recovering only in 2009 and then starting to rise again. What is interesting is that the markup reverses its trend always before GDP movements.

[2] OECD, https://stats.oecd.org/index.aspx?queryid=3501#.
[3] Estimating the US labor share, *Monthly Labor Review*, Bureau of Labor Statistics, February 2017. Data from Figure 2: https://www.bls.gov/opub/mlr/2017/article/estimating-the-us-labor-share.ht.

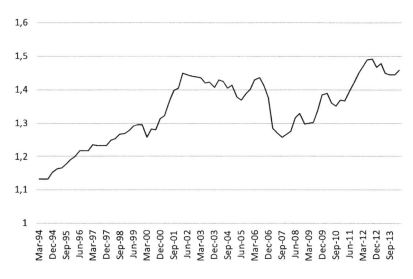

Figure 5.4 The dynamic of the markup

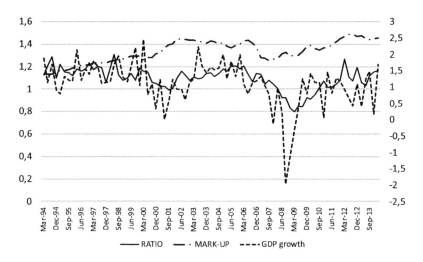

Figure 5.5 GDP dynamic–markup–births/deaths ratio of the enterprises

Finally, the three indexes are shown together in Figure 5.5, where we can see the co-movements among the three series in the recent years. The path of the GDP is clearly associated with the birth-death index, and meanwhile there is a clear negative correlation between

Table 5.1 *Correlation matrix*

	Markup	GDP dynamic	Ratio
Markup	1	−0.1341712	−0.2116298
GDP dynamic		1	0.53767038
Ratio			1

Table 5.2 *Granger causality: Markup, GDP dynamic*

Null Hypothesis	Observations	F-statistics	Probability
GDP dynamic Granger causes Markup	82	7.8737	0.0008
Markup does not Granger cause GDP dynamic	82	0.14778	0.8629

the markup and GDP growth. These hypotheses are confirmed by calculating the correlations, shown in Table 5.1.

The signs of the correlations are consistent with the implications of the theoretical model and simulations shown in the previous chapters of this book. The markup is negatively correlated with the changes in GDP. The correlation between the birth-death index of companies and the macroeconomic fluctuations is positive and shows a high value. According to our initial expectations, the correlation should be positive because the increase in the birth rate of firms is induced by optimistic shocks on the expectations of aggregate demand and generates itself increases in the aggregate demand and GDP. Finally, the correlation between the markup and the birth-death index of companies is negative; intuitively, if the birth-death index of companies is positively correlated to GDP while the markup is negatively correlated with increases in GDP, indirectly, the markup should be negatively correlated also with the birth-death index.

In Table 5.2, the correlation between the economic growth and the markup is unidirectional. The correlation between these two variables is relatively weak, but anyway negative. This implies that in periods of sustained economic growth, there will be a reduction of the markup that could correspond to the principle of Kuznets (1946), according to which the "tide brings all boats to the surface." In times of rapid

Table 5.3 *Granger causality: Markup, ratio*

Null Hypothesis	Observations	F-statistics	Probability
Markup does not Granger cause Ratio	82	0.77186	0.4657
Ratio does not Granger cause Markup	82	0.14744	0.8632

Table 5.4 *Granger causality: GDP dynamic, ratio*

Null Hypothesis	Observations	F-statistics	Probability
Ratio Granger causes GDP dynamic	82	9.9736	0.0001
GDP dynamic does not Granger cause Ratio	82	0.147	0.2363

economic growth, the share of profits on total surplus would fall in favor of labor. On the other hand, in times of recession, due to the concentration of capital and a high level of unemployment, the redistribution of the surplus would be to the advantage of the owners, with a greater share of the total surplus.

In Table 5.3, the negative correlation between the birth-death index of companies and the markup does not seem to be significant according to the reported statistics. The Granger causality test suggests that there is neither unidirectional nor bidirectional correlation. The result is consistent with our expectations, because the birth-death index of the companies does not directly impact the markup.

Finally, in Table 5.4 the Granger test suggests that there is a one-way causality between the birth-death index of enterprises and the economic growth. Intuitively, more companies should also increase GDP. Note that the value of this correlation is very high compared to the other two, suggesting a strong link between the variables. The correlation direction is also consistent with our theoretical model and simulations. It is the birth-death index of companies that modifies growth, not vice versa. In fact, if many businesses die, the GDP will fall as a result. The opposite would not make sense, as our model and simulations predict, by focusing on the impact of entry and exit on the determination of the GDP.

The data shown in the last table are consistent with the hypotheses of the model described in the book. The probability of entry, for the firms, would be determined by the idiosyncratic information shocks following equation (2.30) of Chapter 2:

$$\text{Pr(entry)}_t = \int_0^{n_t(1-h_t)} (\text{Pr}(w_t < E_{t-1,i}(\Phi_t)))_i \, di$$

These shocks depend on the variance of expectations $E_{t-1,i}(\Phi_t)$, which is the probability that the wage is set at a lower level than the expected present discounted value of the future profits as an entrepreneur in case of entry. This expectation, in its turn, is strongly linked to the "shift parameter" Ψ_t of aggregate demand in equation (2.21) of Chapter 2:

$$\Psi_t = \sum_{i=0}^{\infty} \frac{E[n_{t+i}(W_{t+i} + h_{t+i}^{in} E(\Pi_{t+i}^{in}) + h_{t+i}^e E(\Pi_{t+i}^e))]}{[1 + E(r_{t+i})]^i}$$

The variance of shift parameter Ψ is therefore dependent on future monetary policy expectations (the denominator), on inflation (since the variables in square brackets are expressed in nominal values), wages, and profit expectations (both of new entrants and incumbents), since their value appears inside the square brackets in the numerator. So, our model suggests that there should be a link among nominal values of wages, profit, and interest rate, and the entry/exit of enterprises. In our model, the parameter Ψ influences the number of entrepreneurs directly, according to equation (2.36) of Chapter 2:

$$H_t = H_{t-1}[Pr(\Pi^{in} \geq 0)] + (n_{t-1} - H_{t-1})\beta(var(\Psi_t)) -$$
$$- \xi(1 + \iota)(1 + r_{t-1})F_R(n_{t-2} - H_{t-2})\beta(var(\Psi_{t-1}))$$

The Granger causality test shows evidence of causation from GDP changes to births/deaths enterprises. This means that GDP trend (i.e., the total sum of profits and wages) influences the expectation about future GDP, and in its turn, the entry decisions. Shocks on the real GDP, i.e., on the sum of profits and wages, influences births/deaths firm as described in these equations of our model.

Furthermore, it is interesting to point out that the US data on markup show a countercyclical behavior. The current literature in this regard is rather mixed; however, we have calculated a simple correlation index. In order to verify this hypothesis, we have considered the same time series of Figure 5.1, cut off by 1997. From 1993 to 1997, the births-deaths index for the firms is lower than in the following years, and the correlation index for that period is positive (0, 1528).

Conclusions

Even in economics, research is meant to answer one or more questions about individuals' behavior. The question we have dealt with and – we believe – answered with this book is the following.

Do entry, exit, and strategic interactions among oligopolists and changes in market structure affect the macroeconomy?

In this book we introduce a new approach in macroeconomics where market structure is endogenous, its changes generate macroeconomic fluctuations, and its configuration is, in its turn, affected by the nature and features of the macroeconomic equilibrium. In particular, the theoretical chapter of our book provides a modeling framework, that plug oligopolistic firms' strategic interactions in a macromodel may also allow us to keep track of social mobility and income distribution.

Since the focus of our theoretical framework is on the subjective decisions of interactive agents, a logical consequence of this assumption is choosing a methodology for simulations that is founded on the premises of realistically modeling the actual behavior of individual agents.

The agent-based modeling (ABM) technique has its starting point in populations of agents, representing individuals or more generally *entities*. From there, we construct our models via computer code operating in dedicated software environments, with each agent represented by a component of the whole code. As in the Introduction, we underline that an ABM does not introduce equations governing the effects of the agents' behavior at the macro level, but it allows us to observe the emergence of those effects, e.g., analyzing individual and global outcomes generated by the agents' actions.

Thanks to ABMs, we can manage boundedly rational behavior and non-equilibrium dynamics.

An interesting implication of our theoretical analysis and simulations is the fact that expansions are, in general, associated with social mobility, which is generated by entry and higher birth of new firms compared to failed companies. In this sense, our work can also be interpreted as a theory of social mobility over the business cycle.

A Summary

We now briefly summarize the main achievements of the different chapters of this book.

In Chapter 1, we explored the premises of the whole work, including the theoretical pillars of the relationships between the industrial structure and the macroeconomy.

In Chapter 2, the algebraic framework of a new macro-model is analytically *dissected*, to prepare a sound basis for the experiments in simulation.

In Chapter 3, starting from the model outline reported in Figure 3.1, we developed a detailed description of the steps the simulation undertakes over its course with the actions of the different kinds of agents.

In Chapter 4 we discovered the results emerging from the simulation experiments, in the perspective both of the presence of the countercyclical markup phenomenon and of the different market structures generated by the simulation.

In Chapter 5 we examined some actual data related to the GDP cycle and to the income components, observing a significant presence of the countercyclical markup.

Appendix A produces a key explanation about the way a decentralized market based on agents actually works. Those pages are worthy to be read also independently from the other parts of the book.

In Appendix B we report the collection of the parameters (names and values) used in this book.

In Appendix C we offer the technical details useful for repeating the experiments of the book or developing new ones.

Future Research

We hope that the theoretical framework of this book may be a useful tool for further research and extensions, where the endogeneity of market structure in a macromodel and its potential implications are analyzed in their macroeconomic implications.

An interesting development for future research could deal with the macroeconomic implications of the interactions between increasing/decreasing returns to scale, with respect to capital, variable barriers to entry, and market structure, i.e., a richer and more extended formalization of the way firms' technology interacts with capital, capital markets, and the macroeconomy.

We trust that our framework could be used for a new kind of policy analyses, based on the link among entry of new firms, social mobility and economic expansions. We do hope that this little and *modest proposal* may be of some help to the work of other colleagues and fellow economists.

Appendices

Appendix A

The Structure of an Atomistic Simplified Hayekian Market

MATTEO MORINI AND PIETRO TERNA

We propose a simplified version of the Hayek's decentralized market hypothesis, considering elementary processes of price adaptation in exchanges.

As a theoretical framework, we refer to the paper of Bowles et al. (2017).

Section A.1 reports the structure of the model and its *warming up* phase. In Section A.2 we introduce an elementary agent-based model of a market, with emergent (quite interesting) price dynamics.

A counter-example is also introduced in Section A.3, showing that – with tiny modification – we generate implausible price dynamics.

In Section A.4 we report some technical analyses of the cases with unmatching numbers of buyers and sellers. These analyses are strongly related to the ratio between sellers and buyers in Sections 3.6 and 3.7.

In Section A.5 we deepen the problem of the agents that seem to be idle, having the level of their reservation price too low to buy. The analysis is relevant to increase the number of sub-steps in the phases of market interaction, as described in Section 3.7.

Codes and sources:

- The simulation generating the Figures A.1 to A.19 are run using `demandOfferCurvesBW2.ipynb`.
- All the material of this Appendix is online at `https://terna.github.io/microHayekianMarket/`.

A.1 The Structure of the Model and the *Warming Up* Phase

Our agents are simply prices (a number, the price, represents the agent in the agent vector), to be interpreted as reservation prices.[1]

---

[1] The *max* price a buyer could pay and the *min* one a seller could accept are kept reserved, i.e., not declared.

The agents act over the time that we organize in cycles; within a *cycle*, all the buyers act once, in random order.

We have two price vectors: pL^b with item pL^b_i for the buyers, and pL^s with item pL^s_j for the sellers. The ith or the jth elements of the vectors are prices, which we use here also as agents.

Both in the simplified Hayekian perspective (Section A.2) and in the unstructured one (Section A.3), we have to pre-run a *warning up* action.

With the *warming up* phase, we define:

- d_0 – the lower bound of the random uniform numbers, both for the buyers and the sellers, in the warming up phase;
  in the running phase, the lower bound is 0;
- d_1 – the upper bound of the random uniform numbers for the buyers;
- d_2 – the upper bound of the random uniform numbers for the sellers;
- $nCycles$ – number of simulation cycles;
- $nBuyers$ – number of the buyers;
- $nSellers$ – number of the sellers;
- $seed$ – the seed of the random numbers;
- the initial buyer i reservation price, different for each buyer: $p_{b,i} = \frac{1}{1+u_i}$ with $u_i \sim \mathcal{U}(d_0, d_1)$;
- the initial seller j reservation price, different for each seller: $p_{s,j} = 1 + u_j$ with $u_j \sim \mathcal{U}(d_0, d_2)$;
- $buyersSellersRatio$ – the ratio $\frac{nBuyers}{nSellers}$;
- $sellersBuyersRatio$ – the ratio $\frac{nSellers}{nBuyers}$;
- $usingRatios$ – a logic variable activating limitations to d_1 or d_2
- $squeezeRate$ – always < 1, as further compression of d_1 or d_2
- $usingSqueezeRate$ – a logic variable to further squeeze d_1 or d_2

With $d_0 = 0.1$, $d_1 = 0.2$, $d_2 = 0.2$, sorting in decreasing order the vector pL^b and in increasing order the vector pL^s, we obtain in Figure A.1 two not overlapping price sequences that we can interpret as a demand curve (black) and an offer one (gray), but actually are buyers' price and sellers' price curves.

A.2 The Atomistic Hayekian Version

The buyers and the sellers meet randomly. Buyer i and seller j exchange if $pL^b_i \geq pL^s_j$; the deal is recorded at the price of the seller pL^s_j.[2]

---

[2] In the *mall*, sell prices are public.

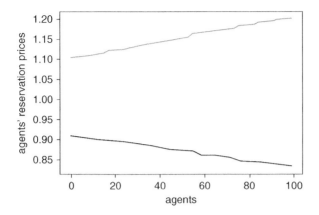

Figure A.1 An example of initially not overlapping buyers' price curve (black) and sellers' price curve (gray)

In this version, representing the key point in this note, the running prices are multiplied in each cycle by the following correction coefficients:

- for the buyer: (i) $c_b = \frac{1}{1+u_b}$ if the deal succeeds (trying to pay less next time) or (ii) $c_b = 1 + u_b$ if the deal fails (preparing to pay more next time); in (i) and (ii) we have $u_b \sim \mathcal{U}(0, d_1)$;
- for the seller: (iii) $c_s = 1 + u_s$ if the deal succeeds (trying to obtain a higher revenue next time) or (iv) $c_s = \frac{1}{1+u_s}$ if the deal fails (preparing to obtain a lower revenue next time); in (iii) and (iv) we have $u_s \sim \mathcal{U}(0, d_2)$.

With $seed = 111$, $d_0 = 0.1$, $d_1 = 0.2$, $d_2 = 0.2$ and $nCycles$ set to 10,000, we obtain sequences of mean prices (mean within each cycle) quite realistic, with a very low variance within each cycle (see Figures A.2 and A.3).

The *coefficient of variation* at time t is calculated as:

$$\frac{standard\ deviation_t}{mean_t}.$$

Note we have a plausible series of mean prices, with a complicated behavior, and with a high stability of the dispersion of the values within each cycle.

The right side of the buyers' price and sellers' price curves shows another plausible situation: that of the presence of agents not

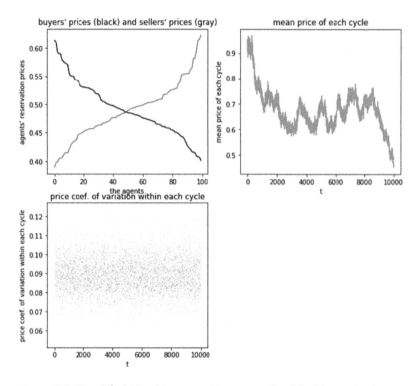

Figure A.2 Simplified Hayekian case: (i) an example of final buyers' price and sellers' price curves, (ii) the history of mean prices tick-by-tick, (iii) their coefficients of variation within each tick (cycle)

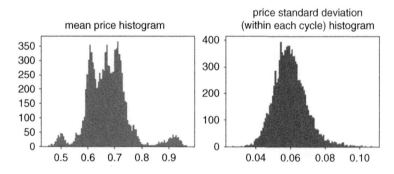

Figure A.3 Simplified Hayekian case: (i) the distribution of mean prices of each cycle (i.e., tick-by-tick) and (ii) that of their standard deviations within each tick (cycle)

exchanging. This note is linked both with Section A.5 and, most of all, with Section 3.7.

In Section A.4 we will also investigate the cases of a not balancing number of buyers and sellers.

A.3 The Unstructured Version

The buyers and the sellers meet randomly as in Section A.2. Buyer i and seller j exchange in any case; the deal is recorded at the mean of the price of the seller pL_j^s and of the price pL_i^b of the buyer.

In this version the running prices are multiplied in each cycle by the following correction coefficients:

- with the same probability for the buyer: (i) $c_b = \frac{1}{1+u_b}$ or (ii) $c_b = 1 + u_b$; in (i) and (ii) we have $u_b \sim \mathcal{U}(0, d_1)$;
- with the same probability for the seller: (iii) $c_s = 1 + u_s$ or (iv) $c_s = \frac{1}{1+u_s}$; in (iii) and (iv) we have $u_s \sim \mathcal{U}(0, d_2)$.

With $seed = 111$, $d_0 = 0.1$, $d_1 = 0.2$, $d_2 = 0.2$ and $nCycles$ set to 10,000, we obtain exploding sequences of the means of the prices (mean in each cycle), and exploding standard deviations within each cycle (see Figures A.4 and A.5).

The *coefficient of variation* at time t is calculated as above.

Note, this counter-example shows that, missing the *intelligence of the theory* in the correction of the prices (implicitly propagating among all the agents), a system of pure random price corrections is absolutely far from being plausible.

Note, in Figure A.4, (iii) plot, we have three evident attractors, appearing from time 7,000 around the levels 6, 7 and 10; we are in the space of the coefficients of variation of the prices. We have no hypothesis about the origin of the attractors, always emerging running the simulation with other seeds of the random number series.

A.4 Two Triple Cases of Not Balancing Numbers of Buyers and Sellers

A.4.1 Case $nBuyers \gg nSellers$

With $nBuyers \gg nSellers$ (e.g., $nBuyers = 100$ and $nSellers = 50$, as in Figure A.6), we have three possible paths of analysis.

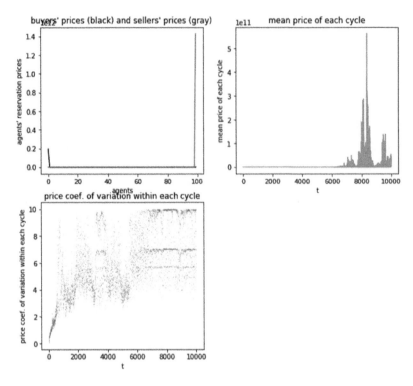

Figure A.4 Unstructured case: (i) an example of final buyers' price and sellers' price curves, (ii) the history of mean prices tick-by-tick, (iii) their coefficients of variation within each tick (cycle)

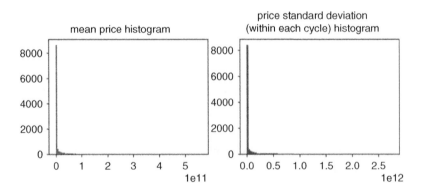

Figure A.5 Unstructured case: (i) the distribution of mean prices of each cycle (i.e., tick-by-tick) and (ii) that of their standard deviations within each tick (cycle)

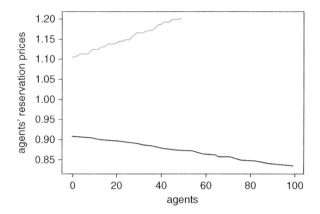

Figure A.6 An example of initially not overlapping buyers' price and sellers' price curves, case $nBuyers \gg nSellers$

A.4.1.1 Case $nBuyers \gg nSellers$, with Different Rates of Per-Capita Correction

We can observe that in Figures A.7 and A.8 the prices are – in the end – lower than in Figures A.2 and A.3 and, most of all, the price tendency has a strong negative slope. We always have $d_0 = 0.1$, $d_1 = 0.2$, $d_2 = 0.2$ and $seed = 111$.[3]

This result is inconsistent with the microeconomic theory, where we could expect that an excess of demand will generate the rise of the prices.

A.4.1.2 Case $nBuyers \gg nSellers$, with Unequal Rates of Per-Capita Correction, with Equivalent Effects

Again, with $nBuyers \gg nSellers$, and always having in each cycle one call – in mean – to a *seller* from each *buyer*, the number of per-capita actions of the *sellers* in each cycle is greater of the number of per-capita actions of the *buyers*.

In this second version of the case $nBuyers \gg nSellers$, we always have $d_0 = 0.1$, $d_1 = 0.2$, $d_2 = 0.2$ and $seed = 111$.

The novelty is that of setting $usingRatios = True$, so we are activating limitations to d_1 or d_2.

---

[3] *usingRatios* and *usingSqueezeRate* set to *False*.

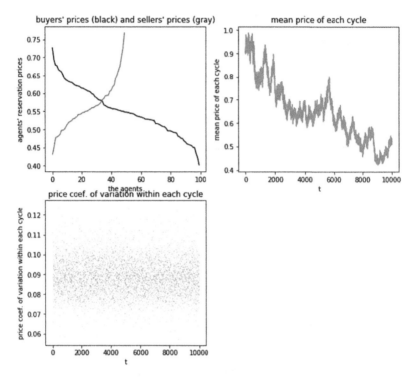

Figure A.7 Simplified Hayekian case, with $nBuyers \gg nSellers$: (i) an example of final buyers' price and sellers' price curves, (ii) the history of mean prices tick-by-tick, (iii) their coefficients of variation within each tick (cycle)

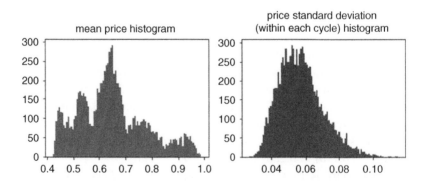

Figure A.8 Simplified Hayekian case, with $nBuyers \gg nSellers$: (i) the distribution of mean prices of each cycle (i.e., tick-by-tick) and (ii) that of their standard deviations within each tick (cycle)

The limitations work as follows:

- if the $\frac{nBuyers}{nSellers} > 1$ (our case in this example), d_2, i.e., the upper limit of the rate of correction of the price of the sellers, is multiplied by $\frac{nSellers}{nBuyers}$.[4]
- if the $\frac{nSellers}{nBuyers} > 1$, d_1, i.e., the upper limit of the rate of correction of the price of the buyers, is multiplied by $\frac{nBuyers}{nSellers}$.

We have now unequal rates of per-capita correction, with equivalent effects. The interpretation is that if the number of sellers is smaller than the number of buyers, the sellers act with a slow pace of price correction (proportional to $\frac{nSellers}{nBuyers}$) because in this way they can cherry-pick the best buyers (those with the higher reservation price). In this way, they avoid to contribute to the fall of the prices.

Always with Figure A.6 as the starting configuration of the prices, in Figures A.9 and A.10 we see now interesting price oscillations roughly confined between the limits of Figure A.6.

A.4.1.3 Case $nBuyers \gg nSellers$, with Unequal Rates of Per-Capita Correction, but Squeezing the Effects

In this third version of the case $nBuyers \gg nSellers$, we always have $d_0 = 0.1$, $d_1 = 0.2$, $d_2 = 0.2$ and $seed = 111$.

The second novelty, after that of Section A.4.1.2, is that of activating further limitations to d_1 or d_2 by setting $usingSqueeze = True$, introducing the $squeezeRate = 0.3$ and always setting $usingRatios = True$, as in Section A.4.1.2:

- if the $\frac{nBuyers}{nSellers} > 1$ (our case in this example), d_2, i.e., the upper limit of the rate of correction of the price of the sellers, is multiplied by $squeezeRate$;
- if the $\frac{nSellers}{nBuyers} > 1$, d_1, i.e., the upper limit of the rate of correction of the price of the buyers, is multiplied by $squeezeRate$.

Always with Figure A.6 as the starting configuration of the prices, in Figures A.11 and A.12 we see a limited price dynamic, very close to the top band of Figure A.6.

---

[4] An example to clarify: in this section we have $nBuyers = 100$ and $nSellers = 50$, so $\frac{nBuyers}{nSellers} \equiv 2$ and $\frac{nSellers}{nBuyers} \equiv 0.5$; d_2 is reduced of the 50%.

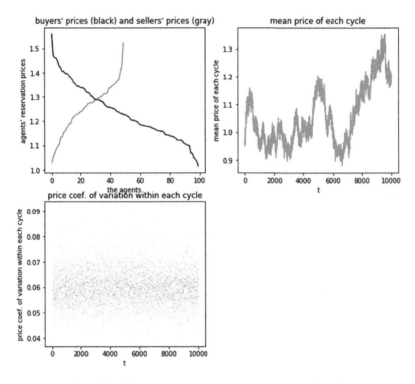

Figure A.9 Simplified Hayekian case, with *nBuyers* ≫ *nSellers* but with equivalent effects: (i) an example of final buyers' price and sellers' price curves, (ii) the history of mean prices tick-by-tick, (iii) their coefficients of variation within each tick (cycle)

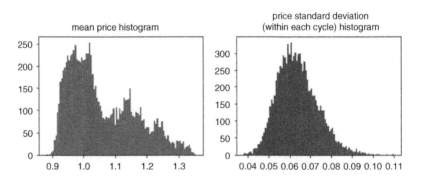

Figure A.10 Simplified Hayekian case, with *nBuyers* ≫ *nSellers* but with equivalent effects: (i) the distribution of mean prices of each cycle (i.e., tick-by-tick) and (ii) that of their standard deviations within each tick (cycle)

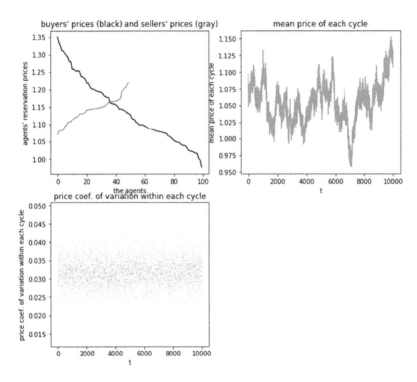

Figure A.11 Simplified Hayekian case, with $nBuyers \gg nSellers$ but squeezing the effects: (i) an example of final buyers' price and sellers' price curves, (ii) the history of mean prices tick-by-tick, (iii) their coefficients of variation within each tick (cycle)

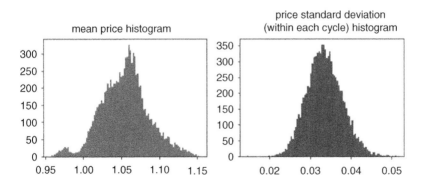

Figure A.12 Simplified Hayekian case, with $nBuyers \gg nSellers$ but squeezing the effects: (i) the distribution of mean prices of each cycle (i.e., tick-by-tick) and (ii) that of their standard deviations within each tick (cycle)

The sellers' price curve is winning and the result is perfectly consistent with microeconomic theory, having a few sellers with a lot of buyers.

Building the macroeconomic oligopolistic model of this book, we do not use directly the *squeeze* technique, but indirectly we introduce it via the parameters that we defined in Section 3.6 and that we used in the ASHAM experiments.

A.4.2 Case $nBuyers \ll nSellers$

With $nBuyers \ll nSellers$ (e.g., $nBuyers = 50$ and $nSellers = 100$, as in Figure A.13), we again have three possible paths of analysis.

A.4.2.1 Case $nBuyers \ll nSellers$, with Different Rates of Per-Capita Correction

If $nBuyers \ll nSellers$, we have in each cycle one call – in mean – to a *buyer* from each *seller*, the number of per-capita actions of the *buyers* in each cycle is greater of the number of per-capita actions of the *sellers*.

As a consequence, the probability that a *buyer* increases her price to meet that of a *seller* is greater than the probability that a *seller* decreases her price to meet that of a *buyer*.

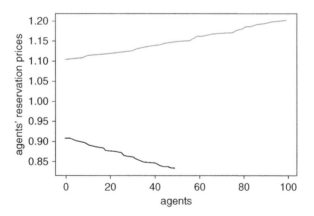

Figure A.13 An example of initially not overlapping buyers' price and sellers' price curves, case $nBuyers \ll nSellers$

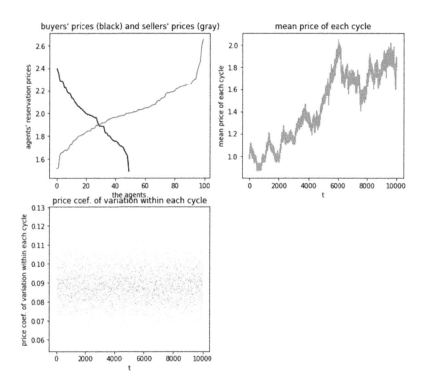

Figure A.14 Simplified Hayekian case, with *nBuyers* ≪ *nSellers*: (i) an example of final buyers' price and sellers' price curves, (ii) the history of mean prices tick-by-tick, (iii) their coefficients of variation within each tick (cycle)

We can observe that in Figures A.14 and A.15 the prices are – in the end – greater than in Figures A.2 and A.3 and, most of all, the price tendency has a strong positive slope. We always have $d_0 = 0.1$, $d_1 = 0.2$, $d_2 = 0.2$ and *seed* $= 111$.[5]

This result is inconsistent with the microeconomic theory, where we could expect that an excess of offer will generate the fall of the prices.

A.4.2.2 Case *nBuyers* ≪ *nSellers*, with Unequal Rates of Per-Capita Correction, with Equivalent Effects

In this second version of the case *nBuyers* ≪ *nSellers*, we always have $d_0 = 0.1$, $d_1 = 0.2$, $d_2 = 0.2$ and *seed* $= 111$.

[5] *usingRatios* and *usingSqueezeRate* set to *False*.

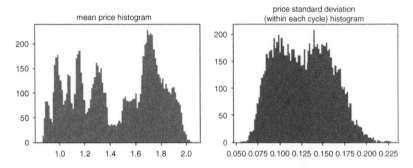

Figure A.15 Simplified Hayekian case, with $nBuyers \ll nSellers$: (i) the distribution of mean prices of each cycle (i.e., tick-by-tick) and (ii) that of their standard deviations within each tick (cycle)

As in Section A.4.1.2, the novelty is that of setting $usingRatios = True$, so we are activating limitations to d_1 or d_2. The limitations work as follows:

- if the $\frac{nBuyers}{nSellers} > 1$, d_2, i.e., the upper limit of the rate of correction of the price of the sellers, is multiplied by $\frac{nSellers}{nBuyers}$;
- if the $\frac{nSellers}{nBuyers} > 1$ (our case in this example), d_1, i.e., the upper limit of the rate of correction of the price of the buyers, is multiplied by $\frac{nBuyers}{nSellers}$.[6]

We have now unequal rates of per-capita correction, with equivalent effects. The interpretation is that if the number of buyers is smaller than the number of sellers, the buyers act with a slow pace of price correction (proportional to $\frac{nBuyers}{nSellers}$) because in this way they can cherry-pick the best sellers (those with the lower reservation price). In this way, they avoid to contribute to the rise of the prices.

Always with Figure A.13 as the starting configuration of the prices, in Figures A.16 and A.17 we see now a compressed price oscillations roughly close to the bottom limits of Figure A.13.

---

[6] An example to clarify: in this section we have $nBuyers = 50$ and $nSellers = 100$, so $\frac{nSellers}{nBuyers} \equiv 2$ and $\frac{nBuyers}{nSellers} \equiv 0.5$; d_1 is reduced of the 50%.

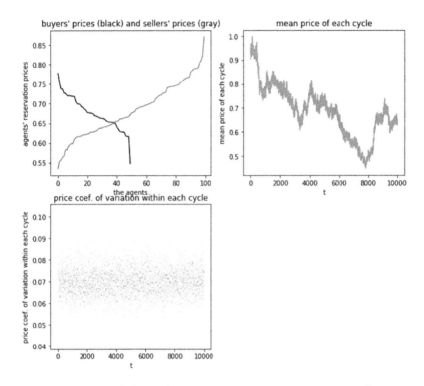

Figure A.16 Simplified Hayekian case, with $nBuyers \gg nSellers$ with equivalent effects: (i) an example of final demand and offer curves, (ii) the history of mean prices tick-by-tick, (iii) their coefficients of variation within each tick (cycle)

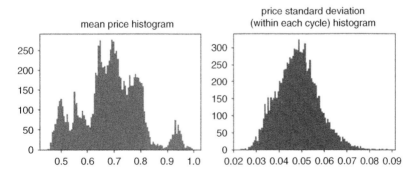

Figure A.17 Simplified Hayekian case, with $nBuyers \gg nSellers$ but with equivalent effects: (i) the distribution of mean prices of each cycle (i.e., tick-by-tick) and (ii) that of their standard deviations within each tick (cycle)

A.4.2.3 Case $nBuyers \ll nSellers$, with Unequal Rates of Per-Capita Correction, but Squeezing the Effects

In this third version of the case $nBuyers \ll nSellers$, we always have $d_0 = 0.1$, $d_1 = 0.2$, $d_2 = 0.2$ and $seed = 111$.

The second novelty, after that of Section A.4.2.2, is that of setting $usingSqueeze = True$ (and setting $usingRatios = True$ as in Section A.4.2.2), so we are activating further limitations to d_1 or d_2. We also have $squeezeRate = 0.3$.

- if the $\frac{nBuyers}{nSellers} > 1$, d_2, i.e., the upper limit of the rate of correction of the price of the sellers, is multiplied by $squeezeRate$;
- if the $\frac{nSellers}{nBuyers} > 1$ (our case in this example), d_1, i.e., the upper limit of the rate of correction of the price of the buyers, is multiplied by $squeezeRate$.

Always with Figure A.13 as the starting configuration of the prices, in Figures A.18 and A.19 we see a limited price dynamics, very close to the bottom band of Figure A.13. This result is perfectly consistent with microeconomic theory.

The buyers' price curve is winning and the result is perfectly consistent with microeconomic theory, having a few buyers with a lot of sellers.

As noted above, building the macroeconomic oligopolistic model of this book, we do not use directly the *squeeze* technique, but indirectly we introduce it via the parameters that we define in Section 3.6 and that we use in the ASHAM experiments.

A.5 Activating Idle Agents

In all the runs of the model up to this point, looking at the buyers' price and sellers' price curves, we can see that the larger part of the agents is not acting: specifically, all the sellers with reservation price greater than that of the crossing point of the curves and all the buyers with reservation price lower than that value.

A.5.1 Corrupting the Simplified Hayekian Market Model to Activate the Idle Agents: An Ingenuous Quest for the Solution

Trying to activate the idle agents, we add two new parameters:

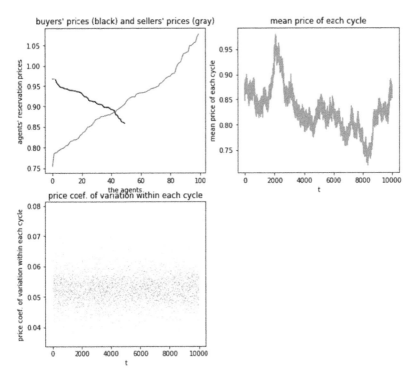

Figure A.18 Simplified Hayekian case, with $nBuyers \gg nSellers$ but squeezing the effects: (i) an example of final buyers' price and sellers' price curves, (ii) the history of mean prices tick-by-tick, (iii) their coefficients of variation within each tick (cycle)

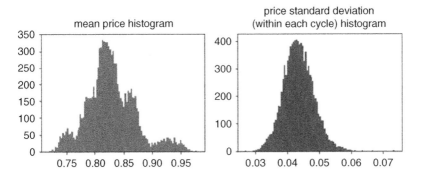

Figure A.19 Simplified Hayekian case, with $nBuyers \gg nSellers$ but squeezing the effects: (i) the distribution of mean prices of each cycle (i.e., tick-by-tick) and (ii) that of their standard deviations within each tick (cycle)

- *buyerThreshold* – over this number of failures, a special price correction occurs, multiplying the buyer price by $c_b = 1 + u_b$ with $u_b \sim \mathcal{U}(0, d_{1_{overT}})$;
- *sellerThreshold* – over this number of failures, a special price correction occurs, multiplying the seller price by $c_s = \frac{1}{1+u_s}$ with $u_s \sim \mathcal{U}(0, d_{2_{overT}})$.

With *seed* = 111, $d_0 = 0.1$, $d_1 = 0.2$, $d_2 = 0.2$ and *nCycles* set to 10, 000, we add *buyerThreshold* = 5, *sellerThreshold* = 50, $d_{1_{overT}} = 0.4$, and $d_{2_{overT}} = 0.4$. We also have *nBuyers* = *nSellers* = 100, so none of the corrections of Sections A.4.2 and A.4.1 are working here.

At `https://github.com/terna/microHayekianMarket`, the notebook is `microCorruptedHayekianMarket\_baseBW.ipynb`.

We count for each agent the number of consecutive failures in buying or in selling. In case of success, the counter is set again to 0.

If the counter is *greater than* one of the thresholds, *buyerThreshold* or *sellerThreshold*, the buyer or the seller make a special correction of their reservation prices, multiplying the buyer price by $c_b = 1 + u_b$ (with $u_b \sim \mathcal{U}(0, d_{1_{overT}})$) or the seller price by $c_s = \frac{1}{1+u_s}$ (with $u_s \sim \mathcal{U}(0, d_{2_{overT}})$).

The idea behind this construction is that of forcing the *idle* agents to operate, amplifying their price corrections. The effect is quite disappointing.

Considering that as a starting point we always have the situation of Figure A.1, in Figures A.20 and A.21 we simply see that in our case, with *buyerThreshold* = 5 and *sellerThreshold* = 50, the price series is quite higher than in Figure A.2 and that a lot of buyers (and sellers too, but here we focus on the buyers) still are not operating. Our attempt of *corrupting* the simplified Hayekian market to force the buyers to buy has been a complete failure. But … the next paragraph shows that it has been a source of inspiration.

Observing now the Figure A.22, we discover that the agents not operating are distributed in the whole range of the possible prices of Figures A.20 and A.21. Consequence: the idle agents continuously change and, in a given instant of the time, the idle ones are not necessarily the same of the previous tick.

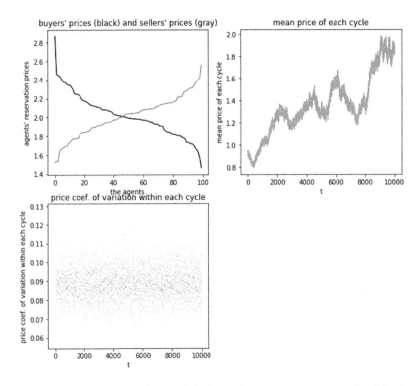

Figure A.20 Corrupting the simplified Hayekian case: (i) an example of final buyers' price and sellers' price curves, (ii) the history of mean prices tick-by-tick, (iii) their coefficients of variation within each tick (cycle)

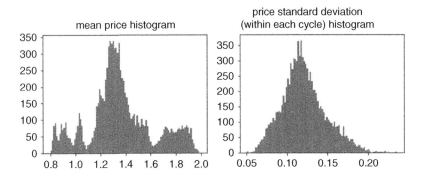

Figure A.21 Corrupting the simplified Hayekian case: (i) the distribution of mean prices of each cycle (i.e., tick-by-tick) and (ii) that of their standard deviations within each tick (cycle)

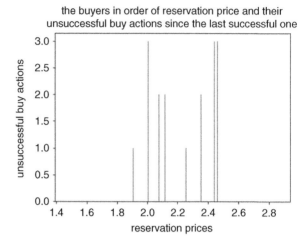

Figure A.22 Extending the simplified Hayekian case: after 10,000 actions we see here a *flash* image of the buyers ordered following their reservation prices, with the number of recent consecutive unsuccessful buying attempts

A.5.2 A Fundamental Unexpected By-Product: The Solution Is Here, Under Our Eyes

The solution of the quest for *the enigma of the idle agents'* was right before our eyes. Due to the continuous price corrections, the buy (or sell, but here we focus on the buyers) actions are quite uncertain, and in the 50% of the cases they fail. Why 50%? Let us analyze the buyers' price and sellers' price curves on the right of their crossing point.

Let us generate a new case, as a by-product of the disappointing model run of Section A.5.1.

With $seed = 111$, $d_0 = 0.1$, $d_1 = 0.2$, $d_2 = 0.2$ and $nCycles$ now set to 20,000, we also have $nBuyers = nSellers = 100$; so, none of the corrections of Section A.4 are working here. Also, *buyerThreshold*, *sellerThreshold*, $d_{1_{overT}}$ and $d_{2_{overT}}$ are not in use here.

The notebook is `microCorruptedHayekianMarket_by-productBW.ipynb` at `https://terna.github.io/micro-HayekianMarket/`.

We now count for each agent the number of successful cases, and we never set it again to 0.

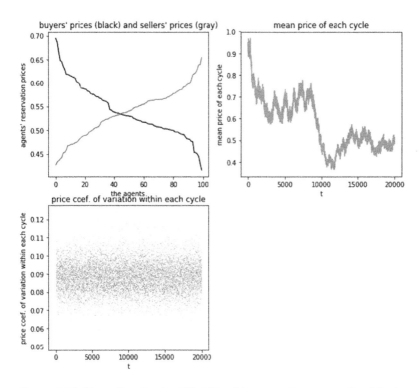

Figure A.23 Extending the simplified Hayekian case: (i) an example of final buyers' price and sellers' price curves, (ii) the history of mean prices tick-by-tick, (iii) their coefficients of variation within each tick (cycle)

Effects have as a starting point the situation of Figure A.1: in Figures A.23 we have in the first half (10,000 cycles) exactly the same result of Figure A.2 (same *seed* and same scheme) and in the second half (until the final value of 20,000 cycles) a consistent continuation of the same dynamic. Figure A.24, with its bimodal price distribution and the low values of the standard deviations within each tick, confirms what we saw in Section A.2.

Most of all, the bar plot in Figure A.25 shows that all the agents are effectively very close to succeed in buying in the 50% of the possible cases. This result is consistent with the plot of the buyers' price and sellers' price curves, with about one half of the agents on the right of the crossing point, remembering that those agents are never the same.

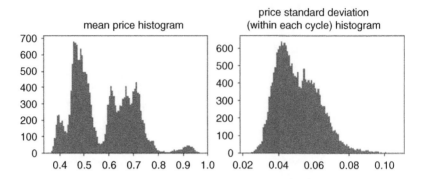

Figure A.24 Extending the simplified Hayekian case: (i) the distribution of mean prices of each cycle (i.e., tick-by-tick) and (ii) that of their standard deviations within each tick (cycle)

Figure A.25 Extending the simplified Hayekian case: after 20,000 actions, each buyer (here the buyers are ordered following their reservation prices) has been successful in concluding a deal only in about 10,000 cases

Appendix B

The Acrostics of the Simulation Model and Its Parameters

MATTEO MORINI AND PIETRO TERNA

Table B.2 describes all the parameters of the simulation model, both in SMAC and in ASHAM mode. With each parameter, we also include the section where it is initially defined.

The simulation model experiments use the set of parameters of Tables B.3 and B.4. The sign "-" means the *Parameter is not used in this case*; for actual use of the model, reproducing the different cases for verification purposes and, most of all, modifying them, see Section C.2.

Technically, the parameters of Table B.2 are defined via commonVar.py at https://github.com/terna/oligopoly, but four of them, defined interactively: mySeed, consumption-Quota, Q and nCycle.

Table B.1 *The acrostics identifying the phases or modes of the simulation model*

ASHAM	Atomistic Simplified HAyekian Market
SMAC	Simple Market Aggregate Clearing mechanism

Table B.2 *Parameters of the agent-based model*

Parameters	Descriptions and reference page
a1	consumption behavior: a_1, Section 3.5
a2	consumption behavior: a_2, Section 3.5
a3	consumption behavior: a_3, Section 3.5

Table B.2 *(cont.)*

Parameters	Descriptions and reference page
absoluteBarrierToBecomeEntrepreneur	absolute barrier to become entrepreneur, max number in a time step, Section 3.11.1
b1	consumption behavior: b_1, Section 3.5
b2	consumption behavior: b_3, Section 3.5
b3	consumption behavior: b_3, Section 3.5
checkResConsUnsoldProd	infos on sub-step output management, Section 3.7
consumptionQuota	max quota (base 1) of the consumptions in each sub step of a cycle, Section 3.5
consumptionRandomComponentSD	consumption random component (SD), Section 3.5
cumulativelyMeasuringNewEntrantNumber	measuring the new entrant number in a cumulative way, Section 3.12.2
decreasingRateRange	decreasing rate range of the prices, *quasi* ASHAM, Section 3.10.2
entrepreneursMindIfPlannedProductionFalls	entrepreneurs mind if plannedProduction falls (True/False), Section 3.10.2
extraCostsDuration	new entrant extra costs duration, Section 3.11.1
fullEmploymentThreshold	full employment threshold, Section 3.12.1
hParadigm	ASHAM sell price modification *full* or *quasi*, Section 3.7
increasingRateRange	increasing rate range of the prices, *quasi* ASHAM, Section 3.10.2
initShift	shift in individual starting prices (ASHAM), Section 3.6
initShock	shock in individual starting prices (ASHAM), Section 3.6

Parameters	Descriptions and reference page
jump	jump in seller prices (*full* and *quasi* ASHAM), Section 3.10.1
laborProductivity	labor productivity, Section 3.2.1
maxAcceptableOligopolistRelativeIncrement	trigger level (relative increment of oligopolistic firms), Section 3.12.2
maxDemandRelativeRandomShock	total demand relative random shock, uniformly distributed between -maxDemandRelativeRandomShock and maxDemandRelativeRandomShock, Section 3.8
mySeed	the seed of random n. (if 1 gets it from the clock), Appendix C
newEntrantExtraCosts	new entrant extra costs, Section 3.11.1
nCycle	number of cycles of the simulation, Section 3.1.3
penaltyValue	price penalty for the firms suffering work troubles, Section 3.9
pJump	prob. of a jump in seller prices (*full* and *quasi* ASHAM), Section 3.10.1
priceSwitchIfProfitFalls	price switch if profit falls, in *quasi* ASHAM, Section 4.7.1
productionCorrectionPsi	production correction (lost production) due to work troubles, between productionCorrectionPsi/2 and productionCorrectionPsi, Section 3.4
profitStrategyReverseAfterN	price reverse action after N cycles, no other action in the while, in *quasi* ASHAM, Section 3.10.2
Q	Q and $1 - Q$ as the weights to be attributed to the consumption at time $t - 1$ and $t - 2$, with $0 \leq Q \leq 1$, Section 3.2.2

Table B.2 *(cont.)*

Parameters	Descriptions and reference page
quasiHchoice	quasi ASHAM choice to drive sellers' price modification, Section 3.10.2
randomComponentOfPlanned Production	random rel. component of planned production uniformly distributed between -random ComponentOfPlanned Production and randomComponentOfPlanned Production, Section 3.2.2
reUseUnspentConsumption Capability	reuse unspent consumption capability, with a quota in the interval [0, 1], Section 3.5
rho	expected employment ratio at $t = 1$, Section 3.2.1
runningShiftB	shift in individual buyer running prices in ASHAM, Section 3.7
runningShiftS	shift in individual seller running prices in ASHAM, Section 3.7
runningShockB	range of the correction of agent (as buyers) running prices in ASHAM, Section 3.7
runningShockS	range of the correction of agent (as sellers) running prices in ASHAM, Section 3.7
socialWelfareCompensation	social welfare compensation, Section 3.5
soldThreshold1	*quasi* ASHAM sold threshold to lower the prices, Section 3.10.2
soldThreshold2	*quasi* ASHAM sold threshold to raise the prices, Section 3.10.2
startHayekianMarket	cycle to start the ASHAM phase, Section 3.2.2
temporaryRelativeWage IncrementAsBarrier	wage relative increment as an entry barrier, Section 3.12.2
thresholdToDecreaseThePriceIf TotalPlannedPFalls	threshold to decrease the price if total planned production falls, case (i), Section 3.10.2

Parameters	Descriptions and reference page
thresholdToEntrepreneur	relative profit threshold to become entrepreneur, Section 3.11.1
thresholdToWorker	relative threshold to lose the entrepreneur status (becoming an unemployed worker), Section 3.11.2
wage	wage base, Section 3.2.1
wageCutForWorkTroubles	penalty applied to the wages of the worker of the firm suffering work troubles (True/False), Section 3.4.1
wageStepInFullEmployment	wage step up in full employment, Section 3.12.1
! from schedule, p. work troubles	probability of work troubles, Section 3.4.1 and Appendix C

The file `parameters.py`, again at `https://github.com/terna/oligopoly`, generates the outputs of the values when a *run* of the project *oligopoly* starts (see Appendix C).

Table B.3 *Values of the parameters [1,26] of the experiments*

experiments	a1	a2	a3	absoluteBarrier ToBecomeEntrepreneur	b1	b2	b3	checkKResCons UnsoldProd	consumptionQuota	consumptionRandom ComponentSD	MeasuringNewEntrantNumber cumulatively	decreasingRateRange entrepreneurs	MindIfPlanned ProductionFalls	extraCostsDuration	fullEmployment Threshold	bParadigm	increasingRate Range	initShift	initShock	jump	laborProductivity	Oligopolist maxAcceptable maxDemandRelativeIncrement	RandomShockRelative	mySeed	newEntrant ExtraCosts	nCycle
0a	0.4	0.3	0	20	0.55	0.65	1	-	-	0.3	-	-	-	3	0.05	-	-	-	-	-	1	0.2	0.15	111	60	50
0b	0.4	0.3	0	0	0.55	0.65	1	-	-	0.3	-	-	-	3	0.05	-	-	-	-	-	1	0.2	0.15	111	60	50
1	0.4	0.3	0	20	0.55	0.65	1	-	-	0.3	-	-	-	3	0.05	-	-	-	-	-	1	0.2	0.15	111	60	50
2	0.4	0.3	0	20	0.55	0.65	1	-	-	0.3	-	-	-	3	0.05	-	-	-	-	-	1	0.2	0.15	111	60	50
3	0.4	0.3	0	20	0.55	0.65	1	-	-	0.3	-	-	-	3	0.05	-	-	-	-	-	1	0.2	0.15	111	60	50
4	0.4	0.3	0	20	0.55	0.65	1	-	-	0.3	-	-	-	3	0.05	-	-	-	-	-	1	0.2	0.15	111	60	50
5	0.4	0.3	0	20	0.55	0.65	1	-	-	0.3	-	-	-	3	0.05	-	-	-	-	-	1	0.2	0.15	111	60	50
6	0.4	0.3	0	20	0.55	0.65	1	-	-	0.3	-	-	-	3	0.05	-	-	-	-	-	1	0.2	0.15	111	60	50
7	0.4	0.3	0	20	0.55	0.65	1	True	0.1	0.1	True	-0.2	False	5	0.05	full	0.02	-0.15	0.1	0.0	1	0.2	0.15	111	60	75
7b	0.4	0.3	0	20	0.55	0.65	1	True	0.1	0.1	True	-0.2	False	5	0.05	full	0.02	-0.15	0.1	0.0	1	0.2	0.15	111	60	75
8	0.4	0.3	0	10	0.55	0.65	1	True	0.1	0.1	True	-0.2	False	5	0.05	full	0.02	-0.15	0.1	0.1	1	0.2	0.15	111	60	50
8b	0.4	0.3	0	10	0.55	0.65	1	True	0.1	0.1	True	-0.2	False	5	0.05	full	0.02	-0.15	0.1	0.1	1	0.2	0.15	111	60	50
9	0.4	0.3	0	10	0.55	0.65	1	True	0.1	0.1	True	-0.1	True	5	0.05	quasi	0.01	1.1	0.1	0.1	1	0.2	0.15	111	60	50
9b	0.4	0.3	0	10	0.55	0.65	1	True	0.1	0.1	True	-0.1	True	5	0.05	quasi	0.01	1.1	0.1	0.1	1	0.2	0.15	111	60	50
10	0.4	0.3	0	10	0.55	0.65	1	True	0.1	0.1	True	-0.1	True	5	0.05	quasi	0.01	1.8	0.1	0.2	1	0.2	0.15	111	60	50
11	0.4	0.3	0	10	0.55	0.65	1	True	0.1	0.1	True	-0.1	True	5	0.05	quasi	0.01	1.8	0.1	0.05	1	0.2	0.15	111	60	50

Table B.4 Values of the parameters [27,52] of the experiments

experiments	penaltyValue	pJump	priceSwitchIfProfitFalls	productionCorrectionPsi	profitStrategyReverseAfterN	Q	quasiHchoice	randomComponentOfPlannedProduction	reUseUnspentConsumptionCapability	rho	runningShift	runningShifts	runningShockB	runningShockS	socialWelfareCompensation	soldThreshold1	soldThreshold2	startHayekianMarket	temporaryRelativeWageIncrementAsBarrier	thresholdToDecreaseThePriceIfTotalPlannedDPFalls	thresholdToEntrepreneur	thresholdToWorker	wage	wageCutForWorkTroubles	wageStepInFullEmployment	wageStepInFullEmployment from schedule, p. work troubles
0a	0	-	-	0.1	-	-	-	0.1	-	-	-	-	-	-	0.3	-	-	51	0.15	-	0.15	-0.2	1.0	False	0.1	0.05
0b	0	-	-	0.1	-	-	-	0.1	-	-	-	-	-	-	0.3	-	-	51	0.15	-	0.15	-0.2	1.0	False	0.1	0.05
1	0	-	-	0.1	-	-	-	0.1	-	-	-	-	-	-	0.3	-	-	51	0.15	-	0.15	-0.2	1.0	False	0.1	0.05
2	0	-	-	0.1	-	-	-	0.1	-	-	-	-	-	-	0.3	-	-	51	0.15	-	0.15	-0.2	1.0	False	0.1	0.05
3	0	-	-	0.1	-	-	-	0.1	-	-	-	-	-	-	0.3	-	-	51	0.15	-	0.15	-0.2	1.0	False	0.1	0.05
4	0	-	-	0.1	-	-	-	0.1	-	-	-	-	-	-	0.3	-	-	51	0.15	-	0.15	-0.2	1.0	False	0.1	0.05
5	0	-	-	0.1	-	-	-	0.1	-	-	-	-	-	-	0.3	-	-	51	0.15	-	0.15	-0.2	1.0	False	0.1	0.05
6	0	-	-	0.1	-	-	-	0.1	-	-	-	-	-	-	0.3	-	-	51	0.15	-	0.15	-0.2	1.0	False	0.1	0.05
7	0	-1	raise	0.1	5	0.5	unsold	0.1	0	0.9	0.1	0.1	0.2	0.05	0.7	0.9	0.99	1	0.15	0.05	0.08	-0.25	1.0	False	0.1	0.05
7b	0	-1	raise	0.1	5	0.5	unsold	0.1	0	0.9	0.1	0.1	0.2	0.05	0.4	0.9	0.99	1	0.15	0.05	0.08	-0.25	1.0	False	0.1	0.05
8	0	0.05	raise	0.1	5	0.25	unsold	0.1	0.5	0.9	0.1	0.1	0.2	0.05	0.7	0.9	0.99	1	0.15	0.05	0.1	-0.25	1.0	False	0.1	0.05
8b	0	0.05	raise	0.1	5	0.25	unsold	0.1	0.5	0.9	0.1	0.1	0.2	0.05	0.4	0.9	0.99	1	0.15	0.05	0.1	-0.25	1.0	False	0.1	0.05
9	0	0.1	raise	0.1	5	0.25	unsold	0.1	0.5	0.9	0.1	0.1	0.0008	0.05	0.7	0.9	0.99	1	0.15	0.05	0.1	-0.25	1.0	False	0.1	0.05
9	0	0.1	raise	0.1	5	0.25	unsold	0.1	0.5	0.9	0.1	0.1	0.0008	0.05	0.4	0.9	0.99	1	0.15	0.05	0.1	-0.25	1.0	False	0.1	0.05
10	0	0.1	raise	0.1	5	0.25	randomUp	0.1	1.0	0.9	0.1	0.1	0.01	0.05	0.7	0.9	0.99	1	0.15	0.05	0.1	-0.25	1.0	False	0.1	0.05
11	0	0.2	raise	0.1	5	0.25	profit	0.1	0.75	0.9	0.1	0.1	0.01	0.05	0.7	0.9	0.99	1	0.15	0.05	0.1	-0.25	1.0	False	0.1	0.05

Appendix C

How to Run the Oligopoly Model with SLAPP

MATTEO MORINI AND PIETRO TERNA

The agent-based simulation of Part 2 of this book uses SLAPP (Swarm-Like Agent-based Protocol in Python)[1] as shell.[2]

SLAPP has an open Reference Handbook in its website, and it is thoroughly described in chapters 2–7 of the Boero et al. (2015) book. Chapter 1 of the Reference Handbook describes how to install and how to run SLAPP (in a trial phase, also without installing it).

Run the *Oligopoly* project[3] with the Python 3 version of SLAPP. Exception: for the two cases of Section 4.1, see the notes in that section.

We introduce the starting phase in a detailed way. Please read the following notes in front of your computer.

- We can launch the SLAPP shell in several ways.
  - As better described in the Reference Handbook[4] quoted above, we can start SLAPP from a terminal, with:
    `python3 runShell.py`
    via the `runShell.py` file, that we can find in the main folder of SLAPP;
  - We can use IPython, mainly in a `Jupyter notebook`: we go to the main folder of SLAPP and we start `jupyter notebook` from there; then we can launch SLAPP via the `iRunShell.ipynb` file, simply clicking on it and then starting the execution with `shift+Enter` in the first cell of the notebook.

---

[1] https://terna.github.io/SLAPP/.
[2] Swarm is the root of many agent-based simulation tools: the article of (Minar et al., 1996) represents a *manifesto* of Swarm; we have also two books related to Swarm (Luna and Perrone, 2002; Luna and Stefansson, 2012) and we can find some information online at http://www.swarm.org.
[3] http://terna.github.io/oligopoly/.
[4] Please see chapter 1 of the Handbook about installing and running SLAPP.

- In both the cases, we are immediately requested to choose a *project*:
  `Project name?`
- We can predefine a default project placing a file named `project.txt` in the folder 6 `objectSwarmObserverAgents_` `AESOP_turtleLib_NetworkX` or in the main SLAPP folder; the content of the file is the path to the folder of the project we are working on (`oligopoly` in our case, with `/Users/pt/GitHub/oligopoly` as an example). The initial message of SLAPP becomes:

```
path and project = /Users/pt/GitHub/oligopoly
do you confirm? ([y]/n):
```

- Resuming the explanation, we receive a few technical messages and then the request:

```
random number seed (1 to get it from the clock)
```

  - We have to enter an integer number (positive or negative) to initialize the sequence of the random numbers used internally by the simulation code.
  - If we reply 1, the seed used to start the generation of the random series comes from the value of the internal clock. So, it is different anytime we start a simulation run.
    This reply is useful to replicate the simulated experiments with different outcomes.
  - If we chose a number different from 1, the random sequence would be repeated anytime we will use that seed.
    This second solution is useful while debugging, when we need to repeat exactly the sequence generating errors, but also to give to the user the possibility of replicating exactly an experiment.
  - The seeds used to run the experiments of the book are reported via the variable `mySeed` in Appendix B.
- Parameters: we set the parameters of the model both interactively or within the file `commonVar.py`.
  The program reports several messages about the project parameters, following the content of the file `parameters.py`; both this file and `commonVar.py` are in the folder of the project.
  The first message reports the version of the project.

Table C.1 *Interactive inputs*

Case	Seed	ConsumptionQuota	Q
0a, 0b, Sec. 4.1	111	not in SLAPP 2	not in SLAPP 2
1, Sec. 4.2.1	111	any value (e.g., 0.1)	any value (e.g., 0)
2, Sec. 4.2.2	111	any value (e.g., 0.1)	any value (e.g., 0)
3, Sec. 4.2.3	111	any value (e.g., 0.1)	any value (e.g., 0)
4, Sec. 4.2.4	111	any value (e.g., 0.1)	any value (e.g., 0)
5, Sec. 4.2.5	111	any value (e.g., 0.1)	any value (e.g., 0)
6, Sec. 4.2.6	111	any value (e.g., 0.1)	any value (e.g., 0)
7, Sec. 4.4.1	111	0.1	0.5
7b, Sec. 4.4.1.1	111	0.1	0.5
8, Sec. 4.4.2	111	0.1	0.25
8b, Sec. 4.4.2.1	111	0.1	0.25
9, Sec. 4.5.1	111	0.1	0.25
9b, Sec. 4.5.1.1	111	0.1	0.25
10, Sec. 4.6.1	111	0.1	0.25
11, Sec. 4.7.1	111	0.1	0.25

- The message:

```
Max quota (base 1) of the consumptions in each sub step
of a cycle (enter any value in a non-hayekian simulation):
```

requires a reply related to Section 3.5, setting the maximum consumption quota per sub-step of each cycle in ASHAM case. You can use any value in the SMAC case.
- The message:

```
Quota (0 <= Q <= 1) of the consumption quantities in
hayekian phase
(Q is the weight of the quantity at t==-1;
(1 - Q) is the weight of the quantity at t==-2:
```

requires a reply related to the variable Q of Section 3.2.2.
- Table C.1 reports the replies for the cases of Chapter 4.
- The message:

```
How many cycles? (0 = exit)
```

requires the number of cycles of the simulation (see Section 3.1.3); we can see the values of the variable nCycles, in Appendix B (always 50).

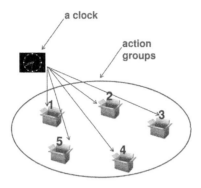

Figure C.1 The representation of the schedule

- The message:

```
verbose? (y/[n])
```

asks if we want more or less messages in output.

C.1 Time Management

To manage the time, we split it into several (consistent) levels of scheduling.[5]

The general picture is that of Figure C.1: in an abstract way, we can imagine that a clock opens – in due time – a series of containers or boxes. Behind the metaphor of the boxes, we have the *action groups*, where we store the information about the actions to be done.

The structure is highly dynamic, because (i) we can associate a probability to each action, and (ii) an agent of the simulation can be programmed to add or eliminate one or more actions into one or more of the boxes (*action groups*).

In the *Oligopoly* simulation model, the actions in the different boxes are the items of the Figure 3.1 of Chapter 3; the same chapter explains the behavior of those items.

---

[5] You can find the files quoted in this section within the package at https://github.com/terna/oligopoly, as referenced at http://terna.github.io/oligopoly/.

C.1.1 *The* Schedule.xls *Formalism*

The choice of SLAPP is that of using the spreadsheet formalism to define the sequence of the events in a detailed way.

The file schedule.xls, which is in the folder of each project, reports this kind of information. SLAPP translates its content in plain text, reported into the file schedule.txt; if we eliminate the file schedule.xls, we can use directly the schedule.txt one, but it is a more difficult task than working via the spreadsheet.

- This kind of script does not exist in Swarm, so it is a specific feature of SLAPP, introduced as implementation of the AESOP (Agents and Emergencies for Simulating Organizations in Python) idea: a layer that describes in a fine-grained way the actions of the agents in a simulation model. More details are in the SLAPP Reference Handbook at https://terna.github.io/SLAPP/.
- The file schedule.xls can be composed of several sheets, with: (a) the first one with schedule as mandatory name; (b) the other sheets with any name (those names are *macro instruction* names). We can recall the macro instructions in any sheet, but not within the sheet that creates the macro (that with the same name of the macro), to avoid infinite loops.
- Within the sheets, we have the action groups, as introduced above (Figure C.1), starting with the sign #, followed by a group identifier which is also its position in the time sequence.

In schedule.xls we have:

- the first column reporting the acting agent/agents;
- the second column reporting the action/instruction;
  - if in the second column we find a (positive) number,[6] it represents the probability of activation of the action/instruction reported in the third column;
  - if in the second column we read computationalUse, the order of the third column is a special computational use of the WordState of the first column. WordState has to be interpreted as an abstract agent;

---

[6] In the above quoted Handbook of SLAPP, we also introduce negative numbers in this position, but we never use that feature within the *Oligopoly* model.

- optional comments are placed in the fifth column (here not reported).

Our schedule is:

```
#    1    100
entrepreneurs      makeProductionPlan
entrepreneurs      adaptProductionPlanV6
entrepreneurs      hireFireWithProduction
entrepreneurs      0.05                     workTroubles
entrepreneurs      produceV5
entrepreneurs      planConsumptionInValueV6
workers            planConsumptionInValueV6
all                setInitialPricesHM
macro              act
WorldState         computationalUse         setMarketPriceV6
entrepreneurs      evaluateProfitV6
entrepreneurs      nextSellPriceJumpFHM
entrepreneurs      nextSellPricesQHM
workers            toEntrepreneurV6
entrepreneurs      toWorkerV3
WorldState         computationalUse         fullEmployment
                                            EffectOnWages
WorldState         computationalUse         incumbentAction
                                            OnWages
```

In `schedule.xls` we have a second sheet named `act`, reporting the content of the macro:

```
all                actOnMarketPlace
all                actOnMarketPlace
all                actOnMarketPlace
all                actOnMarketPlace
all                actOnMarketPlace
...
```

The number of repetition of the method `actOnMarketPlace` in each cycle is determined by the number of rows in the macro sheet `act`.

`#  1    100` means from $t = 1$ to $t = 100$, but the experiments reported in the book are limited to 50 or 75 steps.

If the row starts with:

- `entrepreneurs`, the instruction of the script is operating with the entrepreneurs;
- `workers`, the instruction of the script is operating with the workers;

- `all`, the instruction of the script is operating both with the entrepreneurs and the workers;
- `macro`, the script jumps to the sheet with the specific name, to execute the actions reported there;
- `WorldState`, the instruction of the script is operating with the abstract agent `WorldState`, as in Sections 3.8, 3.12.1, and 3.12.2.

The instructions are:

- `makeProductionPlan`, defined in Section 3.2.1 and reported as item 1 in Figure 3.1;
- `adaptProductionPlanV6`, defined in Section 3.2.2 and reported as item 2 in Figure 3.1;
- `hireFireWithProduction`, defined in Section 3.3 and reported as item 3 in Figure 3.1;
- `workTroubles`, defined in Section 3.4.1 and reported within item 4 in Figure 3.1;
- `produceV5`, defined in Section 3.4 and reported as item 4 in Figure 3.1;
- `planConsumptionInValueV6`, defined in Section 3.5 and reported as item 5 in Figure 3.1;
- `setInitialPricesHM`, defined in Section 3.6 and reported as item 6 in Figure 3.1;
- `act`, the *macro* activating `actOnMarketPlace`;
- `actOnMarketPlace`, defined in Section 3.7 and reported as item 7 in Figure 3.1;
- `setMarketPriceV6`, defined in Section 3.8 and reported as item 8 in Figure 3.1;
- `evaluateProfitV6`, defined in Section 3.9 at and reported as item 9 in Figure 3.1;
- `nextSellPriceJumpFHM`, defined in Section 3.10.1 at and reported as item 10 *full* in Figure 3.1;
- `nextSellPricesQHM`, defined in Section 3.10.2 and reported as item 10 *quasi* in Figure 3.1;,
- `toEntrepreneurV6`, defined in Section 3.11.1 and reported as item 11 in Figure 3.1;
- `toWorkerV3`, defined in Section 3.11.2 and reported as item 11 in Figure 3.1;
- `fullEmploymentEffectOnWages`, defined in Section 3.12.1 and reported as item 12 in Figure 3.1;

- `incumbentActionOnWages`, defined in Section 3.12.2 and reported as item 12 in Figure 3.1;

C.1.2 The observerActions and modelActions as High Level Schedule Formalisms

Formalism of *observerActions*.

- The file `observerActions.txt` reports the first high-level schedule formalism; the content (row changes are not relevant in this kind of files) is:
  - version *without pauses* contained in `observerActions no pause.txt`, to be copied to `observerActions.txt` to run it:
    ```
    collectStructuralData modelStep collectTimeSeries
    visualizePlot visualizeNet clock
    ```
  - version *with pauses* contained in `observerActions with pause.txt`, to be copied to `observerActions.txt` to run it:
    ```
    collectStructuralData modelStep collectTimeSeries
    visualizePlot visualizeNet pause clock
    ```
  The interpretation is the following.
  - The execution of the contents of the file is "with repetition," until an `end` item will appear (see below).
  - `collectStructuralData` collects the number of workers and of entrepreneurs *at the beginning* of each period, both as a basis for internal calculations and for the final output of the model, when two files of data are generated.
  - `modelStep` orders to the model to make a step forward in time.
  - `collectTimeSeries` collects the data of the outcomes of the simulation *at the end* of each period, both as a basis for the action `visualizePlot` and for the final output of the model, when two files of data are generated.
  - `visualizePlot` update the plot of the time series generated by the model.
  - `visualizeNet` updates the plot of the links connecting entrepreneurs and workers, on a network basis.
  - `pause`, if any, puts the program in wait until we reply to the message `Hit enter key to continue`, e.g., hitting the key

⏎. This action is useful to examine the graphical outputs step by step.

- clock asks to the clock to increase its counter of one unit. When the count will reach the value we have entered replying to the How many cycles? query, the internal scheduler of the Observer will add the end item into the sequence of the file observerActions.txt. The item is placed immediately after the clock call. The end item stops the sequence contained in the file.
- We can also consider a potential prune item, eliminating the links connecting entrepreneurs and workers on the basis of their weight (optionally asking for a threshold below which to make the elimination); weights could be introduced to measure the seniority, the skills, or the experience of the workers.

Formalism of *modelActions*.

- The file modelActions.txt reports the second high-level schedule formalism; the content (row changes are not relevant in this kind of files) is:

```
reset read_script
```

The interpretation is the following:
- Also at the Model level the execution of the content of the file is "with repetition," never ending. It is the Observer that stops the simulation run, but operating at its level.
- reset orders to the agents to make a reset of their variables, if necessary.
- read_script orders to the Model to execute the sequence of instructions of the file schedule.xls.

C.2 Running a Specific Experiment, with Backward Compatibility

- To run the experiments of the cases 0*a* and 0*b*, we need to use the Oligopoly code version V5 or V5bP2_fd,[7] running the project with

---

[7] At https://github.com/terna/oligopoly/releases/tag/V5 or at https://github.com/terna/oligopoly/releases/tag/V5bP2_fd.

SLAPP 2.0, which is at `https://github.com/terna/SLAPP2` and controlling that the parameters are those of rows 1 and 2 of Tables B.3 and B.4. In this case, using that SMAC specific version of the *Oligopoly* project, the *startHayekianMarket* parameter is not used, while in the Table B.4 is set to 51 by default.

To set the correct parameters, for the cases 0*a* and 0*b*, you can simply modify the parameter `absoluteBarrierToBecomeEntre` `preneur` at row 123 of the file `commonVar.py` of the above releases of Oligopoly, setting it to 20 (case 0*a*) or to 0 (case 0*b*).

The path to the folder containing the Oligopoly code has to be included in a file named `project.txt`, to be placed into the main folder of SLAPP.

- For all the cases below, please use the Oligopoly code of the release *V6book*, or directly the branch `master`, running the project with SLAPP 3.0 or higher, which is at `https://github.com/terna/` `SLAPP3`.

As above, the path to the folder containing the Oligopoly code has to be included in a file named *project.txt*, to be placed into the main folder of SLAPP.

- To run the experiments of the cases from 1 to 6:

  a) delete the file `schedule.xls`;
  b) duplicate the file `schedule5.xls`;
  c) rename the result as `schedule.xls`;
  d) for each specific experiment:

    – delete the files `commonVar.py`, `workers.txtx`, `entrepre` `neurs.txt` (if any), `entrepreneurs.txtx` (if any);
    – for case *X*, duplicate the files `commonVar.py.caseX`, `workers.txtx.caseX`, `entrepreneurs.txt.caseX` or `entrepreneurs.txtx.caseX`;
    – rename the results as `commonVar.py`, `workers.txtx`, `entrepreneurs.txt` or `entrepreneurs.txtx`.

- To run the experiments of the cases 7 and 7*b*:

  a) delete the file `schedule.xls`;
  b) duplicate the file `schedule6.xls.backwardCompatibily`;
  c) rename the result as `schedule.xls`;
  d) for each specific experiment:

    – delete the files `commonVar.py`, `workers.txtx`, `entrepre` `neurs.txt` (if any), `entrepreneurs.txtx` (if any);

- for case *X*, duplicate the files `commonVar.py.caseX`, `workers.txtx.caseX`, `entrepreneurs.txt.caseX` or `entrepreneurs.txtx.caseX`;
- rename the results as `commonVar.py`, `workers.txtx`, `entrepreneurs.txt` or `entrepreneurs.txtx`.
- The experiments from 1 to 7 also run without the modifications above, but producing slightly different results.
- To run the experiments of the cases from 8 upward:
  a) if you made one of the modifications above:
    - delete the file `schedule.xls`;
    - duplicate the file `schedule6.xls`;
    - rename the result as `schedule.xls`;
  b) for each specific experiment:
    - delete the files `commonVar.py`, `workers.txtx`, `entrepreneurs.txt` (if any), `entrepreneurs.txtx` (if any);
    - for case *X*, duplicate the files `commonVar.py.caseX`, `workers.txtx.caseX`, `entrepreneurs.txt.caseX` or `entrepreneurs.txtx.caseX`;
    - rename the results as `commonVar.py`, `workers.txtx`, `entrepreneurs.txt` or `entrepreneurs.txtx`.
- The experiments from 1 to 7 also run without the modifications reported above, but producing slightly different results.
- Each case requires the input of a few parameters in an interactive way. We report them in Table C.1.

C.3 Running the Code Directly Online

It is possible to run the *Oligopoly* project directly online, via `https://mybinder.org`, accessing the file system at `https://mybinder.org/v2/gh/terna/SLAPP3/master` to modify – if necessary – the content of the folder `oligopoly` contained into the folder

`6 objectSwarmObserverAgents_AESOP_turtleLib_NetworkX`.

Then, from the main folder, we launch the `iRunShellOnline.ipynb` file, and finally we follow the instructions contained in it.

The final part of the file `runningSpecificCases.md` at `https://github.com/terna/oligopoly` contains instructions to run the code using other online resources.

References

Acemoglu, D., Carvalho, V. M., Ozdaglar, A., and Tahbaz-Salehi, A. 2012. The network origins of aggregate fluctuations. *Econometrica*, 80(5), 1977–2016.

Aguirregabiria, V., and Mira, P. 2007. Sequential estimation of dynamic discrete games. *Econometrica*, 75(1), 1–53.

Allen, B., and Hellwig, M. 1986. Bertrand-Edgeworth oligopoly in large markets. *The Review of Economic Studies*, 53(2), 175–204.

Aoki, M., and Yoshikawa, H. 2007. *Reconstructing macroeconomics: a perspective from statistical physics and combinatorial stochastic processes.* Cambridge University Press.

Axtell, R. 2000. Why agents? On the varied motivations for agent computing in the social sciences. Center on Social and Economic Dynamics – working paper.

Axtell, R. L., and Epstein, J. M. 2006. Coordination in transient social networks: an agent-based computational model of the timing of retirement. In: Epstein, J. M. (ed), *Generative social science: Studies in agent-based computational modeling*, 146–74. Princeton, NJ: Princeton University Press.

Bagliano, F. C., and Bertola, G. 2004. *Models for dynamic macroeconomics.* Oxford University Press.

Bertoletti, P., and Etro, F. 2016. Preferences, entry, and market structure. *The RAND Journal of Economics*, 47(4), 792–821.

Bilbiie, F. O., Ghironi, F., and Melitz, M. J. 2012. Endogenous entry, product variety, and business cycles. *Journal of Political Economy*, 120(2), 304–45.

Blinder, A. 1986. A skeptical note on the new econometrics. In: Preston, M., and Quandt, R. (eds), *Prices, competition and equilibrium*, 73–83. Oxford: Phillip Allan Publishers.

Boero, R., Morini, M., Sonnessa, M., and Terna, P. 2015. *Agent-based models of the economy – from theories to applications.* Palgrave Macmillan.

Bowles, S., Kirman, A., and Sethi, R. 2017. Retrospectives: Friedrich Hayek and the market algorithm. *Journal of Economic Perspectives*, 31(3), 215–30.

Branch, W. A., and McGough, B. 2010. Dynamic predictor selection in a new Keynesian model with heterogeneous expectations. *Journal of Economic Dynamics and Control*, 34(8), 1492–508.

Branch, W. A., and McGough, B. 2016. Heterogeneous expectations and micro-foundations in macroeconomics. In: Hommes, C., and LeBaron, B. (eds), *Handbook of computational economics*, 3–62. Elsevier Handbooks in Economics Series, Arrow, K., Woodford, M., Rotemberg, J. (eds), vol. 4, Heterogeneous Agent Models. Amsterdam: Elsevier.

Carvalho, V., and Gabaix, X. 2013. The great diversification and its undoing. *American Economic Review*, 103(5), 1697–727.

Christiano, L. J., Eichenbaum, M. S., and Trabandt, M. 2018. On DSGE models. *Journal of Economic Perspectives*, 32(3), 113–40.

Chu, A. C., and Ji, L. 2016. Monetary policy and endogenous market structure in a Schumpeterian economy. *Macroeconomic Dynamics*, 20(5), 1127–45.

Clementi, G. L., and Palazzo, B. 2016. Entry, exit, firm dynamics, and aggregate fluctuations. *American Economic Journal: Macroeconomics*, 8(3), 1–41.

Comin, D., and Gertler, M. 2006. Medium-term business cycles. *American Economic Review*, 96(3), 523–51.

Corbellini, A., Crosato, L., Ganugi, P., and Mazzoli, M. 2010. Fitting Pareto II distributions on firm size: Statistical methodology and economic puzzles. In Skiadas, C. H. (ed), *Advances in data analysis: Theory and applications to reliability and inference, data mining, bioinformatics, lifetime data and neural networks*, 321–8. Springer.

Dasgupta, P., and Maskin, E. 1986. The existence of equilibrium in discontinuous economic games, Part I (Theory). *The Review of Economic Studies*, 53(1), 1–26.

De Grauwe, P. 2011. Animal spirits and monetary policy. *Economic Theory*, 47(2–3), 423–57.

De Grauwe, P., and Kaltwasser, P. R. 2012. Animal spirits in the foreign exchange market. *Journal of Economic Dynamics and Control*, 36(8), 1176–92.

Delli Gatti, D., Desiderio, S., Gaffeo, E., Cirillo, P., and Gallegati, M. 2011. *Macroeconomics from the bottom-up*. Vol. 1. Springer Science & Business Media.

Delli Gatti, D., Di Guilmi, C., Gaffeo, E., et al. 2005. A new approach to business fluctuations: heterogeneous interacting agents, scaling laws and financial fragility. *Journal of Economic Behavior & Organization*, 56(4), 489–512.

Delli Gatti, D., Gallegati, M., Greenwald, B., Russo, A., and Stiglitz, J. E. 2010. The financial accelerator in an evolving credit network. *Journal of Economic Dynamics and Control*, 34(9), 1627–50.

Di Guilmi, C., Gallegati, M., and Landini, S. 2017. *Interactive macroeconomics: stochastic aggregate dynamics with heterogeneous and interacting agents*. Cambridge University Press.

Dilaver, Ö., Calvert Jump, R., and Levine, P. 2018. Agent-based macroeconomics and dynamic stochastic general equilibrium models: Where do we go from here? *Journal of Economic Surveys*, 32(4), 1134–59.

Dosi, G., Fagiolo, G., and Roventini, A. 2006. An evolutionary model of endogenous business cycles. *Computational Economics*, 27(1), 3–34.

Dosi, G., Fagiolo, G., and Roventini, A. 2008. The microfoundations of business cycles: an evolutionary, multi-agent model. *Journal of Evolutionary Economics*, 18(3–4), 413.

Dosi, G., Fagiolo, G., and Roventini, A. 2010. Schumpeter meeting Keynes: A policy-friendly model of endogenous growth and business cycles. *Journal of Economic Dynamics and Control*, 34(9), 1748–67.

Dosi, G., and Roventini, A. 2017. Agent-based macroeconomics and classical political economy: some Italian roots. *Italian Economic Journal*, 3(3), 261–83.

Dunne, T., Klimek, S. D., Roberts, M. J., and Xu, D. Y. 2013. Entry, exit, and the determinants of market structure. *The RAND Journal of Economics*, 44(3), 462–87.

Epstein, J. 2008. Why model? *Journal of Artificial Societies and Social Simulation*, 11(4), 12.

Etro, F., and Colciago, A. 2010. Endogenous market structures and the business cycle. *The Economic Journal*, 120(549), 1201–33.

Fagiolo, G., Moneta, A., and Windrum, P. 2007. A Critical Guide to Empirical Validation of Agent-Based Models in Economics: Methodologies, Procedures, and Open Problems. *Computational Economics*, 30(3), 195–226.

Fagiolo, G., and Roventini, A. 2017. Macroeconomic Policy in DSGE and Agent-Based Models Redux: New Developments and Challenges Ahead. *Journal of Artificial Societies and Social Simulation*, 20(1), 1.

Forni, M., and Lippi, M. 1997. *Aggregation and the microfoundations of dynamic macroeconomics*. Oxford University Press.

Gabaix, X. 2011. The granular origins of aggregate fluctuations. *Econometrica*, 79(3), 733–72.

Gaffeo, E., Delli Gatti, D., Desiderio, S., and Gallegati, M. 2008. Adaptive microfoundations for emergent macroeconomics. *Eastern Economic Journal*, 34(4), 441–63.

Galí, J. 2002. New perspectives on monetary policy, inflation, and the business cycle. National Bureau of Economic Research Working Paper No. 8767.

Galí, J. 2008. *Monetary policy, inflation, and the business cycle: an intro-duction to the new Keynesian framework.* Princeton University Press.

Gertner, R. 1985. Simultaneous move price-quantity games and non-market clearing equilibrium. *Essays in Theoretical Industrial Organization.* PhD thesis, Massachusetts Institute of Technology, Department of Economics.

Ghorbani, A., Dechesne, F., Dignum, V., and Jonker, C. 2014. Enhancing ABM into an inevitable tool for policy analysis. *Policy and Complex Systems*, 1(1), 61–76.

Grassi, B., and Carvalho, V. 2015. Firm dynamics and the granular hypothesis. In: *2015 Meeting Papers*, Society for Economic Dynamics.

Harsanyi, J. C. 1973. Games with randomly disturbed payoffs: A new rationale for mixed-strategy equilibrium points. *International Journal of Game Theory*, 2(1), 1–23.

Hayek, F. A. 1994. *Hayek on Hayek: an autobiographical dialogue.* Vol. edited by Stephen Kresge and Leif Wenar. University of Chicago Press.

Jaimovich, N., and Rebelo, S. 2009. Can news about the future drive the business cycle? *American Economic Review*, 99(4), 1097–118.

Kirman, A. P. 1992. Whom or what does the representative individual represent? *Journal of Economic Perspectives*, 6(2), 117–36.

Kreps, D. M., and Scheinkman, J. A. 1983. Quantity precommitment and Bertrand competition yield Cournot outcomes. *The Bell Journal of Economics*, 326–37.

Kuznets, S. 1946. *National product since 1869.* National Bureau of Economic Research.

Lee, Y., and Mukoyama, T. 2018. A model of entry, exit, and plant-level dynamics over the business cycle. *Journal of Economic Dynamics and Control*, 96, 1–25.

Lengnick, M. 2013. Agent-based macroeconomics: A baseline model. *Journal of Economic Behavior & Organization*, 86, 102–20.

Lorenzoni, G. 2009. A theory of demand shocks. *American Economic Review*, 99(5), 2050–84.

Loury, G. C. 1979. Market structure and innovation. *The Quarterly Journal of Economics*, 93(3), 395–410.

Lucas, R. J. 1976. Econometric policy evaluation. A critique. In: Brunner, K., and Meltzer, A. (eds), *The Phillips curve and labour market, vol. 1, Carnegie-Rochester Series on Public Policy, Journal of Monetary Economics, Suppl.*, 10–46. North-Holland.

Luna, F., and Perrone, A. 2002. *Agent-based methods in economics and finance: simulations in Swarm.* Vol. 17. Springer Science & Business Media.

Luna, F., and Stefansson, B. 2012. *Economic simulations in Swarm: Agent-based modelling and object oriented programming.* Vol. 14. Springer Science & Business Media.

Madden, P. 1998. Elastic demand, sunk costs and the Kreps–Scheinkman extension of the Cournot model. *Economic Theory,* 12(1), 199–212.

Malleson, N. 2018. *Validating ABMs (SIMSOC discussion).* http:// surf.leeds.ac.uk/announce/2018/10/02/Validation_of_ ABMs.html, accessed October 13, 2018.

Manjón-Antolín, M. C. 2010. Firm size and short-term dynamics in aggregate entry and exit. *International Journal of Industrial Organization,* 28(5), 464–76.

Maskin, E. 1986. The existence of equilibrium with price-setting firms. *The American Economic Review,* 76(2), 382–6.

Mazzoli, M., Morini, M., and Terna, P. 2017. Business cycle in a macromodel with oligopoly and agents' heterogeneity: an agent-based approach. *Italian Economic Journal,* 5, 1–29.

McCallum, B. T., and Nelson, E. 1999. An optimizing IS-LM specification for monetary policy and business cycle analysis. *Journal of Money, Credit, and Banking,* 31(3), 296–316.

Minar, N., Burkhart, R., Langton, C., and Askenazi, M. 1996. The Swarm Simulation System: A toolkit for building multi-agent simulations. SFI Working Paper, 06(42).

Newell, A., and Simon, H. A. 1972. *Human problem solving.* Prentice-Hall.

Osborne, M., and Rubinstein, A. 1994. *A course in game theory.* MIT Press.

Romer, P. 2016. The trouble with macroeconomics. *The American Economist.*

Sutton, J. 1998. *Technology and market structure: theory and history.* MIT press.

Sutton, J. 2002. The variance of firm growth rates: the 'scaling' puzzle. *Physica A: Statistical Mechanics and Its Applications,* 312(3–4), 577–90.

Sutton, J. 2003. The variance of corporate growth rates. *Physica A: Statistical Mechanics and Its Applications,* 324(1–2), 45–8.

Sutton, J. 2007. Market share dynamics and the "persistence of leadership" debate. *American Economic Review,* 97(1), 222–41.

Trichet, J.-C. 2010. *Reflections on the nature of monetary policy non-standard measures and finance theory.* Opening address at the ECB Central Banking Conference, Frankfurt, November 18, 2010. http:// ww.ecb.europa.eu/press/key/date/2010/html/sp101118. en.html, accessed December 1, 2018.

Veracierto, M. 2008. Firing costs and business cycle fluctuations. *International Economic Review,* 49(1), 1–39.

Veracierto, M. L. 2002. Plant-level irreversible investment and equilibrium business cycles. *American Economic Review*, **92**(1), 181–97.

Vives, X. 2001. *Oligopoly pricing: old ideas and new tools*. MIT Press.

Walsh, C. E. 2017. *Monetary theory and policy*. MIT Press.

Weidlich, A., and Veit, D. 2008. Agent-based modeling of oligopolistic competition in the German electricity market. In: Möst, D., Fichtner, W., Ragwitz, M., and Veit, D. (eds), *New methods for energy market modelling: proceedings of the First European Workshop on Energy Market Modelling Using Agent Based Computational Economics*, 3–13. KIT Scientific Publishing.

Wiesner, K., Birdi, A., Eliassi-Rad, T., et al. 2019. Stability of democracies: a complex systems perspective. *European Journal of Physics*, **40**(1), 014002.

Author Index

Subject Index